WHERE THE PAVED ROAD ENDS

WHERE THE PAVED ROAD ENDS

One Woman's Extraordinary Experiences in Yemen

CAROLYN HAN

Potomac Books
Washington, D.C.

Library of Congress Cataloging-in-Publication Data
Han, Carolyn, 1941–
Where the paved road ends : one woman's extraordinary experiences in Yemen / Carolyn Han.
    p. cm.
ISBN 978-1-59797-725-8 (hardcover : alk. paper)
ISBN 978-1-59797-726-5 (electronic edition)

1. Han, Carolyn, 1941—Travel—Yemen. 2. Women travelers—United States—Biography. 3. Women travelers—Yemen—Biography. 4. Yemen—Description and travel. I. Title.
 G226.H35A3 2012
 915.304'53—dc23

                                             2012014705

Printed in the United States of America on acid-free paper that meets the American National Standards Institute Z39-48 Standard.

Potomac Books
22841 Quicksilver Drive
Dulles, Virginia 20166

First Edition

10 9 8 7 6 5 4 3 2 1

For Daood and Kamal

Thanks for the memories

Contents

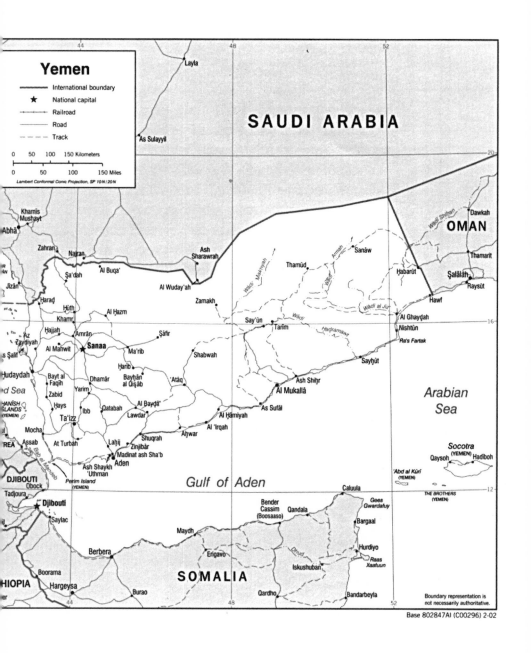

Yemen

- International boundary
- ★ National capital
- ┼─┼─┼ Railroad
- Road
- Track

0 50 100 150 Kilometers

0 50 100 150 Miles

Lambert Conformal Conic Projection, SP 10 N / 20 N

SAUDI ARABIA

OMAN

Layla

As Sulayyil

Khamîs Mushayt

Abhā

Zahrān

Najrān

Al Buqa'

Ṣa'dah

Al Wuday'ah

Zamakh

Ash Sharawrah

Sanāw

Thamūd

Wādī Masīlah

Wādī Armah

Wādī al Jīz

Dawkah

Wādi Shihan

Thamarît

Ḥabarūt

Ṣalālah

Raysūt

Hawf

Jizān

Haraḍ

Ḥūth

Al Ḥazm

Say'ūn

Tarîm

Wādī

Ḥaḍramawt

Al Ghaydah

Nishṭūn

Ra's Fartak

Khamr

Amrān

Ṣāfir

Ḥajjah

Az Zaydiyah

Al Maḥwit

Sanaa

Ma'rib

Shabwah

Sayḥūt

s Ṣalīf

Ḥudaydah

Bayt al Faqîh

Zabid

Dhamār

Yarim

Ḥarîb

Bayḥān al Qiṣāb

'Atāq

Ash Shiḥr

Al Mukallā

ʽABIAN Sea

Arabian Sea

HANISH ISLANDS (YEMEN)

d Sea

Hays

Ibb

Qatabah

Al Bayḍā'

Lawdar

Ta'izz

Al Ḥāmiyah

As Sufāl

Mocha

At Turbah

Laḥij

Shuqrah

Zinjibār

Madînat ash Sha'b

Aḥwar

Al 'Irqah

Assab

REA

Bāb al Mandab

Ash Shaykh 'Uthmān

Aden

Perim Island (YEMEN)

Socotra

Qaysoh (YEMEN)

Hadîboh

'Abd al Kūrī (YEMEN)

THE BROTHERS (YEMEN)

DJIBOUTI

Obock

Tadjoura

Djibouti

Saylac

Gulf of Aden

Caluula

Bender Cassim (Boosaaso)

Qandala

Gees Gwardafuy

Bargaal

Maydh

Hurdiyo

Raas Xaafuun

Berbera

Erigavo

Iskushuban

Boorama

HIOPIA

Hargeysa

Burao

SOMALIA

Qardho

Bandarbeyla

Boundary representation is not necessarily authoritative.

Base 802847AI (C00296) 2-02

Author's Note

"Let the beauty we love be what we do." I am grateful for Rumi's words; they have encouraged me to travel uncharted paths. Fate surely created the path to Marib, Yemen, and without question, I followed. Words in the book are merely swirls of dust kicked up as I journeyed over an ancient caravan route, finding pieces of myself, but that was not the plan. I went to teach English. The journey took me to a little-known part of our world, but a place long ago of ancient renown. Answers to unasked questions involved struggles and sacrifices, which I could not have known at the beginning of the journey.

The book is not about Yemen but a thin slice of life within a brief period of time viewed through a narrowly slit window showing the landscape and people of Marib. Watching others, I came face to face with myself. In the desert, I kept notes to make sense of the often-mystifying experience. Otherwise, I might have disappeared. When things got too crazy, I told Mohammed, my bodyguard, that I would write about him. He laughed, believing no one would be interested in reading about him or Yemen. After dusting off my notes, I combined them with remembered moments. Some names are changed for various reasons because it seemed wise.

I am thrilled to welcome you to Marib. Together we can gaze out a small window and, if we are lucky, catch a glimpse of a desert wildcat or camels on the horizon. Or perhaps by looking from the other side, we can discover a new awareness of ourselves.

A Note on Transliteration

I had to make choices about rendering Arabic words into English. In the book, I have used the generally accepted English spellings of Arabic terms. After using an Arabic word, I have explained its meaning. If I was not sure how to render a word, I consulted my Yemeni teachers. I take full responsibility for any errors that may have occurred.

PART I

A Far-Off Corner
of the World

1

THE JOURNEY

That which we do not confront in ourselves we will meet as fate.
—CARL JUNG

In Marib, I disappeared. Although I did not drink a magic potion like Alice in *Alice's Adventures in Wonderland*, I grew smaller and smaller. The desert bleaches bones chalky white, turning them to dust. Sandstorms twist day into night. Winds wear away rock. Raindrops vanish in sand, and like them, one day—*poof*—I was gone.

I had not planned to disappear in Marib. I went to teach English.

Marib was once the famed capital of the Sabaean kingdom—the greatest city-state in all of South Arabia—and home to the legendary Queen of Saba, from which we get the name "Sheba." Yemenis refer to the queen as Bilqis, a name of unknown origin. The Bible tells the story of the auspicious meeting of the Queen of Sheba and King Solomon, and the Koran gives a vivid account of the Queen of Saba's travels north delivering gifts of gold, gems, and incense to King Sulayman's court in Jerusalem.

For nearly three thousand years, the retold stories have included romance and mystery as underlying themes, but in part, the meeting between two sensible leaders may have been an economic endeavor for the international distribution of frankincense and myrrh. The Sabaeans controlled the southern portion of the incense route, and King Solomon maintained territories in the north. An alliance would benefit both leaders.

Trade in frankincense and myrrh brought vast riches to Marib. Incense (made from gum resin) was a major commodity essential for religious and secular uses and exported from the southern tip of Arabia. Transported on donkeyback to gathering centers, the incense was later loaded onto camels for winter caravans traveling north to the marketplaces of Petra, Jerusalem, Damascus, Alexandria, Rome, and onward. Used in ancient ceremonies, burning

incense carried prayers to the sky gods: sun, moon, and morning star. Phara-
onic Egypt required huge quantities of frankincense and myrrh for embalm-
ing. Incense was burnt before the Tabernacle, the portable sanctuary in which
the Jews carried the Ark of the Covenant. Frankincense perfumed King Solomon's couch, as mentioned in Song of Solomon. Gifts to baby Jesus included
gold, frankincense, and myrrh—treasures worthy of a king. Incense perfumed
clothing and masked odors of an ancient world.

Camel caravans loaded with incense traveled the recognized trade routes,
stopping to pay tributes or taxes at important cities. Keeping to well-known
routes was necessary for survival. Caravans attempting to avoid Marib or other
established sites faced certain death. Stories, of course, traveled with goods on
the ancient trading routes, including tales of Marib's fabled Sabaean queen.

Through the ages, legends of the Queen of Sheba have endured. When
stories persist, they hold truth—a collective memory bank—creating possibilities. Retold stories help overcome the transitory quality of life by providing
continuity. They allow us to kick dust along ancient footpaths, listen to music
of camel's bells, smell incense and spices in marketplaces, experience wonders
of the world, and perhaps, if we are lucky, taste forbidden fruit. Stories act as
maps—connecting us to the past, helping us find our way in the present, and
guiding us into the future. They tell us everything if we are still and willing
to listen.

Like the Queen of Sheba, heroes in stories often leave places of comfort
and venture into the unknown. Life presents travelers with at least two paths.
One way appears easy and secure. The other looks difficult and uncertain, but
the risky path may lead to hidden truths. As heroes in our own stories when
faced with situations we never dreamed possible, we must confront ourselves.
This takes courage because ten thousand distractions lurk along the way. Pres-
sured by unseen forces, we need to take a hard look and have faith that our
intuition is directing us to become whom we are destined to be. We must
quiet ourselves enough to listen. Listen and leap.

With this in mind, I wanted to someday travel to Yemen and stand in the
Queen of Sheba's footsteps, to walk the same land, and to write stories in the
shadows of her temples. In Arabia, there is a saying: "That which is inscribed
on our foreheads we must obey."

2

PLACES FIND US

There are years that ask questions and years that answer.
—ZORA NEALE HURSTON

Since the 1980s, I had traveled the silk and incense routes through China, India, and the Middle East collecting and writing stories. Yemen was not next on my agenda; it was far down on the list, or so I thought. Destiny sometimes tugs at our consciousness, and other times it actually drags us to the place we need to experience.

During my journeys, I let whatever happened happen, and in that way the journey was my teacher. I was constantly delighted to find myself in new situations being swept up in the dust of the moment. Not understanding what it is I am supposed to do or learn—that comes later.

In 1999 I rented a closet-like room in a downtown hotel in Amman, Jordan, after collecting Bedouin tales in Petra by moonlight. When the hotel clerk brought tea, he spoke about teaching mathematics in one of the oldest capitals of the world, Sana'a. He said, "It's where you go next." I followed his advice.

Sana'a, legends tell us, was established by Noah's eldest son, Shem. After the biblical flood, Noah sent his three sons to populate the world. Shem traveled south until he found a suitable location to begin a city. At the base of the mountain, he took out his plumb line, but a bird picked up the line and flew away. Shem followed. The bird dropped the plumb line where Sana'a stands today, and the rest is history.

I dreamed of standing at the base of Jabal Nuqum, the very mountain where the bird picked up Shem's line. In 2000 I came to Sana'a and stayed to study Arabic. By learning the language, I hoped to achieve as direct a relationship with the people as possible in order to collect stories.

Kamal, my first-year Arabic instructor and later friend, was endlessly patient. However, after six weeks of total frustration and feeling dyslexic, I took a break and traveled. Traveling in Yemen is complicated—foreigners are required to have letters of permission at the numerous military checkpoints to leave the city. The difficulties did not stop me from traveling but further heightened its appeal. The institute where I studied Arabic frowned on travel outside Sana'a. "Yemen's a dangerous place," warned Jamal, the institute's director. I did not listen.

Fate, as often happened, introduced me to Abdulmalik, a Yemeni driver who for money would take me to forbidden sites. Yemen was my destiny, and I gave myself up to it without a second thought. Before leaving Sana'a, a classmate reminded me to pack extra underwear and medicine. "You never know, you might be kidnapped," he said. "Then your Arabic will improve." That week in the *Yemen Times* newspaper, I read in an article that a German student had been kidnapped but luckily released unharmed.

Yemen's much-publicized kidnappings are usually pleas for education (schools) and services (hospitals). Tribesmen hope to extract concessions from the government by using hostages as bargaining chips. Since 2000 the kidnappings often happen to put pressure on the government for the release of prisoners. It is an age-old tribal practice—nothing new—and gets the Yemeni government's—and more recently the Western media's—attention. Captives are usually treated well and freed unharmed. However, hostages have been injured and killed caught in crossfire. With a stronger al Qaeda presence in Yemen, kidnapping foreigners may end differently. Undaunted by warnings, I traveled to Marib.

Unfortunately, much had changed in the city since its Sabaean heyday. The once-thriving Marib (M R Y B from ancient inscriptions—vowels were not written) had flourished in what today could only be described as a desolate desert region. The fabulous kingdom of the Queen of Sheba is no more. Marib is a run-down, dusty town.

Abdulmalik drove his Toyota Land Cruiser—nicknamed "Monica" because of its oversized fenders resembling Lewinsky's hips—on a bumpy unpaved road to the Land of Two Paradises Hotel, a neglected inn named for the Koran's description of the two gardens of ancient Saba. There I stayed locked behind the hotel's metal gates. Bedouin stood on opposite sides of the hotel's rooftop keeping watch and aimed automatic rifles at anyone approaching the gate until afternoon when it was time to chew *qat.*

Qat-chewing in Yemen has been a social pastime and universal habit among men and now women. The magic elixir said to cure Yemeni ills is at the same time condemned for depleting water resources. In fact, criticizing qat is often the topic at qat sessions. Although I had been to sessions before, this meeting at the hotel was my first time chewing qat myself. I sat with the Bedouin on the floor of the box-like concrete guardhouse carpeted with dusty goat-hair rugs. Of course, I sat on a separate rug.

Without touching me, a man passed fistfuls of leaves, dropping them into my open hands. Men and foreign women do not touch except to shake hands, but the ultraconservative religious men might consider handshaking taboo. Some Yemeni men stepped backward and shook their head when I extended my hand or covered their hands by pulling down a sleeve or putting their hands in pockets so as not to touch me directly. If men had washed for prayer, they could not shake my hand without having to wash again.

Western men—usually Americans new to Islam—avoided shaking my hand. They studied Arabic at institutes and converted to Islam either before or after coming to Yemen. Some had reverted, believing that we are all born Muslims. What intrigued me were reverts—more males than females—dressed in Arab or Pakistani clothes with American accents unwilling to acknowledge me.

Other converts/reverts showed great openness and respectful tolerance discussing Islam's philosophical and historical relationships with other religions. These students tended to study Arabic to read the Koran in its original language. They would bridge the ever-widening gap between the misconceptions and stereotypes growing in the Western world that Islam is a war-like religion. Associating violence with Islam is inaccurate and ignorant and feeds social divisions of misunderstanding. Relating Islam with extremism would be the same as connecting Christianity with fanaticism; both views are radical interpretations of religious doctrines on the extreme conservative ends.

Since it was my first time chewing qat, I watched the men before I put leaves into my mouth. I knew to chew the leaves and not swallow them but rather store a ball of masticated leaves in my cheek. That sounds easy, but bits of leaves slid down my throat, causing me to choke and cough. Drinking water or soda is necessary because the leaves dry your mouth, but swallowing and keeping the leafy mass in my cheek became a challenge.

Sitting across the room, a handsome Bedouin with kohl-rimmed eyes handed me the Al-Momtaz milk can. I held the can by the half-opened serrated top as a handle, and to my surprise, inside was homemade strawberry wine. The more I chewed, the more I smiled. While disconnected thoughts floated through my elastic mind, I watched the Bedouins grab their weapons and run out the door.

In Marib assault rifles are standard attire. The desert Arab lives by his rifle and may die without it. Guns equal honor and symbolize male virility. No boy past the age of twelve (sometimes younger) and certainly no man can be without weapons—usually Kalashnikovs or Chinese-made AK-47s slung over shoulders, along with *jambiyas* (wide-bladed curved daggers) tucked into belts. Weapons settled disputes.

After realizing it was a false alarm, the Bedouins returned and settled again, tucking thin, brown, sinewy legs under *futas*, the wraparound woven skirts Yemeni men often wear, or *thobes*, the long shirt-like garments, and propping one leg up with elbows resting against folded blankets as bolsters, keeping weapons within easy reach. They resumed padding their cheeks with leaves.

Abdulmalik rapped on the blue metal door, and as if choreographed, the Bedouin jumped up and grabbed rifles, plastic bags of qat, and water bottles. Within five minutes, we were in the Toyota, bouncing over an unpaved road heading across the open desert to one of the ancient wonders of the world, Marib Dam.

Filled with anticipation approaching the dam and remembering that the Sabaeans constructed it in approximately the seventh century BCE, I felt transported to an earlier age. Abdulmalik parked at the bottom of the dam's sluice gates in the middle of what was once a thriving garden mentioned in the Koran.

My sandals filled with hot sand when I stepped out of the car, but I hardly noticed the heat, transfixed by the grandeur. Followed by armed men, I climbed the massive hand-hewn stones, peered into now desiccated desert land, and tried to imagine what it might have looked like with flowering orchards and fields of green. The dam is so big and so wide that my camera lens could not capture it. Climbing down, I aimed my camera at a man whom I believed was posing, when in fact he had squatted to pee.

Bedouin led me to stone canal systems at different heights that once de-livered water to the surrounding fields and explained proudly of their ances-tor's work, as if they had witnessed the construction. Over the centuries, the dam had been patched and repaired, but its final collapse in the sixth century CE coincided with Prophet Muhammad's birth. The Koran's account of the dam's destruction states that the Sabaeans who farmed the fabled gardens turned away from God, and to punish them, He destroyed the dam. In Yemen, the past is ever present in the forms of stories, history, fact, and fantasy, all intertwined. Captivated, I wanted to find out more.

Marib storytellers tell of King Amr of Saba:

The King dreamed that a small, gray mouse dug stones at the base of the dam. Since he had the dream repeatedly, he wanted it interrupted and sought the advice of a fortune-teller. The seer explained that his dream was a sign that the dam would collapse. King Amr rode his camel to the dam and witnessed a tiny mouse moving an enormous stone. Amazed by its strength he watched as the mouse moved another stone and yet another . . . and as predicted, the following day the dam collapsed.

3

EMBRACING ADVENTURE

Adventure is worthwhile in itself.
—AMELIA EARHART

Although Yemen is one of the oldest inhabited regions of the world, it remains cloaked in mystery as one the least known places. While in Yemen, I wanted to see as much as possible. Abdulmalik, like other Yemeni drivers, carried a handgun when traveling outside Sana'a. He stashed his pistol in his wide leather belt, between a jambiya and mobile phone.

On the day we traveled to Baraqish, an ancient fortified kingdom established in the early seventh century BCE, I watched Abdulmalik's assistant load an assortment of weapons under the car seats, and he crammed rifles in the trunk. I wondered what they were expecting.

At the al-Jawf turnoff, the halfway point to Marib, truckloads of scruffy-looking armed men waited by the side of the road. Abdulmalik quickly tied his turban in a way that said he was from the region. Few people visit Baraqish since warring tribal skirmishes and government conflicts, fear of dying or kidnapping, keep travelers and law-abiding Yemenis away. Outside Sana'a, there is an even greater sense of lawlessness and of venturing backward in time.

Welcomed by the Shaykh of Ma'in and truckloads of his militia, we followed the procession in Abdulmalik's car to Baraqish. On foot, we toured the towering walls made from blocks of cut-stone decorated with carved inscriptions using the ox-turn style, where the first line reads from right to left, the next line from left to right, and so on, a method of writing used in ancient South Arabia. Hard on our heels were the tribesmen holding each other's hands; they were likely descendents of those who had inscribed the stones.

During the first summer, I traveled with Abdulmalik and his Yemeni friends, who showed me out-of-the way places and introduced me to charming and sometimes alarming Yemenis. Summer was coming to an end, but before leaving, I wanted to find a way to return to Yemen the following year.

"Please, say that again," I said to the receptionist on the telephone. "*Naam* (yes), Gamal Street and go straight until I see a spice shop, and then *luf yameen* (turn right). *Shukran* (thank you)," I said, hanging up the phone and staring at my English and Arabic scribbles on paper. A lecture at the American Institute for Yemeni Studies (AIYS) in Bir al-Azab would be that evening. If I understood correctly, the lecture was on qat.

Rewriting the directions—turn right at the spice shop and then left at a laundry. Go straight until you see a narrow alley. Turn right, you will come to two blue gates, then knock at a wooden door.

The evening shadows grew long as I walked to Tahrir (Liberation) Square. Old alabaster windowpanes in the stone tower-houses cast golden glows on the cobblestone walkways. The *qamariya* (half-moon), jewel-patterned, colored-glass windows sparkled in daylight, but by evening darkened to gleaming gems. Trash scattered along the pathways disappeared into deepening shadows.

On Gamal Street, I found the Military Museum. If the museum was on my left, I was going the right direction. I did not see a spice shop. Looking at my watch, it was half past seven o'clock. Light quickly faded. Boys pushed wheelbarrows on the broken, narrow sidewalk selling towels, t-shirts, sleepwear, bras, panties, cosmetics, ringing alarm clocks, prickly-pear cactus fruit, and chocolate bars.

A hand tapped my arm. Shocked that someone would touch me on the street, I looked into a female Chinese face. "Where are you from?" she asked. Hawaii, I answered in English. "It's difficult for women in Yemen," she said as we walked. "Lucky my daughter studies in America, but my son doesn't work. He chews qat everyday."

Her family had emigrated from Vietnam to Yemen as refugees. She asked shopkeepers directions in Arabic, and we doubled back, turned at an unmarked street, and found the laundry. While she spoke with the laundry worker, a lanky, bony-faced Yemeni entered the shop. Tossing the flowing end of his turban over his shoulder with a theatrical flip of his hand, he said "*Amereeka*" and motioned for me to follow.

The Chinese woman and I zigzagged with him across the street, dodging cars, and then followed him through a dark narrow alleyway. We stopped at an opened arched wooden door, and I looked into a courtyard of potted plants. The people inside greeted each other in English. *"Ma'a salaama*. Go in peace," the Yemeni man said, saluting before he disappeared into evening shadows. When I turned to thank the Chinese woman, she had gone.

After the lecture on qat, I stayed for punch and cookies and introduced myself to Dr. Chris Edens, the director of the AIYS. He agreed to meet me the following week, which he did, and explained how to apply for an AIYS grant and encouraged me to try.

My idea was to retell Yemeni Sufi stories so that American children could travel to Yemen in their imaginations, the way reading folk tales helps introduce children to different cultures. Judaism and Christianity once flourished in Yemen, and these religions along with Islam share ancient wisdom—mysticism—of the heart stories, Sufism.

Mohammed, a Yemeni scholar who specialized in Islamic architecture, told me he had access to a library of old Sufi tales and would gladly help. Sufism is alive in Yemen but not openly practiced. Followers remain secretive because religious fundamentalists frown upon Sufism. Books about Sufis who lived long ago in Yemen are available in bookshops, however, finding a living Sufi to answer questions would be difficult. Mohammed did not reveal his beliefs, nor did I ask. I applied for an AIYS 2001 summer fellowship to collect Sufi stories for children. The wait was agonizing, but in mid-May, I heard yes.

4

TRAVEL AWAKENS

What you get by reaching your destination isn't nearly
as important as what you become by reaching it.
—ZIG ZIGLAR

On a June morning after traveling more than halfway around the world, I returned to Yemen. Golden sunlight lit the jagged mountains encircling Sana'a, the capital, as the plane touched down. Legend has it that the mountains left the Sinai when Moses asked to see God's face. Shocked and embarrassed by Moses's words, the mountains picked themselves up and flew south—to Yemen.

Inside the terminal, I lined up with men to process my passport to clear immigration. At that moment, I envied the black veiled women seated off to the sides while fathers, husbands, or sons dealt with the paperwork and authorities.

My Yemen visa was in my passport, but the immigration officer examined every page in detail, as if it were the first passport he had seen. He commented to a man seated next to him and finally signed his name across two pages and stamped his signature. I was free to collect my luggage.

While I was clearing customs, the official asked what was in my largest suitcase. "Makeup," I replied, tired and not thinking clearly. He smiled and marked my bag with an "X" using a piece of white chalk.

Thankfully, the AIYS driver showed up, and I followed him to the car.

At the AIYS hostel, I watched the slowly turning clock hands until they reached 10:30 a.m., a reasonable time to telephone Mohammed. I hoped he would be excited to hear from me. "Aaloo," a sleepy voice answered on the sixth ring.

"May I speak with Mohammed?" I asked.

"It's he," the yawning voice replied.

"I arrived in Sana'a early this morning," I said. "Can we meet?"

We met that afternoon in the AIYS kitchen, where Mohammed explained that he would do the Sufi translations but could not start work until mid-August, because his daughter needed his help with her studies.

"But I leave Yemen in August," I said disappointed. "Can't you begin earlier?"

"Okay," he agreed. "But, I need the money." We settled on $500 for fifteen Sufi tales delivered in three installments.

Mohammed returned two weeks later with two pointless, half-page, hand-written stories. After reading the pencil scribbles on the pages, I still did not understand them because the stories did not make sense—they were not stories. I asked Mohammed why he had chosen them. He shrugged his shoulders.

"The stories are unclear," I said diplomatically. "A man does a good deed—white light flashes—he becomes a shaykh."

"I like them!" he protested. I wrote and rewrote, but no amount of re-writing could make the Sufi stories interesting. There was no substance.

Our meetings continued, but the stories did not improve. Mohammed produced poorly written, uninteresting, sketchy outlines jotted down on lined notebook paper, probably done while his daughter took a break from her studies.

Since the project was a failure, I decided to return the remaining fellow-ship money to AIYS. I walked to the home of Kamal, my Arabic teacher and friend, in the old city to tell him I was leaving Yemen. We sat on low cushions in his *mafraj* ("the room said to chase away worry"), drinking tea. Kamal was neatly dressed in a long-sleeved, light blue shirt and blue and gray woven futa, as if he had been expecting visitors. His receding hairline and glasses made him look distinguished and older than his twenty-nine years. A well-groomed, dark brown beard and mustache added to his handsomeness. When speaking, he gestured with solidly built hands that emphasized his well-chosen words.

"You can't quit," Kamal argued and took off his glasses when I explained why I had come to say goodbye.

"It's not right for me to use AIYS money since I'm not doing the work," I said.

"Why not collect folk tales," he asked, "like you did in China? Write about our Yemeni stories. We have thousands. I'll help you."

"Thanks," I said. "But I can't pay you. I've promised the money to Mo-hammed."

"Money," he replied dismissively as if he had sacks of gold instead of empty pockets. "What's important is you stay in Yemen." That is how Kamal and I began collecting Yemeni tales. Lessons in life, like our journeys, choose us.

The following week, Kamal collected folk tales from day laborers on the streets of Sana'a. The workers sat on street corners holding paintbrushes and carpentry tools; they came from all over Yemen. Kamal bought the men tea and qat, and they were happy to share tales, which he wrote in his notebook or memorized and retold to me. We met several times a week, and after six weeks, we had more than twenty drafts of Yemeni folk tales. I could not thank Kamal enough for his help. "It's for me to thank you," he replied. "You made it possible for me to understand my culture."

Preparing to leave Yemen and return to Hawaii for the academic year was increasingly difficult. I packed the stories Kamal collected, but I could not pack the feeling of well being I found in Yemen—a feeling of being in the right place at the right time. I find great generosity from the people of an enigmatic land branded a terrorist state by many who have never been there. International media often gives inaccurate information to readers/viewers unfamiliar with Yemen. They repeat catchphrases that promote negative views: "Yemen is the poorest country in the Arab world." "Yemen is the ancestral home of Osama bin Laden." Consider Aldous Huxley's words: "To travel is to discover that everyone is wrong about other countries." Surely this fits for Yemen. Although things do not always go as expected—like Mohammed and the Sufi stories—the results often end up even better.

PART II

ACROSS THE DESERT

5

CAMEL SHADOWS

Our truest life is when we are in our dreams awake.
—HENRY DAVID THOREAU

In June of 2003, sunlight streamed through the qamariya, stained-glass, fan-shaped windows of the room I stayed in at AIYS. Patterns of colored light danced on the well-worn red carpet runner from Afghanistan. My bare feet settled on the wool carpet, and I walked to the window. Opening the shuttered window, I looked out onto the neighbor's mud rooftop and into his walled garden and noticed trees with ripening yellow figs and pinkish apricots. I was in Yemen, but the grant money had not been awarded, or at least not yet.

With the impression of sliding down the rabbit hole, I decided to pursue my dream of crossing the desert by camel. Before, I was not choosy about which desert, but now that I was infatuated with Yemen, its desert seemed right. Dreams take time, of which I have less and less. Following footsteps of desert explorers through books they had written, I traveled through sandy deserts, experiencing hardships and highlights while crisscrossing drifting sands. Closing volumes by Thesiger, Lawrence, Bell, Stark, Snyder, and others on my sixty-first birthday in Hawaii, I thought, "Someday. Someday better be soon," or I will be too old to ride a camel.

"Travel to Marib isn't a good idea this summer," Tim Mackintosh-Smith, a British author living in Yemen, cautioned when we spoke on the telephone. He has more experience in Yemen than any non-Yemeni I know.

Everyone I asked said, impossible—it was not good timing—wait. Two American researchers sporting bushy black beards had told Yemeni authorities in Sayun that they were from Afghanistan in order to board the bus to Sana'a— Americans without believable disguises could only travel in well-protected tourist cars with armed military escorts.

16

The reasoning behind restricted travel in Yemen for westerners was sound. In November of 2002, the CIA launched a Hellfire missile from a U.S. Predator drone (an unmanned aircraft), killing an alleged leader and five suspected al Qaeda terrorists in Marib. Unmanned aerial drones are modern-day tools for deadly warfare. The Predator's "pilots" sit in rooms thousands of miles away and control the attacks of Hellfire missiles by satellite links. They identify and destroy targets known in military jargon as the kill chain. Drones are typically limited to war zones, but not in this case. Bombing Yemenis in Marib did not make America or Americans popular.

If America were seeking popularity, building modern schools and hiring educators to teach critical thinking skills would be far more effective than sending Hellfire missiles. Killing Yemenis does not accomplish America's goals. It makes people angry and creates more activists apt to join organizations that America has struggled to eradicate.

Few al Qaeda suspects actually come from Marib, but fugitives driven out of Saudi Arabia, Afghanistan, Pakistan, and elsewhere seek refuge in the desert's mountainous terrain because tribesmen, out of a sense of tribal honor, must protect those who need protection. Poverty, illiteracy, and hatred of the Yemeni government are reasons why people in Marib give shelter. There is a saying in Marib: "Where the paved road ends, al Qaeda begins." Marib has few paved roads.

The camel trip seemed doubtful.

"Okay, I will study Arabic." Although my Arabic sentences are grammatically incorrect, Yemenis are good at deciphering my tangled syntax. A willingness to put themselves in the other person's place is tribute to their intelligence and sensitivity. My lack of language skills in no way reflects on Kamal or my Arabic instructors.

On my way to Arabic class with Sina, a female teacher, I stopped at Fares' Internet shop to check my e-mail. On the screen appeared a message from Abdulmalik, the Yemeni driver whom I had not heard from in two years. "It's a sign," I thought.

At half past eight that evening, Abdulmalik stepped through the arched wooden AIYS gate. Instead of a typical Yemeni thobe and suit jacket, he wore a long-sleeved plaid shirt, blue cable-stitched sweater-vest, and dark blue slacks. His stooped shoulders sagged. "Times are difficult," he explained. "My last paying tourist was sixteen months ago. Tourism's down because of America's war in Iraq and recent kidnappings."

Times were indeed tough for everyone in the travel industry—few if any tourists were in Yemen. Negative news spreads quickly, and fear-based journalism keeps tourists away. Falling on hard times, Abdulmalik drove a city bus to feed his wife and six children.

Apologizing for his lack of English, he walked with me up the stone steps to the kitchen. Serving tea, I expressed regret for knowing so little Arabic—after all, I was in his country. While seated at the kitchen table, we laughed about our earlier misadventures: the sandstorm in Ma'in that nearly obliterated the car, chewing qat, and drinking homemade strawberry wine in Marib. The Bedouin at the Salaam Restaurant who asked me where I was from and slammed his Kalashnikov on the table before I answered, shouting that he would kill any American that set foot in Marib.

Abdulmalik confessed that he had been frightened while we escaped from the rock throwers in Na'it by speeding away in the car. It had felt dangerous, even though we laughed about it at the time. He admitted he had not slept the night before traveling to Baraqish. I remembered the collection of weapons in his car. "Were you worried?" I asked.

"Of course, the men in Baraqish could have killed us," he answered.

Later, after we had separated, Abdulmalik had visited the institute where I studied Arabic and asked for me, but no one gave him information. Cleaning his wallet, he found my e-mail address and decided to write. Fate.

"Can you take me to Marib?" I asked smiling at our earlier mishaps. "I'd like to ride a camel across Yemen's desert."

"Well, why not," he replied. "I'll call a friend." Abdulmalik's approach to life opened possibilities.

The next day, I visited travel agencies in Sana'a to check prices for my journey. They were reluctant to take a woman to the desert, and none would do so without military escorts. My goal was to experience the desert's peacefulness. For a long time, I had felt empty and required a dose of spiritual nourishment, which I hoped to find in the desert. Finding peacefulness would be impossible with a half-dozen armed military men crowded into a Toyota pickup truck following my camel.

"Who is Abdulmalik?" Kamal quizzed me the next day. His dark eyes were already narrowed from when I told him of my desert plan. "How do you know this Yemeni?" I explained that he was the driver who had taken me traveling my first year in Yemen. Listening to my reply, Kamal looked concerned. "Do you trust him?"

I nodded yes.

"Okay, if you go to the desert, I'll call you several times a day." An absurd picture of me sitting on a camel talking on a mobile phone popped into my head, but perhaps the desert would be out of telephone range.

In tribal society, Kamal is my self-appointed designated caretaker; he is responsible for me since I do not have a Yemeni family. He, of course, is responsible for his mother, wife, sisters, and female aunts and cousins—he comes from a long line of responsible men. If anything or anyone should harm "his women," he is the one to settle the tribal score. Yemeni men are very serious about protecting women—it is an honor-bound and sacred duty in society.

Abdulmalik called and agreed to pick me up at seven o'clock, and we would go to dinner. I figured eight o'clock, because he was habitually late, as people generally tend to be in Yemen. At eight thirty, I called his mobile phone.

"I'm coming," he replied.

At nine o'clock, I called again.

"I'm near," he said. Since he no longer had his own transportation, he borrowed a huge white bus from a friend and parked it blocking the alleyway with the motor running. "Is the fish restaurant okay?" he asked, as I clambered aboard.

While he parked the bus, I looked into the restaurant located across the street. Its fluorescent tubes glowed icy blue, but it looked empty. I followed Abdulmalik as he crossed two lanes of snarled, honking traffic, and we waited on the concrete center divider for traffic coming the other direction to slow before we continued weaving our way through slowly moving cars.

At this hour, we were the only diners in the very basic restaurant, and we sat facing each other on wooden benches. For Yemenis, lunch is the main meal of the day. They fortify themselves for the upcoming qat sessions. Qat dulls the appetite—no need for dinner.

Workers in dirty aprons hunched over short straw brooms and swept the splattered concrete floor, but no one approached. Finally, a waiter slapped newspaper on the blue-and-white Formica tabletop. He returned carrying three fish hooked on his fingers; Abdulmalik choose two.

We washed our hands with laundry soap heaped on the ledge above the dirty washbasin in the corner of the restaurant. By the time we returned, a great round of freshly baked flat bread covered the newspaper. Two dented aluminum plates held spicy sauce made by grinding soft cheese, tomatoes, onions, and green chili peppers together in a hand-operated meat grinder. We tore pieces of hot bread with our right hands and dipped chunks into the delicious sauce. Two blackened fish arrived, sizzling. "What do you drink?" Abdulmalik asked.

"Coca-Cola," I answered. He sent the waiter to a nearby store to buy bottled drinks. Yemenis no longer drank Coca-Cola, showing displeasure at the American war in Iraq by boycotting American products. Abdulmalik drank Canada Dry ginger ale, thinking it was from Canada.

An orange-bodied flying insect landed on Abdulmalik's long-sleeved shirt. He brushed it into his hand. "It's an *anab* [grape] bug," he said, smiling and letting it go. "They fly when the grapes ripen." He told a story about the anab bug that his grandmother had told him as a child. "Oh, I know another," he said, and began a tale about a butterfly. I listened but did not write down the stories, since I was stuffing bread and fish into my mouth. Abdulmalik gestured with his hands while telling stories, and I understood about half, but I was thoroughly entertained. "Did you like them?" he asked.

"You're a storyteller," I replied feeling grateful that the art of storytelling was alive. Yemenis—taxi drivers, store clerks, bank tellers—are willing to tell tales. As a boy growing up in Dhamar, Abdulmalik spent evenings with his grandmother, and she would gather the children and tell stories. The tales were ongoing, and each night she added details to keep the children's interest like Scheherazade. "Do you think many grandmothers continue this custom?" I asked.

"A few," he answered. "Yemen has changed, and nobody has time." Perhaps oral traditions become less appealing in an age of high-speed Internet and cell phone communications. It is a high price to pay. Storytelling allows dreaming and connects us to our intuition. Stories are vital to well being and are as necessary as food and shelter. Children brought up on television and video games forfeit an imaginative inner world.

"The same is true in America—people don't have time," I explained. "I had hoped Yemen was different."

"You can still find storytellers," he said. "But not like before."

The waiter cleared the remaining food by efficiently bundling the newspapers on the table. He served hot, sugary tea in small, tulip-shaped glasses. "Did you speak with the people in Marib?" I asked. My mouth fell open when he told me the price. Abdulmalik looked wounded. "I'm sure the price is fair for them," I gasped. "But it's way too much for me."

"Traveling by camel is expensive," he replied. "Maybe you can ride a camel from Marib to Shabwa and return by car. That would be cheaper."

My original plan was to cross the desert, starting in Marib; going to Shabwa, Shibam, and Sayun; and finishing in Tarim. Listening to the price, I could only afford the first leg of the journey.

6

CROSSING THE *RAMLAT AS-SAB'ATAYN*

And the time came when the risk to remain tight in a bud
was more painful than the risk it took to blossom.
—ANAÏS NIN

AIYS had not yet agreed to sponsor my fellowship. To finance the camel trip, I sold my gold jewelry: three bracelets and my wedding band.

"You sold your wedding ring," Fouad, a young Yemeni friend and student studying at Sana'a University, exclaimed when I mentioned selling my jewelry as we drank tea in Tahrir Square one evening. "I'll buy your wedding ring back." Fouad did not have enough money to buy more than two cigarettes at a time, and I wondered what he would have done if I had asked him to buy back my wedding ring.

"It's gone," I said, feeling surprisingly sad even though the marriage had ended twelve years earlier.

Fouad and I met my first year in Yemen while he worked part-time for Abdulmalik, and we had recently met again at the Internet shop. He worked nights at a small hotel and would graduate with a degree in English literature the following year. A Dutch couple paid his school fees. I valued his candid insights and enjoyed meeting him for tea. "You have to be careful around Yemeni men," he warned. "They think Western women are easy. We see American films."

"I know young unmarried women might be 'tickets' out of Yemen," I said. "But don't believe everything you see in films."

"Of course, we all want out," he replied laughing. "Yemen is a restrictive society, and men don't and can't have girlfriends. They naturally want to have relationships with women. You think because your age they would not be interested to make a relationship. Yemeni men, including me, find you attractive." His directness caused me to blush. "I respect you and why I speak honestly," he said looking at his watch.

"Who do I pay for the tea?" I asked, realizing it was almost eleven o'clock.

"The boy," he replied and nodded to a boy not over nine years old. "That was me, when I first came to Sana'a."

"You worked in Sana'a as a child?" I asked, surprised. "I thought you lived in Taiz."

"My family was very poor, they sent me to Sana'a when I was that boy's age. Life is hard on the streets." Seeing discomfort in Fouad's eyes, I waited for him to continue. "One night, I slept in a room and a man came in and took off his belt and started to whip me when I wouldn't do what he said. I promised myself that night if I lived, I would change my life."

Fouad and I said goodnight. We planned to meet again, but neither of us knew when. He would return to Taiz for summer. I would cross the desert. Walking through Tahrir, I saw a boy seated on the curb with a bathroom scale next to him as he waited for a paying customer. I smiled when I passed and pressed coins in his small hand.

The next morning I spoke with Dr. Chris Edens about the camel trip. "Why does it have to be Yemen's desert?" he asked, shaking his head as I signed a letter absolving the institute of any responsibility. "There're other deserts." The AIYS wanted nothing to do with my camel journey and washed its hands of me.

Maybe I appeared stubborn, but I did not want to miss the opportunity of a lifetime. If we do not risk anything, we risk everything. In my deepest heart of hearts, I knew riding a camel across the Ramlat as-Sab'atayn desert was right.

Three days later, Abdulmalik and his uncle picked me up in an old Land Cruiser that looked as if it would not make it across the street, let alone travel to Marib. Surprisingly, the uncle's dashboard did not have fake fur like most Yemeni cars. An orange velvet cloth dotted with sequins and edged with gold fringe made the dashboard festive. He had been one of the Yemeni guerrilla fighters known as mujahedeen, who had been set adrift from Afghanistan and were now back in Yemen, abandoned by the West. Fighting in Afghanistan for Yemenis was less about religious beliefs and more about running the Communists out of the country. Retaliation is a strong motive in Yemen, and the

Communists had taken land and family holdings mostly from south Yemenis. Abdulmalik's uncle probably bought the colorful cloth for his dashboard while he was waging war for America.

The uncle—a dashing, proud-looking, rugged, unshaven tribesman—was indifferent to his passenger. When he talked with Abdulmalik, I noticed that his pair of Armani sunglasses were broken, with the right earpiece missing, but he never looked at or spoke to me.

Dressing as a Yemeni woman in a black *baltu* (a long cloak), black *hijab* (headscarf), and black *lithma* (face veil) made travel outside of Sana'a easier, but Abdulmalik had the official traveling papers. The uncle stopped the car at Nehm, the first checkpoint outside Sana'a, where we waited at the side of the road. A teenager with green-colored, kohl-rimmed eyes carried an aluminum tray of sesame seed candy cut into even rectangles. He stared through our rolled-up car window as he passed. His dusty, matted hair stuck out from under his loosely tied turban. The suit jacket he wore over his thobe was new, and he walked as if he were a prince.

The military policeman asked Abdulmalik questions, and I overheard him say I was Canadian. Although I wondered why, I did not correct him. A skinny soldier wearing a rumpled uniform two sizes too big shouldered an assault rifle, opened the rear door, and got in the backseat. He grinned. Yemenis lead difficult lives, but that does not stop them from smiling or being friendly.

My phone rang. It was Kamal. "Naam, yes," I said, hoping he would understand it was not a good time to talk. He did. The police waved us through, and we were on our way to Marib.

Heat waves bounced on the blistering road and created mirages. Dust clouds twirled on the desert landscape as *jinn* (invisible spirits), taking the form of whirlwinds as they danced. Yemenis believed that some jinn were friendly, but most wreaked misery and misfortune.

Although I was thirsty, drinking water was out of the question, as there was no place for a woman to stop and pee. At the next checkpoint, the soldier who rode with us was ordered out of the car; military could not ride inside tourist's vehicles. Apparently, soldiers stole money and cameras while sorting through traveler's luggage. Several checkpoints down the road, a soldier spoke to Abdulmalik and told him to sit in back. He climbed over the seat and sat by me. Two soldiers wearing ill-fitting uniforms cinched at the waist squeezed in the front seat next to the uncle. Seemingly, the rule had changed again, and we needed protection.

In Yemen, several layers of reality happened at the same time, and I understood few of them—even when I paid attention. It was not only my lack of Arabic. Something different happened than what was expected. We parked on the side of the road at the al-Jawf–Marib crossroads for over an hour, waiting for a military convoy to escort us to Marib. The black polyester clothing became an oven—I lifted the black veil, flapping it up and down, hoping to create a breeze and dry the perspiration trickling down my neck. "It is best to ignore the heat," I thought.

Outside the window, heat waves shimmered on the horizon, creating a gauzy, curtain-like blur. One humped camels floated on the sunburned haze, which reminded Abdulmalik of a story:

A Bedouin noticed that one of the camels was especially fat while the others grew thinner each day. He followed the camel to see where it went, but each night he lost sight of the camel among the sandy dunes.

One evening the Bedouin tied himself to the camel and fell asleep. Awakened, he looked down at land rushing by far below—the Bedouin had tied himself to a flying camel. The camel stopped in a forest of green things to eat. Waterfalls cascaded down the steep mountains, creating refreshing pools. The man could not believe his eyes because never in his wildest imagination could he have dreamed such a paradise. When the camel finished eating and drinking, it took to the air and returned to the desert.

The Bedouin explained to the tribe what had happened and what he had seen. The camel listened to the man's words and ran away because it was so ashamed that it had not shared with the others. It ran and ran until it could run no further and collapsed in a big heap. The camel turned to stone. Its hump is still visible in the sand near Marib, as a reminder to those who do not share.

"I'll show you the camel's hump," Abdulmalik said and smiled, pleased with his story. My telephone rang. "We're halfway to Marib," I said to Kamal, but the phone connection was weak. "If you don't hear from me, it's because

I'm out of telephone range." Another soldier squeezed in the backseat next to Abdulmalik. Two Toyota trucks—one in front and one in back—loaded with military police escorted us.

In Marib, Abdulmalik paid the military men protection money. Buying security, meals, and qat for the soldiers was expected—part of the expense of traveling in Yemen.

The uncle drove to the outskirts of Marib where three Bedouin waited at a prearranged site in an old, tan-colored truck. The uncle parked his Land Cruiser behind them. I watched the youngest, a teenager with curly ringlets, get out of the cab and jump in the back of the truck. Two men in the cab sat motionless.

I scooted in next to a stick-thin Bedouin inside the cab who was wearing a once-white thobe. Neither the stick-thin man nor the driver looked at or spoke to me. Abdulmalik jumped in back and sat with the young Bedouin, his turban flapping in the wind as we barreled across stony desert, dirt and sand flying. Looking out the window, I watched the uncle's car become a vague spot and vanish in the cloud of dust kicked up by our tires.

Pounding on the truck's roof startled the driver, and he swerved. The Bedouin sitting next to me grabbed his rifle. "That's the camel's hump!" Abdulmalik yelled in English through the window, gesturing to a stone in the sand.

More pounding, but this time the young Bedouin was shouting for the truck to stop. A permit paper had blown out of his hand—the truck turned around and retraced its tracks. Looking for a piece of paper blowing across the desert seemed impossible; Abdulmalik said the goats would eat it, and of course, I thought he was kidding. He spotted the permit a few minutes later and pounded on the truck's roof.

Stopping to retrieve the paper gave me an opportunity to get out, and I disappeared behind a bush some distance away. While squatting, I saw a herd of goats.

An hour or more outside Marib, the truck stopped, and the men set up camp at the edge of rolling dunes. The driver—named Mohammed al-Baraki, I later discovered—shook out a long brown goat-hair rug and tossed it on the sand, along with a pile of woolen blankets. I sat on one end of the rug and removed the black face veil but kept my hair covered. None of the men looked in my direction.

Salah, the oldest, with a hawk-like nose, dark leathery face, sparse henna-tinted hair, and well-shaped dark beard, made a fire for tea. Talib, the youngest, with dark curly locks dusted with sand, brought me a plastic bottle of water and piece of flat bread. I noticed he wore crossed bandoleers stuffed with cartridges over his sand-colored vest. His inquisitive eyes held a feral intensity even when he smiled. The men, including Abdulmalik, sat together—facing away—on the far end of the rug. No one spoke to me. Starlight lit the night sky as I watched meandering camel silhouettes on the sandy backdrop. Hobbled camels moved awkwardly.

When it was dark, Mohammed, who was tall and rail-thin, had gleaming, straight white teeth; wore his dark corkscrew hair short; and had a sculpted beard that outlined the lower half of his high–cheekboned face. He unfurled the blankets. The men unfastened belts and lay down on the blankets next to their Kalashnikovs and handguns, forming a semicircle around me. Evidently, it was time to sleep.

Falling asleep, I listened to Abdulmalik snore—snore—snore. Wrapped in my blanket, it dawned on me that I was in the middle of the desert with men I did not know, and tomorrow at first light, I would ride a camel across the Ramlat as-Sab'atayn.

As quietly as possible, I took off the black baltu, removed my headscarf, and rolled them into a ball for a pillow. I would not need the black cloak in the desert. I knew to dress modestly, keeping my arms and legs covered. Sifting through my memory for practical Arabic words, I stared at twinkling stars. I had asked Yemenis about the meaning of the desert's name. Some said it referred to the "area of two Saba's," when the ancient Sabaeans controlled Marib and the vast territories to the east. Others simply replied, "*Sab'atayn* means 'fourteen sand dunes.'" Arabic, a poetic language, can be ambiguous.

Yemen's desert stretches from Marib eastward to the Hadramawt, and from Beihan in the south northward to some vague point where it overlaps the great Rub al-Khali, "The Empty Quarter," the largest sand surface on earth. Why, I wondered, had I waited so long to ride a camel?

Apparently, I slept, because just before daylight I heard rustling and opened my eyes. Mohammed, dressed in a brown long-sleeved shirt and brown-and-black woven futa, had been up before dawn making a fire to boil water for tea. The dark canopy overhead held millions of twinkling stars but

no moon as I clutched my blanket to my chest. At daybreak, I watched Mohammed place his Kalashnikov on the sand and face Mecca. His prayers welcomed a new day as the sun exploded on the horizon and daylight colors
changed from silver to gold.

After praying, Mohammed returned to the fire and without looking at
me poured thick, sugary tea into two cut-off plastic water bottle bottoms. I
unwrapped myself from the blanket and joined him. Words unnecessary, we
sat in silence. Talib, Mohammed's teenage nephew, folded the sleeping blankets and afterward poured himself tea. Sometime during the night, Salah had
disappeared. Abdulmalik was still rolled up in his blanket, sound asleep, but
thankfully no longer snored.

In the distance, the soft rumbling sound of a motor interrupted the silence long before the Toyota truck came into view. Mohammed and Talib
readied their weapons. Automatic rifles were unnecessary because it was Salah
driving the truck, which would serve as transportation for supplies and water
as we crossed the desert. After the men stood face-to-face with noses gently
touching—an age-old traditional custom for Bedouin—Talib loaded the rug,
blankets, Chinese teakettle, and metal bowl in the truck's bed.

Talib poured handfuls of sand on the fire and kicked it with his sandaled
foot, making sure the glowing embers were out. Mohammed walked toward
the camels, and his shuffling gait made scratchy sounds as he crossed the hard-
packed sand. His long, sinewy feet, well grounded to the earth, looked too
large for the rest of him. Talib's long strides followed. The green face of the
watch Mohammed wore on his wrist sparkled in the sunlight. It was the only
green-colored thing in sight.

Mohammed couched the camel by pulling down on the lead rope and
making a guttural noise in his throat: "*khrr, khrr.*" The camel dropped to
its front knees and then swayed backward, settling on its hindquarters and
sinking down in the toast-colored sand. He bound the camel's bent left front
leg with a piece of rope. Mohammed kept his foot on the camel's folded leg,
which prevented the camel from standing, and placed the blankets and then a
wooden A-frame camel saddle on its back.

Saddling is noisy business, and my camel roared and snarled in protest.
When Mohammed removed his foot and the rope from the camel's leg, it
leaned backward, gaining momentum. Stretching out its front legs, it rocked

forward and then backward, coming to standing position. Mohammed led *Ata Allah*—meaning God's gift in Arabic—on a long lead line, checking to make sure the girth strap was secure. Evidently it was not snug, so he tugged downward on the lead rope and made the *khrr, khrr* sound again, and the camel lowered itself to the sand. Keeping his foot on the bent leg, he tightened the girth strap and then motioned me over with his hand.

Deciding what to wear had been difficult, because I had not planned to ride a camel when I left Hawaii, or I would have packed a straw hat and sensible clothes. Dressed in a long brown cotton skirt, underneath it I wore a pair of khaki ankle-length cotton pants, with a fawn-colored long-sleeved T-shirt under a long cream-colored tunic—all colors of the desert. Abdulmalik had lent me his blue cotton scarf. He had wrapped it around my head, turban style, and had perched on top of it a small straw hat I had purchased at the basket store in Sana'a. A pair of beige socks and brown, flat-heeled leather sandals covered my feet.

Salah and Mohammed stood on either side of the camel, and I tried unsuccessfully to swing my leg over the tall saddletree. Abdulmalik, now fully awake, walked over to watch. After two tries, I sat balanced on the saddle, but not comfortably. My feet dangled. I knew the camel would lean backward and then forward when it stood and I prepared for the jarring, unbalancing, movement. Unfortunately, Abdulmalik thought I was going to fall and, trying to save me, grabbed the back of my tunic and ripped it to shreds, nearly pulling me off the camel's back. There was no way of mending the tattered tunic, and I was just thankful he had not torn off one of the sleeves.

Abdulmalik, red-faced, apologized for ruining my tunic and handed me two pieces of flat bread and packets of cheese triangles wrapped in metal foil as an offering. "Stay away from me," I shouted and laughed.

7

INTO THE HADRAMAWT

The things I thought were so important have turned out to be of small value.
—THOMAS MERTON

A camel's gait takes getting used to, and sitting in one position for hours, thinking that if I moved I might fall off, made it worse. Eventually I relaxed and tried all sorts of positions: Legs stretched in front, balanced on the camel's neck. Legs dangled on each side of the camel. Legs draped while sitting side-saddle. I had ridden horses, but nothing prepared me for camel riding. When muscles in my back ached and felt ready to snap, other muscles compensated for the discomfort. Once, I got off and led the camel, but walking on the burning sand and pulling the camel's head up when it wanted to nibble plants was hard work. I got back on.

The first day, we crossed *ramlats*, or gently undulating sandy plains. We rested in the middle of the day, when the heat was at its worst, and tossed blankets over shrubs, creating spots of shade. Shade and water are vital in the desert. Writing in my notebook, I hoped to capture the essence of the place so I could later elaborate. I wanted a written record of one of the most spectacularly beautiful places on earth, which only a few privileged people see. However, my words lacked the depth to capture the significance of the experience. I wrote thoughts in half-sentences.

Mohammed—with his open-mouthed smile beneath a thick, dark mustache—inched closer when I wrote in my notebook. His head leaned forward as words appeared on paper. On occasion, Mohammed would lean over and gently remove my glasses and put them on his face. His large, expressive, molasses-colored eyes peered through the lenses. He never borrowed my pen—just my glasses, as if they were magic windows to another world.

Our world changed throughout the day. The sharp play of light that past writers have experienced in the desert was indeed profound, but for me, it was the exaggerated sounds. I expected silence and stillness, but grasses hummed. Acacia trees vibrated. Camels' feet plodded. Wind whined. Breezes blew. Sand gritted. Sounds never stopped, and melodies changed pitch depending on the wind's strength moving across the sand.

My cultural upbringing had taught me to fill all gaps of silence with talk and all free moments with busyness. Here I rode into an unknown, surrendering to forces outside my control. I was conscious of something inside me being eroded. I felt transformed, yet, it was hard to identify what was going on. Time in the desert is not measurable except during the magical hours of dawn and dusk.

Days of riding ended at nightfall, when the rug, tossed on the sand, became an island home. As the campfire glowed, visitors appeared as if dropping from the sky, often at mealtime. The fire brought men together as stars twinkled overhead, mirroring the immensity of the desert. There seemed to be as many stars in the sky as grains of sand on the desert. Guests stayed and stared, not impolitely—just curious about the stranger in their midst.

Our evening meals consisted of food cooked in a blackened, dented aluminum pot over a fire—boiled rice mixed with cans of tuna, including the oil. Sometimes a can of beans was added and stirred with a stick because Mohammed had forgotten utensils. Abdulmalik chopped tomatoes and onions with his red Swiss Army knife, explaining each time he used it that he had purchased the knife in Luxemburg on a trip to Europe.

Talib was the bread baker, and the first night I watched him prepare the dough, I could not believe that we would eat bread baked in the sand. First, he emptied handfuls of flour into a metal bowl and poured in water, stirring the wet, sticky dough with his hand. Kneading the big ball of dough until long, rubbery threads appeared, he stretched it arm length. Next, he pulled out fist-sized rounds of dough, flattening them before plopping them on the hot coals. After a few minutes, he turned the bread over and blacked the other side. Moving the hot coals aside with a stick, he dug a hole in the sand and buried the semi-cooked bread, then replaced hot coals on top. After thirty minutes, he dug in the sand, releasing the piping hot sand-covered loaves. Before passing the bread, he hit them together, knocking off loose sand. The bread was salty-tasting and filling.

I ate meals with my right hand from a small metal pan left on my end
of the rug. The men ate with right hands from a communal aluminum pan.
When Mohammed felt generous, he passed me an extra handful of rice or
hunk of bread. Once he gave me a chicken leg, but I gave it back, hoping he
was not offended. I was excluded from eating with men, but we drank water
from the same goatskin bags. Evaporation kept water in the goatskins cooler
than in plastic bottles, but I preferred drinking from the neck of a bottle,
not the neck of a goat. Once when we stopped to fill goatskins, Abdulmalik
explained that Bedouin believed stars falling from the sky created the wells. I
liked the image.

After dinner one night, Talib repeated the bread-making procedure, but
the loaves were larger—camel's bread. While watching steam rise from the
sand, I noticed a man tear a strip from a black plastic bag to clean between
his teeth. I rummaged through my purse, found dental floss, and gave him a
thread. Abdulmalik held out his hand for a sample. Mohammed moved closer
for his thread, and we sat together, cleaning our teeth until the men remembered that I was a woman. They turned away.

One evening Mohammed served dessert. He sawed the top of a can of
pineapple with the dagger that he usually wore tucked in his futa and fed me
chunks with his fingers, as if I were a pet. Whoever travels with Bedouin must
conform. Abdulmalik fished in the can for his share of pineapple, sat next to
me on the rug, and told a story:

> A beautiful, big-eyed Bedouin girl climbed to the top of a tree to pick
> fruit, but once she was up, she could not get down. She asked one hun-
> dred camel riders as they passed in a long caravan if they would help get
> her down from the tree. Only the last rider said to the girl, "I'll catch you
> in my hand if you jump. If you land near my little finger, you will be my
> daughter. If you land near my ring finger, you will be my mother. If you
> land near my index finger, you will be my sister. And if you land near my
> middle finger you will become my wife."
>
> The girl desperately wanted to get down from the tree and jumped
> into the man's hand, landing next to his middle finger and becoming his
> wife. Unfortunately, he was not a kind husband.

When her brother heard about his sister's mistaken marriage, he came to her rescue. The husband murdered the girl's brother. The girl planted a watermelon seed on top of her brother's grave and watered it with her tears. Although the leafy vine grew very long, there was only one watermelon. She believed her brother's spirit lived inside the melon.

When the watermelon ripened, she carried it home and split it open. Instantly her brother appeared. Together they lit a fire in the room, and hot flames burned her sleeping husband, turning him to ashes. He never bothered anyone again.

Abdulmalik stayed on my end of the rug and told me a story about the woman he loved, but circumstance forced him to marry her sister. I listened. Abdulmalik was not feeling well and asked for medicine. I mixed the package of rehydration salts with water. "Please keep this with you," he said and removed his money belt. I gave him two bottles of *Bao Ji Wan* pills, Chinese herbal medicine.

Abdulmalik walked slowly away with his untold stories; he disappeared into the night shadows. I wandered in the opposite direction, knowing Mohammed knew without looking where I was going. I squatted to pee and afterward washed my hands with sand. Before sleeping, I poured water in a bowl and wiped my face with a damp cloth. Using the same water, I brushed my teeth, spitting the frothy toothpaste on the sand.

"Goodnight," I said to the moon and stars, and fell asleep.

The following day, Talib chanted as we followed the path his tribe had used while crisscrossing the desert for thousands of years, but he did not know the meanings of the words. Ancient chants were disappearing, but they still provided maps with elaborate directions so that Bedouin could find their way across unmarked sands. The length of chants indicated distances. Subtle sounds or the repetition of words signaled twists and turns in the paths.

Mohammed said his grandfather knew many chants and he would introduce me to him—*inshallah* (God willing). A pressure-flaked spearhead half covered by sand lay near Mohammed's foot, and he picked it up and handed it to me. Excitedly, I showed the spearhead to Abdulmalik, who deposited it in his pocket. Talib's keen eyes searched for spearheads the following day, but when he found one and gave it to me, I did not show Abdulmalik.

Mohammed, Talib, and Salah had finely honed senses of observation and awareness that had been lost to more settled people. They understood things not evident to Abdulmalik and me. As literate beings, we are less likely to "read" the details of the natural world. Bedouin learn or are born with the language of the desert. They carry knowledge inside them without words. They have an innate sense of direction that allows them to follow *taruq* (unmarked paths) from oasis to oasis. Taruq are etched deeply into the collective consciousness.

Each tribe follows its own *tariqah* (singular) to safely cross the desert, avoiding unnecessary contacts or conflicts. We traveled through friendly tribal territories along narrow passes and desert trails. We crossed bare stretches of land northward and skirted sand dunes using serpentine bends, avoiding the steep climbs and drops of the endless rose-red tinted sand dunes of the Rub al-Khali and then moved south to Shabwa. Maybe Talib's chants guided us, but I had no way of knowing.

Shabwa is the ancient capital of the Hadramawt dating from around 750 BCE. Hadramawt is named Hazarmaveth in Genesis, the first chapter of the Bible. The name is said to mean "enclosure of death." Like many cities on the trade routes, Hadramawt thrived, collecting taxes from camel caravans crossing the desert. Shabwa is the ancestral home of the al-Baraki tribe, a small clan. They are the caretakers of sacred places for untold generations.

Five days crossing the desert went too fast, and from the top of a sand ridge, black goat-hair tents appeared on the horizon. I knew our destination—Shabwa—was in sight. Although change is a way of life, I wished my time in the desert would never end.

Mohammed noticed my tears and turned away so as not to see me cry then motioned with his hand that it was okay to ride around the site, looking at the collapsed temples and broken walls of mud-brick palaces. I stopped my camel next to the salt mine's funnel-like sides, which led to an eerie yellow pool deep within the earth. I inched away from its gaping rim as Abdulmalik told me a story about a French archeological team in the 1980s that accidently drove into the pit.

As I unpacked the camera, Mohammed cautioned me away from the edge of the salt mine by tugging on frayed cloth that dangled from my shredded tunic. Adjusting my clothes and dusting off the dirt did not help my appearance, and I decided to leave Abdulmalik's scarf in place, covering my matted hair. We smiled at the camera, taking turns as photographer.

Mohammed, Talib, and Salah, not by words but deeds, taught me valuable lessons. Up until then, I let people and circumstance define me, but while crossing the desert atop a camel, I stopped listening to the outside world and in noisy silence heard. We need only a few comforts but tend to acquire accessories—which we call essentials—in our lives. The Bedouin showed me true wealth: the sky for a roof and sand for a bed. Our desert home had no walls, doors, or windows. Because of the Bedouin, I made an unspoken promise to return to Marib the following year and teach English, my way of saying thanks to the desert people who have few opportunities for schooling.

Salah led my camel in the direction of the cluster of black goat-hair tents, but I could not watch. The desert was not my home, but it was where I wanted to stay. In fact, I could not say good-bye, so we arranged to walk the desert in two weeks. Deserts change people who live in them, even for short stays, and it had changed me. The journey into the desert was not the destination but rather a stop at an oasis to view the world from a new perspective. To return to the desert, I had to first travel to Sana'a, secure a Yemeni visa extension and an exit visa in my passport, and change the date on my return flight.

8

WALKING THE DESERT

The real voyage of discovery consists not in seeking new landscapes,
but in having new eyes.
—MARCEL PROUST

In Sana'a, I changed the airline booking and took my passport to the Yemeni
authorities for the visa extension and an exit visa. Processing a new visa would
take two weeks, but the man assured me a photocopy of my passport and cur-
rent visa, which had not expired, would suffice.

After much pleading with Kamal, he agreed to accompany me to Marib so
that I could walk the desert. However, he made it abundantly clear he would
only travel to Marib once in this lifetime. Kamal telephoned Mohammed al-
Baraki and arranged to collect chants and poetry from his grandfather, and this
gave Kamal an added incentive to make the disagreeable trip.

Ali, a driver, would take us to Marib and bring Kamal back the same day.
I would stay with Mohammed and Talib and walk the desert, and Ali would
return for me in seven days. Since I would wear the same clothes for a week,
I did not need to carry much, just a small backpack for medicines, toiletries,
a cup, and a towel.

On a cloudless morning, a day during which you think nothing could
go wrong, we left Sana'a and headed for Marib. We ate lunch in the Salaam
Restaurant in Marib before going to the Land of Two Paradises Hotel to meet
Mohammed, Talib, and the grandfather. In the corner of the restaurant, tables
were stacked to the ceiling and shook violently when a man jumped from the
top where he had been sleeping, missing our table by inches. Kamal raised his
eyes briefly toward the ceiling and then glanced at me, and he seemed to be
saying, "Only in Marib."

At the hotel Mohammed introduced Abdullah, his grandfather, a biblical
character with a flowing white beard and a lavender-colored turban embroi-

dered with gold and red threads. He was dressed in a roomy course-linen homespun robe the color of rinsed rice. The open-necked robe revealed white, wire-like hairs on his ruddy chest. Around his narrow waist, he wore a wide, black leather cartridge belt stuffed with bullets. Grandfather Abdullah's regal presence filled the room—sparks seemingly ignited in a halo above his head. He sat on the dark, leather-like sofa, arranged his robe, and smoothed out the wrinkles. It was impossible to guess his age, but his wise, dark, penetrating eyes and deeply lined face suggested he had crossed many deserts in his lifetime. His massive, gnarled hands stayed in his lap as Mohammed introduced us to him. Talib set the tray with six glasses of tea on a table and handed one to his grandfather.

Kamal sat next to Grandfather on the sofa, took out his notebook, put the tape recorder on the table, and turned it on. While Grandfather chanted ancient melodies, Arabic script flowed from Kamal's pen onto pages of a yellow lined notebook. When Kamal did not understand an antiquated word, Grandfather lost patience—he squeezed Kamal's thigh with his sinewy hand, scolding him for not knowing Arabic. "What's that?" Grandfather shouted upon seeing the tape recorder, his eyes ablaze and eyebrows rising.

Kamal rewound the tape and let him listen. At first, grandfather looked puzzled and then greatly disturbed. He pushed the tape recorder out of Kamal's hand, knocking it to the floor. It took twenty minutes for Mohammed to convince his grandfather that jinn did not live in the "talking" machine. He was probably not convinced. I glanced at Ali, who was smiling.

Two uniformed soldiers without laces in their boots were sitting in chairs, watching us from the opposite side of the room. I busily photographed Grandfather. Ali asked if I wanted tea. I shook my head. The box-type air conditioner quit working because the electricity stopped. Windows and doors were thrown open to let in air, but only heat and dust entered.

I asked to use the toilet. A hotel clerk said, "Room 104," and handed me the key. It was the same room I had stayed in after the camel journey. The towel from two weeks ago hung on the bathroom door hook where I had left it. My abandoned, ragged tunic crumpled in the pink plastic trash basket, looking sadly forlorn.

Returning the key to the desk clerk, I saw a portrait of Ali Abdullah Saleh, Yemen's president who came to power in 1978, in a gold frame on the wall.

The clerk took the key from me and placed it in a cubbyhole. When he glanced up, his eyes widened. I turned to see what was wrong.

Standing in the lobby entrance were a dozen armed soldiers. The leader shouted at Kamal, "Stop! You don't have permission to interview Bedouin." He ordered Mohammed and Talib out of the hotel at gunpoint, rifles trained on their backs. I looked around for Grandfather Abdullah, but he had disappeared.

Kamal asked for the man's name and extended his hand. "Abdullah Shaykh," he answered but did not shake Kamal's hand. Calmly Kamal explained he had escorted me to Marib so that I could to walk the desert with Mohammed and Talib and write an article to encourage tourism in Yemen. He was to collect chants for a cultural project before poems disappeared. Abdullah Shaykh's expressionless eyes stared at Kamal, but he did not allow him to complete his next sentence. "You can't trust Bedouin," he yelled.

"I've spent time in the desert with Mohammed and Talib," I said to Abdullah Shaykh, whom I was sure understood English. "They're trustworthy men, I trust them."

"Your passport," he ordered, holding out his hand.

"It is in Sana'a," I replied. "I needed a visa extension to stay in Yemen. Here are photocopies of my passport and Yemeni visa. The dates are still good."

"Where is the original visa?" he asked, his strong, chiseled features turning the color of stone.

"It's stamped in my passport, which is at the Public Security Office in Sana'a, getting a visa extension so I can stay in your country," I replied.

The soldiers wearing boots without laces slouched in chairs, busily chewing qat until Abdullah Shaykh slapped the backs of their chairs and ordered them to accompany us—in our car—to al-Jawf turnoff. "Get in the car now," he yelled in Arabic. The two soldiers, cheeks bulging, jumped to attention.

"I'm not leaving until I know Mohammed and Talib are okay," I said to Kamal. "What happened to Grandfather Abdullah?"

"They'll be fine," Kamal answered, opening Ali's car door. "They know Marib better than we do."

"I didn't get to say good-bye."

"It wasn't meant to be," Kamal replied.

Driving to Sana'a, Kamal told Ali to stop the car when we reached the sand dunes that marched toward Saudi Arabia. The unwilling soldiers got out of the car and followed me up and over the dunes. Sinking with each step, they stopped to empty sand from their boots. We did not get far, but I did get to walk the desert.

PART III

BACK TO YEMEN

9

An Unmarked Path

I see my path, but I don't know where it leads.
Not knowing where I'm going is what inspires me to travel it.
—Rosalia De Castro

Just before leaving Sana'a, I made an appointment to meet with the American ambassador to Yemen, who was sympathetic to my idea of teaching English in Marib. The U.S. Embassy in Sana'a—with fortified sandbagged defense points, Yemeni military armed guards, iron gates, metal detection machines, and U.S. Marines—appeared impenetrable. But appearances can be misleading.

Standing outside the embassy, I showed a Yemeni guard my passport. Inside, a female clerk checked my name on the clipboard to make sure I had an appointment. After the metal detector and body search was completed, I sat in a waiting room with barred windows until my name was called. I clipped a plastic badge to my cloak, and a guard escorted me to the public affairs officer's office before meeting the ambassador.

"Your name came across my desk," the officer greeted me without saying hello. He held a clipboard in his hand; my name was printed in black letters in the rectangular space. "What were you doing in Marib? It's dangerous."

I explained that I had ridden a camel across the desert. Abdulmalik had mistakenly registered me as a Canadian, and, of course, the embassy would not know about the camel crossing.

"We have no mention of that," he replied, studying my face. "It's serious. The Yemeni police filed a report, and why didn't you have your passport?"

It was looking darker by the moment, but he would not stop talking so I could explain. "You have freedom to travel in taxis and do whatever you want in Sana'a," he said between his clenched teeth. "I can't even leave the embassy grounds without armed guards. What were you thinking? Yemen's not safe. . . . "

Fortunately, an aide knocked on the door. "The ambassador can see you," he said. I thanked the officer and followed the aide down a long, linoleum-tiled corridor.

The ambassador's western-style waiting room was decorated fashionably, and a female secretary seated behind one of the two large wooden desks in the reception area said, "Go on in," in a warm American way and gestured with a wave of her hand toward an open door. "He's expecting you."

After the encounter with the public affairs officer, I was not sure what to expect from the ambassador, but he greeted me kindly and asked what I wanted to drink. Seated on a beige-and-green nubby-plaid sofa, I folded my hands in my lap.

The ambassador sat in a high-backed wooden chair opposite me. Reaching for the telephone, he ordered tea for me and water for himself. His goal, he explained, was to promote a positive view of America in the region. Neither of us acknowledged the credibility lost under the Bush administration, especially the president's teenager-like response in declaring "war against terror" and bombing Afghanistan, which played right into the hands of the people who disliked America and now made America unpopular throughout the world. Perhaps the ambassador wanted to counter the growing anger toward the war in Iraq and quiet the ongoing debates regarding the assassinations of Yemenis carried out by the CIA's unmanned Predator drones on Yemen's soil. But none of these topics were mentioned.

We discussed a safer subject: the qamariya, or half-moon—signs visually marking America's economic aid in Yemen. The signs resembled the colorful, traditional fan-shaped windows found in north Yemeni tower-houses. Writing on the signs was in Arabic and English, announcing, and thus advertising, U.S. projects. However, Yemenis living in desert regions as a rule could not read, and when they could read, they shot the signs full of bullet holes.

While we discussed the idea of my teaching English in Marib, the ambassador leaned over and pressed a button on the speakerphone, and shortly afterward, his assistant joined us. "We've spent millions of dollars building the President's Hospital in Marib. It would look good to have an English teacher working with doctors," he said to his assistant, and she nodded her agreement.

"Stay in touch with my assistant and work out the details," he said, turning to me. "Teaching English in Marib is a good idea." His assistant gave me her business card. She excused herself and left the office.

While saying good-bye to the ambassador, he expressed interest in my camel journey, asking questions about how to arrange a crossing. He wished someday to do the same, but he would not be able to do so for a long time—maybe ever. He asked for the names and telephone numbers of the Bedouin, but I could only give him names. Outside his office, he introduced me to his wife, who waited on the lime-green sofa. I shook her hand and said good-bye.

A sinking feeling settled in the pit of my stomach, as if I had swallowed chunks of lead as I walked the long corridor to the exit. I had not mentioned the camel journey to the ambassador, which meant the public affairs officer must have informed him. Neither of them had known about the camel trip until today because I was "Canadian." Both knew I had been in Marib without my passport and sent back to Sana'a by the Yemeni police. My excuse of being in Marib to walk the desert with the Bedouin seemed flimsy, even to me. I had foolishly volunteered names.

A week later at the airport, I lined up at the immigration counter to exit Yemen and handed the official in a booth my passport, pink departure card, and boarding pass. He asked me to stand to the side but did not return my documents. Two uniformed men escorted me to a room. "You don't have an exit visa," a man seated behind the desk informed me.

"Yes, it's stamped in my passport," I replied. Since my passport was on the desk, I picked it up and turned to the page.

"This is not an exit visa," he said. "You have a one month visa extension."

"Well, I asked for an exit visa," I answered.

"Does your company know you are leaving Yemen?" he asked. Suspicion clouded his dark face. "Did they give you permission?"

"I don't work in Yemen," I answered, feeling suddenly panicked. "I work in Hawaii."

"Can you prove that?" he asked. I could not. Finally, I showed him my Hawaiian driver's license, and he let me go with a lecture about exit visas and waived the fine.

Back in Hawaii, I taught fall and spring semesters, all the while communicating with staff at the embassy in Sana'a by e-mail. My run-in with the Yemeni police was hopefully forgotten. In early May I received a telephone call from the public affairs officer. He would send employment forms, and I was to submit them via fax. The semester was ending, and even though I was busy with finals and grades, I packed for Yemen. My colleagues cautioned that the university would not take me back if I quit. "The universe will take care of me," I reminded them. My dream was coming true. So true to my word, I quit my job.

10

JOURNEY TO MARIB

It is only in adventure that some people succeed in knowing themselves—in finding themselves.
—ANDRE GIDE

In June 2004 I traveled to Yemen with boxes of textbooks and hopes of making a difference. In Sana'a I was told there were no funds for teaching in Marib. The ambassador took me aside. "I personally support the project," he whispered and gave me a pat on the back and the telephone number of an American woman running a health project. She would return from meetings in Washington, D.C., the following week. Until then I could call Dr. Ahmed, who worked for the embassy, if I had any questions.

The chief-of-party, Cheri, a petite, blonde woman, had a million more important things to do than waste her time with me. "We'll pay $15.00 an hour," she said.

"That's all?" I asked and looked to Dr. Ahmed, who had accompanied me to the meeting, hoping he could lend support. He did not make eye contact and stared at the carpet.

"If we hired a Yemeni teacher for the Marib Health Department, that's what we'd pay," she said, turning to her computer.

"But I'm not Yemeni," I said to the back of her head.

"That's my offer," she replied. "Take it or leave it."

After quickly working out the numbers, I figured that I would make $180.00 a week for twelve hours work, and since I was in already in Yemen, it was a way to get to Marib. "Okay," I said, "as long as I can volunteer to teach English to Bedouin."

"Do whatever you want on your own time," she said, glancing at her watch.

"Can you help with the Yemeni residence permit?" I asked.

"No," she said without hesitation. "You're not an employee or contractor—you're a purchase order." A purchase order!

Dr. Ahmed walked me back to the embassy, which was across the street from Cheri's office, to see if he could help with a residence permit to stay in Yemen. Since it was not possible, I asked Dr. Chris Edens, the director at AIYS, for help.

The following week, Cheri, her assistants, and the "purchase order" visited Marib to meet with officials. Our military escort consisted of three Toyota pickup trucks; two were crammed with armed military personnel, and a third truck followed our bulletproof car (driven by Mohammed Hani, Cheri's driver) with soldiers and a heavy-caliber machine gun mounted on a tripod.

A Yemeni assistant, working for Cheri, rode with us in the backseat and asked the driver to stop at a qat market outside Sana'a. Cheri unwrapped a bundle of Yemeni rials and gave them to the assistant. Protection was expensive. He bought qat for himself and the soldiers in the military escort. The qat loosened the assistant's tongue, and he went on about how nothing good had happened in Islam since the first years after its founding. "We should return to the pure Islam before it was corrupted by *kafirs*, infidels," he said. "Islam must embrace the teachings of the Koran." After two hours, the qat had the opposite effect, and he became quiet.

Marib's governor was away on business so the deputy governor, who disliked America's war in Iraq and perhaps Americans as well, was not enthusiastic about our visit. His ranting about American imperialism was so clear that translating it to English was unnecessary. When the meeting ended, he turned to me, wiping spittle from his lips. "I'd like to study English with you," he said, his smile revealing a mouthful of straight white teeth.

Dr. Mustafa, director of the Health Department in Marib, was waiting for us in the hallway wearing a morning glory purple–colored shirt with shiny brown trousers and a wide black leather belt laced through all but one of the belt loops. Attached to the belt on its right side was a handgun covered with a sheet of turquoise-green plastic. A dark mole on his clean-shaven, unlined face moved up and down when he smiled.

We followed his slouched, rounded shoulders down the hall. His pistol caught on the half-opened door, and his bodyguard unhooked it from the door's frame. Four armed bodyguards with AK-47s stood behind Dr. Mustafa, who sat opposite Cheri at the conference table. Welcome bottles of cold water and orange Fanta appeared. With the help of translators, the meeting began.

After a three-hour ride from Sana'a, I asked to use the bathroom. "Sorry, we don't have a bathroom for women," the translator apologized. He then spoke with someone standing outside the door.

Two armed guards walked with me up a flight of stairs. I followed them into a room of leather-faced desert-men clad in long thobes with bullet-filled bandoleers strapped over their chests. Faded red-and-white checked scarves tied into turbans covered unruly hair. Their dusty bodyguards dressed in similar fashion stood behind the shaykhs and grabbed rifles when we entered.

One of my escorts spoke to the unsmiling deputy governor, who sat behind a large wooden desk and, without speaking, raised his outstretched finger, pointing to a door at the back of the room. Eyes straight ahead, I crossed the room. Surely once, I would have felt terrified in a roomful of wild-looking tribesmen, but after traveling the desert, I guessed these seemingly violent armed men kissed camels, too.

After Cheri and Dr. Mustafa's meeting ended, we walked to the still-under-construction Health Department building where I would teach. We crossed a towering heap of sand mixed with broken bits of building materials. My sandaled feet disappeared. We waited for Dr. Mustafa to locate the key as the sun made the tops of our heads feel like they were smoldering. No key, so we climbed on broken pieces of cement and peered through dirty windows. We stared into a large, empty, uninviting concrete room. "Is this the classroom?" I asked, assuming it was, but no one answered. Cheri was absorbed in a discussion because she had just found out it was her responsibility to supply the empty building with office and classroom furniture.

We returned to the scorching heat of the car, and the director told the driver to take us to the newly built but still incomplete Health Institute, a place where I could live while teaching in Marib. The director stressed that I would not need to pay for the accommodation. Built with German money, the institute would eventually house female nursing students. Someone banged on the metal gate, and it creaked open. We stepped into what looked like a rock-strewn prison yard.

My face could not hide the disappointment. "No problem," the health director said. "You won't have to walk. There's a van to take you to and from the classroom."

"It's not that. . . . I like—love to walk," I protested. "What about shopping?"

"You can ask the driver to buy whatever you need. Women stay home. They do not go out. Men take care of everything in Marib."

We followed Dr. Mustafa up flights of stairs and glanced into a small room with a bed but no desk. There was a window but no screen in this malaria-infested area. A communal bathroom had showers and toilets but no doors. Downstairs in the kitchen on the first floor, a group of young nursing students grabbed my hands, jumping up and down and squealing about how happy they were that we would be living together. "Is there something else?" I asked.

We bumped along a deeply rutted, unpaved road in town and parked in front of a crumbling concrete building. The first floor consisted of a pharmacy, paint store, electrical shop, and barbershop. A flight of cracked concrete stairs led to a third floor flat. We stepped over torn plastic bags and bits of garbage. "Who has the key?" the director asked.

Loud music and women's laughter came from the flat below. The men suggested that Cheri and I knock, and the door half-opened, and hands yanked us inside. Kisses from old and young women dressed in gaily colored prom gowns with low-cut bodices and gathered skirts. Jet-black arched brows. Red-painted mouths. Turquoise-colored eyelids. Hair—mostly flowing—hennaed from auburn to orange-brown.

It was impossible to see the layout of the flat because so many women claimed our attention. A woman handed us fruit punch in chipped glasses. Women seated on mattresses that lined the walls tugged at our clothes. "Sit," painted lips said in Arabic.

Saying good-bye to a roomful of women—who were now disappointed because we weren't staying at the party—takes time, and by then someone had found the key to the empty upstairs flat. Broken windows, no screens, a kitchen dripping grease, smashed tiles in the bathroom, and a broken sink. I had visions of women visiting me at all hours. "Isn't there something else?" I asked.

There evidently was not, because we went to lunch at the Bilquis Hotel. After lunch, on the return trip to Sana'a, I heard more than once that the flat had potential. "Don't be so picky. . . . When I was in the Peace Corps . . . "

When in doubt, I called Kamal, my Yemeni "family." Although he thought my idea of teaching in Marib was crazy, he never said so to my face. Kamal telephoned Dr. Mustafa. "The health director is guaranteeing your life," Kamal explained when he returned my call. "You can't live just anywhere. . . . Marib is dangerous. . . . You're an American."

The following week, I returned to Marib with Kamal, who never wanted to visit Marib in the first place. A year later, he sat with me in the blistering shade of a blue-and-white striped umbrella at the Bilquis Hotel discussing my fate in Arabic with Hisham, the hotel's assistant manager.

The American ambassador, who had compared me to John the Baptist (either "the voice crying in the wilderness" or "head on a platter"), suggested that I live at the President's Hospital, but the unfinished apartments would not be completed by mid-July.

The hotel seemed the best option. I sipped my iced lime drink.

A tiny room and attached bathroom in the one-story hotel annex that housed less-affluent guests—usually budget travelers and tour drivers—would cost an outrageous $350.00, nearly half my monthly income. I did not ask the price of a room in the main hotel. "You'll be staying for two years," Hisham added. "Inshallah," I answered. Kamal rolled his eyes.

While Kamal and I looked at rooms in the annex, two hotel workers coated the red brick walkway with thick black reused motor oil. The fumes danced in the air, stinging our eyes. "Does it really keep snakes and scorpions away?" I asked Hisham.

Mine was a corner room, Number 408, its window overlooking an unkempt patch of dried ground with yellow grass that waved lazily in the dry heat. The selling point was the room's taupe wall-to-wall carpet had the fewest stains.

"Do you really want to do this?" Kamal asked. I nodded. Traditionally, in Yemen, women belong to a tribe—a clan or family, which protects them. Later that day, Kamal literally handed me to Dr. Mustafa. They shook hands.

The following week, Mohammed Hani drove me to Marib to give placement examinations to the Health Department staff. Oral examinations were first. Potential students pushed and shoved to get into the conference room, but there were too few chairs—men remained standing. Three armed guards wearing military uniforms secured the door. Mazen, a health department employee, introduced himself and volunteered his help, and he fortunately spoke some English.

"What is your name?" I asked the first man. He stared. "Please tell me your name," I repeated slowly. No answer. I waited. Mazen asked the man his name in Arabic. Only a few men could tell me their names or answer simple questions in English.

"Where are the women?" I asked. "Surely, there must be female nurses and midwives who want to study English."

"They would not be in the same room with men," a man sitting at the table answered while the other men nodded their agreement.

"Well, I'm a woman, and I don't want to be alone with men," I said. After a short discussion among the men and a phone call, three veiled women entered the room.

"Please sit down," I said to the women. They sat and answered the questions.

Returning to Sana'a, I asked Mohammed, "Do you think this is the first time that men and women will study together in Marib?"

"Yes," he replied laughing. "No one will believe it!"

11

LANDING HEAD FIRST

*Sometimes you have to jump off cliffs and build
your wings on the way down.*
—RAY BRADBURY

In Sana'a, I bought a made-in-China electric hot plate and a stainless steel teakettle, along with a knife and peeler for fruit and vegetables—I am not a cook, but I could prepare simple meals without a kitchen. One cup, one plate, one bowl—I did not need much. With tea, sugar, salt, pepper, peanut butter, cans of tuna, and a package of crackers, I could manage.

At the National Gallery in the old city, I purchased two black-and-white prints and had them framed. At the frame shop, I bought a mirror. Two Persian rugs to cover the carpet stains, one small, one medium-sized. Three potted plants. One table lamp with a Chinese scene painted on its base and a white lampshade.

Mohammed Hani was busy and could not drive me to Marib, so I hired a car and driver to take me. Abdullah, the driver, placed the framed prints and mirror on the passenger seat next to him, "They'll be safe here," he assured me. Shakeeb, an AIYS gate guard, and three workers digging up pipes in the street loaded my boxes of books and possessions in the back of the Land Cruiser. I sat in the back seat and closed the door. Abdullah started the engine and backed slowly out of the narrow driveway, avoiding the gaping hole in the street. He made a U-turn, and I waved goodbye to life in Sana'a.

"Why is such a beautiful woman going in Marib?" he said, leering into the rearview mirror. We were off to a bad start. "You'll be back in less than a month," he said and took a business card from his wallet and passed it to me. "Call when you're ready to return to Sana'a."

At the first checkpoint, soldiers asked for traveling documents. Abdullah handed them the required photocopied pages. Westerners travel with armed military escorts in caravans. My face was uncovered. The military guards waved the car through. "What did you tell them?" I asked.

"Russian," Abdullah answered in a high-pitched giggle.

We passed vegetable and fruit stands on the sides of the narrow road, which was paved with a solidified layer of discarded plastic bags. Bags carried on the wind lodged in bushes and stunted trees appeared at first glance to be dusty, sagging pieces of fruit. Further along the road were green and purple grapes, real fruit clustered on wire trellises made of old bedsprings propped up on sticks. In the past, Yemeni Jews turned grapes into wine in basements of houses. A few Yemenis, mostly non-Jews, carried on the tradition of wine making, but the majority of the grape harvest is dried and sold as raisins. We drove by a roadside stand selling handmade terra cotta pots, and I asked Abdullah to stop, but he said it was too dangerous and continued.

An hour outside of Sana'a, we came to a large qat market, and Abdullah stopped the car— it seemed that it was no longer dangerous. There were boys—less than ten years old—selling plastic bags of qat. Men and boys haggled over prices as hands reached into bags examining leaves. I watched men burn holes in plastic bags with lit cigarettes so the leaves could breathe. Others emptied the leaves into wet shawls, keeping them fresh for later. Long bundles of qat were carried proudly by men on their way to qat chews. A tense frenzy surrounded the qat market even though qat is legal in Yemen. Abdullah returned with his "bag" and two bottles of water, ready for the journey.

"Why don't you chew qat?" he asked, caressing a leaf before stuffing it into his mouth.

"High blood pressure and drugs don't mix," I said, giving him my simple answer. Lecturing him about the harmful effects of illegal pesticides sprayed on qat plants causing cancer did not seem appropriate. Eighty percent of the illegal pesticides smuggled into Yemen and used by farmers who often cannot read labels are sprayed on qat plants.

Abdullah turned in his seat and faced me. "Qat's not a drug," he said, shaking his head and starting the engine. When his cheek began to bulge, he began to talk. "You should try qat."

"I've tried it," I said, but Abdullah did not listen.

"My wife and I chew every weekend. It makes sex better," Abdullah persisted. "Are you married?" Before I could answer, a loud crack, which sounded like a gunshot, got his attention. The car limped to a halt.

In the sweltering heat of the mid-July desert, he located the tire-changing tools, wrenched loose the flat tire, and replaced it with a spare—which had a puncture. We crossed a considerable section of the desert, stopping every few miles so that Abdullah could pump air into the tire with a hand pump.

At the al-Jawf turnoff, he stopped, and a mechanic repaired the spare. Boys with dark skin and kinky hair stared through the rolled-up windows, pressing runny noses and fingertips against the glass. I wrapped my scarf so it covered my hair and face.

Unfortunately, the patch did not stick. We hobbled to Marib. In Marib I asked Abdullah to stop at a market and buy a case of bottled water before we reached the hotel. Irritated by my additional request, he grumbled but stopped at a small open-air shop. I gave him six hundred rials, and he paid the clerk, who plopped the twenty-bottle case of water in the front seat on top of my framed prints. The glass shattered.

The Bilquis Hotel entrance looked grand and was protected by two tall crenellated, arched gates separated by a guardhouse. As we waited for the guard to open the massive wooden gates and unlock the metal fence to let us pass, the last hiss of air escaped from the tire. Only one of the arched entrances was used for traffic; the other was blocked.

At the hotel Abdullah apologized for the store clerk smashing my art-work. I collected the wilted plants from the back of the car. Two workers from the hotel carried the rest of my belongings to room 408 in the annex. I had arrived in Marib. Abdullah left to find someone to repair the tire.

With the books on the shelf, rugs over the carpet stains, reviving plants on the desk, and two woven baskets on the floor, the room was officially mine. Luckily, the mirror was not broken. I felt happy unpacking my set of gold-rimmed tea glasses. Drinking hot tea in the summer heat seemed illogical, but it was expected. Serving small glasses of sugary tea is part of hospitality. "Who is it?" I said after hearing a knock at the door.

"Abdullah," the voice replied, and I opened the door. He reminded me to call if I needed anything. "Next time I come to Marib, I'll stop by." We shook hands, and he was gone.

I placed the hot plate on top of the cube-like refrigerator next to the hotel's TV. I opened a bottle of water and poured some into the teakettle then set it on the hot plate. I plugged the hot plate into a three-way electrical outlet. Fireworks! Red and blue sparks shot from the plug. When the water boiled, I used a towel to unplug it.

Pulling the drapes aside, I looked out the window; the dust-colored goats with fat, drooping tails returned my gaze. Beyond the goats, green hedges surrounded the garden and, past that, the main hotel building, which was obscured by trees. Guards in military uniforms walked on the footpath and kicked dust into the hot, dry air. I had nothing to do, so I laid down. At dusk, I walked around the hotel grounds and listened to faraway chants from mosques encouraging the faithful to prayer.

Stepping over mounds of broken earth, I followed the fence line and stumbled over tangled pieces of discarded metal wire. I did not see anyone. An enormous generator roared electricity for the hotel while the rest of Marib slept in darkness. Stars shown overhead, and the crescent moon smiled. I returned to my room.

Falling asleep, I felt lonely. I had forgotten how to be brave. What had I gotten myself into? With that thought, I fell asleep.

PART IV

LIFE IN MARIB

12

AWAKING IN MARIB

When I let go of what I am, I become what I might be.
When I let go of what I have, I receive what I need.
—LAO TZU

The next morning someone trashed plastic bottles by stomping on them—
one by one—on the brick walkway outside my window. Stomp . . . stomp . . .
stomp. In Marib, I had no need for an alarm clock.

Again, red and blue sparks shot from the electrical plug when I plugged
in the hot plate to boil water. After a breakfast of tea and crackers, I pushed
the drapes aside. A man dressed in a rumpled military uniform carried what
looked like a wad of clothes as he walked on a dirt path. "He must be one of
the soldiers guarding the hotel gate," I thought. Then I heard a door slam and
footsteps crunching loose gravel on the path. I shut the drapes. Hisham, the
assistant hotel manager, told me he lived in the annex and never missed *The
Oprah Winfrey Show* on television.

I spent the next hour hand-sewing a curtain from gauzy material purchased in Sana'a and attaching it to a string above the window opening held
in place by two nails. Now, I could open the brown drapes and look outside
without anyone looking in. It dawned on me that I had nothing to eat except
the tuna, peanut butter, and a package of crackers. No one had checked on
me. By afternoon, I had eaten all the crackers. "I'll walk to the market to buy
bread and yogurt when it cools," I thought and laid on the bed. After a nap,
I remembered it was Friday—the holy day—and maybe the markets would be
closed.

I did not feel like writing in my journal—there was nothing to say. So I ab-
sentmindedly flipped through pages of a *Self* magazine. I stared out the window.

The next morning was Saturday, the first business day in the Yemeni week.

I woke up hungry and decided to walk to the market after drinking a cup of tea and making a shopping list.

Wearing my baltu and tying a black scarf around my hair, I walked the tree-lined dirt path through dappled sunlight to the hotel gate. The military guard, upon seeing me, grabbed his rifle, and two uniformed men ran after me as I stepped outside the gate. One guard pulled my arm, and two guards yelled words I did not understand. "I'm hungry and want to go to the market," I explained in jumbled Arabic. "Please."

An unsmiling soldier—the one I had seen with wadded clothes—shouldered his rifle and went inside the guardhouse and returned with two round loaves of *kidam*, Turkish wheat bread, the recipe brought to Yemen by the Turkish army when they invaded the country long ago. The bread is still baked daily and distributed to the Yemeni army.

In Sana'a, I bought kidam from a bakery with an ancient beehive-shaped brick oven located in the old city. Now a soldier at the guardhouse handed me the dense brown loaves and pointed to the annex. I followed his finger and retraced my steps. In Marib it was only a short walk for bread, but it was not nearly as friendly as in Sana'a.

In the afternoon, I would teach, but no one explained how I would get to class. Clearly, I could not walk. At noon, a phone call came from a man who introduced himself in English as Abdullah Shaykh. He would be my driver. "Class begins at four o'clock," I said. "I should be there early. Please come at 3:30 p.m."

In the blistering shade of a flowering acacia tree I waited by the annex holding a cassette player in one hand and books in the other at 3:30. The driver arrived at ten minutes after four behind the wheel of an old blue and gray Land Cruiser. I opened the rear door and sat in the backseat. He looked as though he had just woken from a nap, his light-colored hair sticking out of a haphazardly tied turban, but he did not apologize for arriving late.

The governor's compound—where the Health Department was located, surrounded by high walls and military guards on constant patrol—was five minutes by car. Sentries at the gate stood at attention and saluted the driver when his car entered the compound, although he was not dressed in military uniform. Then I remembered where I had seen him. We had met in Marib the previous summer—he was the rude police official who had forced Kamal and me to return to Sana'a with a military escort. I wanted to call Kamal, but it was not the right time.

Now I wondered if he remembered me, but it was a year ago, and I was not wearing a black baltu or headscarf. Abdullah Shaykh was a disturbing man, so it was best to keep away from him. I hoped he had not remembered me.

Keeping my eyes lowered, I thanked him and opened the rear door and stepped into soft, powdery sand. Stamping my sandaled feet on the walkway, I climbed the concrete steps to the health department building. Omar, the building caretaker, wore a green plaid shirt, brown-patterned futa, and a red-and-white checked turban wound around his head. He also had a big wad of qat stuffed in his protruding cheek. He welcomed me and unlocked the classroom door.

In mid-July, the temperature inside the classroom was well over one hundred degrees. When I opened the windows, sand blew in and settled on the conference room table and floor. Students, like the sand, drifted in over the next thirty minutes—male students sat in front, and the three black veiled females sat at the end of the conference table in back. The overhead fans swirled hot air until the electricity stopped. I opened and closed the windows a dozen times.

"Take out paper and pens," I instructed. "Open your books to page one." Only the female students and Mazen followed directions. I asked Mazen to translate my words to Arabic.

"Please write your name at the top of the paper," I said. Names appeared in strange places. A few wrote across the middle of the page. Others wrote at the bottom. Some wrote nothing.

"Please write the numbers from one to ten," I said slowly. Mazen translated. This everyone could do, but some of the numbers were extremely large, covering half the page. They had not planned.

The students copied ABCs from the textbook. For most, an easy assignment, but several took the rest of the class period. During class, the students were to write their names, staying within the lines. Although I could not see the women's expressions behind veils, I knew they were probably bored.

The electricity went off and on, the cassette player useless. As the call to prayer sounded, the electricity went off again. A faint, faraway voice chanted from the mosque. Using cell phones as lights, the male students returned from praying thirty minutes later. By then it was so dark that the homework assignment on the board was unreadable. "Good night," I said.

When Abdullah Shaykh arrived, I asked if he would drive to a market before returning to the hotel. I opened the back door of the car. "Sit in front," he ordered in Arabic and watched my reaction. I sat next to him in the passenger's seat. At a small market, I bought flat bread, jam, yogurt, Pepsi, and cookies. We did not speak as he drove to the hotel annex, and I still did not know if he remembered me.

Inside my room, I opened the package of cookies. "Tomorrow, I will buy fruit and vegetables," I thought, eating the last cookie in the package, "but how will I get to the suq (market). Just then my phone rang. It was Dr. Mustafa wanting to know how the first day of class went.

"Okay," I said. "But I don't want a driver. I would rather walk."

"Walking!" he exclaimed. "No one walks in Marib!"

13

FOLLOWING MOHAMMED

There are some things you learn best in calm, and some in storm.
—WILLA CATHER

While seated on a bench in front of the guardhouse with some of the off-duty hotel staff outside the entrance to the Bilquis Hotel, I first met Mohammed. He was dressed in a green camouflage military uniform and sat down on the bench next to me and positioned his automatic rifle against his thigh, barrel pointed skyward. We exchanged greetings in Arabic. Silently, I went back to staring into the starry night sky.

Deep in thought, I wondered how I could possibly stay in Marib for six months. Six days seemed like a lifetime. Without Abdullah Shaykh's permission, I could not get out of the hotel gate. He was everywhere, sneaking up on me and speaking Arabic, hoping to catch me and apparently thinking I only pretended not to understand the language. He controlled my life.

When Mohammed stood to leave, he asked the typical and dutiful Yemeni question in Arabic, "Any service?"

"Yes," I answered. "I'd like to walk."

"Where to?" he asked.

"There," I said, pointing to the flickering lights of Marib. Mohammed slung the canvas strap of his Kalashnikov over his shoulder and motioned for me to follow. I followed him along a black ribbon of a road leading away from the hotel out of "prison," scarcely feeling the ground beneath my feet. The hotel workers came with us, and together we sat on broken pieces of concrete outside a small shop near the hotel, drinking sodas. "Thank you," I said to Mohammed a dozen times that night. "Thank you!"

In all my life, I never knew a person's back as well as I came to know Mohammed's. I followed him everywhere. Although I am an American, in Yemen I walked behind a man. The subtle shift of Mohammed's gait and slight limp, throwing out one leg stiffly, became so familiar that I could tell if something was bothering him. I watched the blue-and-white vertical stripes on his shirt shift positions as we traveled the road to and from Marib or walked on desert tracks. The flutter of his plaid futa made swishing sounds, rubbing against the backs of his muscular sun-browned legs. I worried about the Kalashnikov, which Mohammed slung over his shoulder, its barrel pointed at the ground. If the gun accidentally fired, would bullets hit his sandaled feet? I watched deep cracks on his calloused heels, like well-worn maps leading the way. I followed.

Strands of black, close-cropped hair curled tightly at the nape of his thick neck. Mohammed's prominent nose resembled those on aristocratic statues or ancient coins. The size of his head matched the bulk of his ample body. His dark, thickly lashed eyes could signal coldness or warmth. They changed abruptly. When walking in intense sunlight, he plopped his black-and-white checked scarf on top of his head and let the ends dangle. When sandstorms changed day into night, he pulled the scarf around his head, covering his nose and mouth and leaving only a slit for his eyes. Once I saw Mohammed twist the scarf and tie it like a headband. But never, in all the time I knew him, did he fashion his scarf in a neatly wrapped turban like other Yemenis.

Mohammed eventually became my *murafik*, Arabic for a companion or bodyguard, although he sometimes seemed like a jailer and was likely a spy. Mohammed was the "key" to getting outside the gate.

14

NO ONE WALKS IN MARIB

A journey brings us face to face with ourselves.
—UNKNOWN

The next morning, I dialed Dr. Mustafa's telephone number, and he finally answered. "Last night, I met Mohammed, a soldier. He works as a guard. Please let me hire a taxi for shopping and going to the Internet shop," I pleaded. "I'm sure he'll escort me. I'll pay whatever it costs."

"Where are you?" he asked.

"At the hotel," I answered, thinking, "Where else could I possibly be?"

"Yes, thank you," he replied. "He will come now." Twenty minutes later, Dr. Mustafa met me in the hotel lobby. "You can go anywhere in Marib—to the dam or sites. It is safe."

Dr. Mustafa would not think of stepping outside his well-guarded office or driving in Marib without protection. Even at the hotel, six armed men guarded him—one at each door and two seated on the sofa. Who was he kidding about Marib being safe?

"If it's so safe, tell Abdullah Shaykh to let me out the gate," I said.

"You will call Abdullah Shaykh and tell him," he replied, his index finger pointed to his chest. I pointed to myself. He shook his head. "Yes, you will call," he replied. He meant he would call. The health director was forever getting "you" and "I" mixed up. He turned on his heel and marched to the front desk to use the telephone. During the conversation, he told Abdullah Shaykh that I was on my own, but of course, that was not true.

Late that afternoon, I answered a knock at my door. "Who's there?" I asked.

"Cheri's driver, Mohammed Hani," a voice replied. "Cheri sent cheese." Opening the door, Mohammed Hani handed me two packages of cheddar—she remembered. There is no cheese in Marib. Cheri wanted to send a bottle of wine, but of course, Mohammed Hani could not deliver alcohol. Getting caught with wine would mean a long jail sentence. "The next time foreigners come, they'll bring the wine," he added.

"Thanks for the cheese. I couldn't open the wine anyway. I don't have a corkscrew."

"Do you need to go anywhere?" he asked. Thinking of many more places than Marib, I nodded. He waited in the car while I dressed in my black baltu and wrapped the hijab around my head, winding it under my chin and fastening it with a pearl-headed straight pin. Glancing in the mirror, I looked modest.

Mohammed Hani drove the bulletproof car along the rutted road to the hotel's arched gate, and two military guards dressed in uniform with automatic rifles got in back. "Is Mohammed working?" I asked the soldiers. They shrugged their shoulders.

We traveled on the paved road to Marib, and in less than ten minutes, we walked in the open-air suq. Shabby stalls made of reused pieces of wood leaned against each other like a house of cards. Thin, dirt-colored chickens cackled helplessly, trapped in tiny yellow plastic cages. Potatoes caked with hardened mud were stacked in blue plastic tubs—a half-kilo of potatoes and a half-kilo of dirt. Bright red tomatoes, skins peeling in blistering sun. Wilted cucumbers slumped on makeshift tables. The lettuce and greens had also seen better days.

A rusted white Toyota truck weighted down with boxes of arrowhead-shaped mangos cut the corner, spraying clouds of dust. "I'm sorry," the driver apologized in English, and he began unloading boxes of fruit. "Welcome to Marib," he said, looking up and smiling.

"Thanks," I said, happy to meet someone who spoke English.

"I lived in Saudi Arabia," he replied, "until the first Gulf War." I knew that Yemenis who worked in Saudi Arabia and Kuwait were forced to leave abruptly because Yemen's government, seated on the Security Council, voted against the American invasion of Iraq. Saudi and Kuwaiti governments influenced by America expelled approximately one million Yemeni workers overnight. Working abroad, Yemenis had sent money home to families, and after they returned to Yemen, the population exploded, unemployment increased, and the economy crumbled.

Before he asked another question, Mohammed Hani signaled concern with his eyes and led me to a stand with small, misshapen, red-and-green striped Yemeni apples. I bought a half-kilo. Yemeni women would not speak above a whisper on the street—what was I doing holding a conversation with an unknown man? Another minute and I would have volunteered my nationality.

Mohammed Hani and I walked around the suq. Although friendly merchants tried to make conversation, I stopped being so friendly. Misunderstandings are bound to occur when people from different cultures meet, especially in a conservative society like Marib. I did not want to cause trouble or send the wrong message.

Our next stop was the Sabafon office for a phone card. The military guards waited at the door, and Mohammed Hani and I went inside. "What are you doing in Marib?" the cheerful clerk asked, obviously startled to see a woman. I smiled widely, surprised he spoke English.

"I'm teaching English at the Health Department," I answered, forgetting that I might be volunteering too much information.

"Can I be your student?" he asked, grinning. "Lots of people in Marib will pay you to study English."

"Inshallah, God willing, there's plenty of time."

15

ANCIENT MARIB

Life is either a daring adventure or nothing.
—HELEN KELLER

Dr. Mustafa waited for me inside the hotel's reception area, and I followed the traditional three paces behind him. We walked outside to the terrace overlooking the pool, and the waiter brought cups of tea, a bowl of sugar, and one teaspoon on a stainless steel tray. Stirring sugar into my tea, I said, "Abdullah Shaykh frightens me," handing the spoon to Dr. Mustafa. "Does he work for the hotel?"

"Yes, Abdullah Shaykh is not a good one," Dr. Mustafa replied, adding sugar to his tea. "Are students coming to class?" he asked, changing the subject.

"Some men dropped out when they realized they aren't paid to come to class," I said. "They're interested in money—not learning. Others quit when they could not chew qat in class. The two men from Shabwa with long black beards dressed in pure white futas stopped coming. One told me speaking English was against Islam, and the other said it is too far to drive."

"How many attend?" he questioned.

"Usually ten," I answered. "The ones that come to class are making progress."

"How's Ahmed doing?" he asked. Ahmed was his younger brother, who attended class when Dr. Mustafa was not sending him on errands.

"Fine," I replied. "Why is Abdullah Shaykh hanging around the annex? He told the guards it was forbidden for me to leave the gate."

"Abdullah Shaykh works for Political Security," he explained. "He thinks you're a spy."

His directness shocked me. Although it was a perfect opportunity to explain that I had met Abdullah Shaykh the previous July in Marib, I kept silent.

Maybe my acknowledgment would raise more suspicion. "Was he angry that I didn't want him to be my driver?" I asked, feeling my face flush.

"Probably," he said. "He expected to make money. When the American archeological team comes to Marib, they hire him. Americans have lots of money."

If he was convinced that all Americans have deep pockets, I am sure Abdullah Shaykh was disappointed. It is true—compared to Yemenis, more than half of whom lived below the poverty line and struggled to make ends meet—that Americans in Yemen are wealthy.

"Do I have your permission to walk to class with Mohammed, the murafik?" I asked. Although Dr. Mustafa thought walking was a very strange thing to do, he approved, but before saying definitely yes, he would check with General Shamlan, the head of Marib's military. We said good-bye.

A young man at the reception desk asked if I needed any help when I passed. "Yes," I answered. "Washing my jeans in the bathroom sink is difficult. May I use the hotel laundry?"

"Of course," he replied and extended his hand. Daood's kindness was evident from his open smile and firm handshake. His short, wavy black hair, deep-set dark eyes, prominent nose, and well-manicured beard balanced perfectly on his handsome face. Most striking aside from his height was his beautiful skin, the color of dark, polished teak.

"I'll be right back," I said and left to get my Levis.

That afternoon Mohammed waited at the hotel gate to walk me to class because General Shamlan had agreed to my request. We got as far as the small store on the highway, "He's a troublemaker," Mohammed said, looking over his shoulder as Abdullah Shaykh's Land Cruiser stopped on the side of the road, blocking our way.

"Get in!" Abdullah Shaykh ordered. "Mohammed, tell her to get in the car. It's dangerous."

"I'm walking," I said to Mohammed. "Ride if you like." The car sped away, kicking up clouds of dust that covered our clothes with talcum-like powder.

Before class started, I walked around the classroom and noticed that several of the male students had inked cloaks and head coverings on the female figures in our textbook. One had drawn a veil over a female face.

Later, I asked Mohammed why the students felt the need to "dress" the females in the book. "Women have to be modest," he said. "Women shouldn't tempt men." "Women blamed for men's desires," I thought. Then I remembered a saying: "If the parts of sex pleasure be counted as ten, nine parts have women and only one part men." A Greek soothsayer long ago knew this as his "truth," and the notion persists.

"But Mohammed," I said, "the book doesn't show photographs of women. They're stick drawings—not real people." He shrugged his shoulders, as if to say, "You will never understand." We walked the rest of the way without talking.

That evening, Dr. Mustafa called. "Tomorrow, you'll see the old city Marib," he said, "as long as you take the murafik. The car will come in the afternoon."

"What time?" I asked, delighted at the thought of an outing.

"After *Asr*," he replied. Time in Yemen was divided according to daily worship.

Outings are rare in Marib. I invited several of the off-duty hotel staff. At four o'clock, after the mid-afternoon prayer, the driver picked us up at the hotel entrance. Clamoring for the front seat, Hani, Mohammed, and Nasser squeezed next to the driver. Daood, Hamid, and I sat in back. Looming on the horizon, an ominous sandstorm darkened the sky and threatened our plans. Dirt gusted through the air. I prayed it would pass so we could continue.

Hani asked the driver to stop and shielded his eyes from the blowing sand when he got out of the car to buy all of us bottled strawberry sodas and Pik One chocolate bars at a small market—a generous offer, considering that his monthly salary was less than fifty American dollars. Our next stop was a gas station before heading to old Marib.

Squinting into the dust-filled wind, ancient Marib appeared on the horizon. A site of crumbling mud skyscrapers, it sits atop an earthen hill and over the many centuries has grown taller as mud houses melted, building up existing ground. Through the sepia-colored sunlight, the polished mud structures shimmered as we approached. Our car bounded up a rutted road, and the driver drove between mud-brick tower-houses with tiny slit windows. Old Marib looked like an ancient movie set.

"Is there something wrong?" Daood asked. His black eyes searched my covered face. "Why aren't you talking?"

I shook my head. When I wore a veil, I seldom spoke.

"Take off the veil," he said. I untied the veil and slipped it in my bag.

The car traveled rapidly up a dirt incline, and dust billowed like smoke through the open windows. "I'd love to live here," I said, clutching the back of the car seat so my head would not hit the roof.

"Why?" Daood asked.

"Living in a mud tower-house would be great," I replied. He did not answer, just stared with a look of concern.

The sandstorm that threatened to cancel our adventure changed direction. We spent the afternoon searching through abandoned mud skyscrapers, crouching through small doorways, and climbing mud steps to second and third floors, but we dared go no higher. From inside the houses, I saw that the ceilings were made of tightly woven palm fronds forming strong bases, allowing the builders to apply the next layer of mud to form additional floors. In the heat of the desert, the rooms with extra-thick walls were cool. Being inside, I knew why the windows were small—to keep out summer's heat, winter's cold, and the persistent blowing sand.

Dust clung to my sandaled feet, but instead of brushing it away, I thought it might be the same dust stirred by the Queen of Sheba's footsteps. Shadows darkened as the sun dipped behind Marib's mountains. "It's not safe," Mohammed shouted, clearly annoyed because we had wandered off. "Get in the car."

"Sorry," I apologized. "We were just having fun."

16

Beginning to Disappear

Misery and joy have the same shape in the world.
You may call the rose an open heart or broken heart.
—Dard

I plugged my hot plate into the socket the next morning but no red-and-blue fireworks shot from the plug. A cup of tea in the hotel cost $2.50. I decided to splurge. Entering the hotel lobby, I saw Abdulkarim, the gardener, chasing a stumbling black cat. Weaving back and forth, the cat managed to reach the front door before it collapsed. "*Taban*—sick," Abdulkarim said, noticing my worried expression. A worker followed with a plastic bag. I left.

Later that day, I returned to the hotel and spoke with Hisham. "My hot plate is broken. Can someone drive me to Marib?"

"You can't go outside, Abdullah Shaykh's orders," he replied.

"A day without hot tea isn't the end of the world, but almost," I blurted out, wondering if I should call Dr. Mustafa over something so insignificant.

Daood at the reception desk called me over. "I'll get tea," he whispered. Daood returned carrying a styrofoam cup of steaming tea. He placed the cup on the desk and with a spoon twisted the teabag. Using the string, he squeezed out the last drops of liquid and tossed the teabag into the trash can with theatrical flair.

Since no one was in the lobby, Daood suggested that we sit outside on the steps. We exchanged words in Arabic and English. "Do you have a note-book?" I asked. "We'll continue our lesson tomorrow."

Later, I saw Mohammed at the gate. He was dressed in a military uniform and wore a blue beret pushed back on his head. "Where have you been?" I asked, sounding desperate.

"Is something wrong?" he asked.

71

"My hot plate is broken," I answered. My eyes stung with tears from the frustration of not being able to take care of such a simple need.

"I can't leave," he said, looking at his unlaced boots and avoiding my face.

At two o'clock, Mohammed knocked at my door, dressed in his blue-and-white striped shirt and black-and-white patterned futa, his Kalashnikov casually slung over his shoulder. "Are you ready?" he said, keeping his eyes on the ground.

"My scarf," I replied. "One minute." I closed the door and checked in the mirror to make sure my hair was hidden beneath the scarf before I placed the lithma over my face. Dark eyes peered out from behind the mask. Wearing layers of black polyester was hot, but I did not want to draw attention to myself.

Walking to Marib, I carried the broken hot plate in a sack, the soles of my black leather sandals making sucking sounds and sticking to the melting asphalt. We passed a small grocery store "Let's get a drink," I suggested. Taking a sip of the Pepsi, I forgot to lift the veil, and fizzy brown liquid poured down the black fabric. The shopkeeper saw but pretended not to notice. Mohammed downed his Pepsi, looking around anxiously, as if someone might suddenly burst through the door and start shooting.

"Why are you so nervous?" I asked.

"Marib is dangerous," he replied. His eyes darted from the door to the windows.

"It doesn't seem dangerous," I laughed.

"That's because I'm protecting you," he said. "Without me, you'd be dead."

I wondered if Marib was really so dangerous, or if people exaggerated.

"How much does the military pay?" I asked. He said that he made seven thousand rials (less than forty U.S. dollars) a month.

"I'll pay you one hundred dollars a month," I said. "A small price for freedom," I thought.

"I'd protect you for nothing," he replied. "I like you."

Near the suq, we found a store that sold electrical appliances. Mohammed placed the broken hot plate on the counter. The store clerk brought a new hot plate in an unopened brown cardboard box. "Plug it in," Mohammed ordered. He plugged it in, and the electric coils glowed orange.

While we waited for the hot plate to cool, I noticed a woman on the street, her short blonde hair uncovered. "Who is she?" I asked, my eyes wide.

"A Russian doctor," Mohammed said, staring at her. "She works at the military hospital."

"Where's her bodyguard?" I asked, even more surprised, if that were possible.

"She's Russian," he said a little too loud, as if that explained it.

"Well, I want to be Russian," I answered. Mohammed's lips tightened, forming a straight line and signaling that he did not think my comment was funny.

I was surprised that the clerk exchanged my hot plate, even though I had not purchased it from his store. Mohammed said I was lucky because the clerk would not do that for a Yemeni or a Russian.

While we were in downtown Marib, I wanted to check if the Internet café was open. "Ahmed drove me to the Internet café last week," I said to Mohammed.

At first, he looked as if he did not understand what I had said. "You don't have to worry with Ahmed," he replied. "No one crosses him, people are afraid." What he said fit with my picture of Ahmed, who for his twenty-three years displayed a casual air of danger. He often laughed, but behind his laughter lurked something unsettling.

"It's here," I said and pointed to the Internet café door secured with a heavy chain and lock. Mohammed asked at the teahouse when the Internet café would open. Shaking his head, he told me, "Not until evening," translating the man's answer. "We can't come to Marib after dark."

"But I want to use a computer," I replied. "To e-mail my parents and friends to let them know I'm okay." Mohammed had already crossed the road before I finished my sentence. I followed him along a dirt track that cut through a dusty vacant lot.

17

SUNFLOWER THE CAT

In ancient times, cats were worshipped as gods. They have never forgotten this.
—TERRY PRATCHETT

Early the next morning, I turned on my computer. I wanted to write. I opened "White Dragon," a Chinese folk tale. In Yemen, I was writing about China.

While rereading the story, I heard high-pitched, ear-splitting wails. For as long as possible, I disregarded the sounds. Whatever it was, I could not help. Finally, I opened the door, and the sunlight nearly blinded me. I shaded my eyes with my hand. Slinking away on the sunburned grass was a desert wildcat. It was so close that I could have stroked the wild animal's sandy-colored back. It disappeared behind the yellowing hedge, its toasted colors blending with the desert.

A wild animal had brought me outside and outside of myself. "What an opportunity, seeing a desert wildcat," I thought, returning to my room. I completed one sentence, and the loud wailing resumed. It was impossible to ignore.

High-pitched mews came from under the basil plants. Pushing the plants aside, I found a powder puff of sandy-colored fur. I looked around for more kittens, but there was only one. I did not touch the newborn kitten. If I did, the mother would reject it. I hid behind a pillar on the walkway and waited for its mother to return. In the furnace-like heat, the crying grew weaker. Its mother did not come back.

Holding the kitten in the palm of my hand, I could see that its eyes were not yet open and its earflaps were plastered against its head. I carried it to my room, wrapped it in a washcloth, and placed it in a basket. It disappeared in the terrycloth folds of fabric. I could not let it die under the sun.

"Why would a mother leave a newborn kitten?" I wondered as I ran to the guardhouse, not knowing what to say in Arabic. "I need Mohammed," I said; it was all I could think to say. The soldier pretended not to understand.

Dr. Mustafa's telephone number was busy when I called, and Ahmed called me back. "I need milk and a medicine dropper for a kitten or it will die," I said. He did not catch my words. I tried again, slowly.

Ahmed knew it was urgent from the tone of my voice. "No problem," he answered. Within five minutes, car tires screeched rounding the annex, Ahmed behind the wheel. Dressed in black, I got in the car. At the gate, Mohammed jumped in the backseat. "Where were you?" I asked.

"Busy," he replied.

Although I thought Ahmed knew what I wanted, he stopped the car at dozens of pharmacies—there are more than eighty in Marib. "Maybe he was not saying 'medicine dropper,'" I thought. Ahmed demanded service from clerks but did not get out of the car; he yelled through the car window. Pharmacists shook their heads.

Finally, I ask him to stop. I climbed the cracked concrete steps that led to the open-front pharmacy. Shocked to see a woman, even one completely covered in black, the pharmacist blushed.

Ahmed followed me inside and explained, "She has a baby and wants milk." The pharmacist opened a cardboard box and handed Ahmed a breast pump. Mohammed, who had joined us, turned to face the wall in embarrassment.

"No, no," I said, forgetting women do not speak in public. "It's for a kitten."

The pharmacist did not understand. Ahmed and Mohammed remained silent.

"A small cat," I said in Arabic showing its miniature size with my black gloved fingers in the palm of my hand. The pharmacist took a green box from the shelf and dusted it off. Inside was an eyedropper. "Yes, that's it!" I said. The pharmacist dropped the medicine dropper in my gloved hand. He would not take any money.

"Don't tell them the milk is for a cat," Ahmed said as I stacked three cans of Al-Momtaz canned milk on the grocery counter. Mohammed waited at the market door.

In my room, I dripped milk into the kitten's tiny pink mouth. That night the alarm went off every two hours, and I fed the kitten and rubbed its furless pink tummy with a moist tissue. I rewrapped it in the washcloth and fell back asleep.

Sleep deprivation lasted ten days, until the kitten's ears came away from its head and its eyes opened. When I went to class, Daood took over feeding duties. On the fifteenth day, the furry wildcat stretched its four squirming legs, fighting the hand towel, full of fury.

From the beginning, it was not a "normal" kitten. I wrapped it in a wash-cloth when I fed it because it struggled. It despised being touched and hated any restraint. Whatever it wanted to do, it did, and it got angry if stopped. Although it was still tiny, when it flattened its ears against its head and emitted angry growls, it was intimidating. I did not know if I would be able to handle a full-grown cat. The cute kitten looked adorable but did not behave that way.

Since the kitten would live, it needed a name. "You can't use Arabic names!" Mohammed warned me. "That would be *haram* (forbidden)!"

"We'll, I'm not naming him after you," I answered.

I called the kitten Waled, "boy" in Arabic. Most ginger-colored cats are male. However, the sandy-colored, extra-long-tailed half desert wildcat and half feral kitten was a girl, and I renamed her Zhara bint Shams, Zhara, the daughter of the Sun in Arabic, or "sunflower." Maybe a sweet name would alter her cantankerous personality. Certainly, she was beautiful with her pointed face; unusual, close-set, big green eyes circled in white; striped legs; and spotted coat in sandy desert colors. She had not inherited her mother's dark markings on her face, ear tips, and tail, but she had her mother's powerful jaw. The pads of her feet were covered with puffs of fur that acted like shoes. She would likely be bigger than her mother, her size would come from her father, one of the larger ginger tomcats who lived at the hotel.

Climbing the curtains was one of Zhara's favorite games, and if removed, she scratched and bit—hard. She swung on the curtains to gain momentum and then hurled herself across the room like an opened-clawed rocket. Zhara was entertaining. At first, the hotel staff played with her, but she grew increasingly vicious, and bites and scratches kept them away. Daood was the exception; he came to see his Flower, the name he called her, most days and brought her slices of English teacake.

Since cat food was unavailable in Marib markets, Zhara ate canned tuna and mackerel. Instead of cat biscuits, I crumbled Abu Waled sandwich cream cookies in her bowl. Each morning she drank Al-Momtaz milk mixed with water.

The desert supplied unlimited sand, and the hotel, with Daood's help, supplied the Hadda water bottle carton bottoms. Covered with plastic, they were just the right size for Zhara's kitty litter box.

Storekeepers knew I bought food for a cat, because secrets are hard to keep in Marib. Mohammed and the clerks exchanged knowing glances as Mohammed paid for the purchases with money from my wallet. "Women don't hand money to men—they might touch them," Mohammed explained. If Mohammed thought I was not looking, he wadded the change and stuffed it into his folded waistband.

Yemeni cats dig through garbage bins for food. Zhara was born with a "digging gene" that gave her the urge to search the trash, even though she was well fed. Each morning the contents of the wastebasket lay scattered on the floor.

Pepsi pop-top aluminum rings were her favorite toys. Zhara carried the aluminum rings in her mouth and stashed them under the carpets, along with chunks of English teacake. She loved plastic bags, which of course were dangerous when she walked off the bookcase trapped inside of one of them.

At three months, Zhara jumped in and out of the litter box, crying and straining to urinate. Blood, instead of urine, colored the sand.

"Are you sure there are no veterinarians?" I asked Mohammed. "Farmers keep goats, sheep, donkeys, and camels in Marib. I see them."

"It's different," Mohammed explained. "They believe sickness will either be cured or not—God's will."

At the pharmacy, Mohammed walked away, not helping to translate. I spoke with a pharmacist and explained why I needed antibiotics. The pharmacist listened and suggested a dose by weight, but he was not sure how much to give a cat. Mohammed stayed hidden around the corner of the building, embarrassed by a woman buying medicine for an animal. I bought ten antibiotic capsules. "That's expensive," Mohammed complained when he saw the receipt. "It's only a cat!" Slowly sinking into silence, we retraced our steps to the hotel.

Alone in my room, I opened one red-and-yellow capsule and emptied a few granules of yellow antibiotic into warm milk. "Please let it be the right amount," I prayed. Zhara drank the milk, licking the saucer clean.

"Don't worry," Ahmed assured me the next day. "I'll take it and bring you a healthy cat."

"Just throw Zhara away?" I asked, shocked he would even suggest such a thing.

"Yes," he replied, wondering why I had started to cry.

Within two weeks Zhara was, again, her unusual self, hissing and biting.

Ahmed's suggestion of throwing Zhara away upset me until I realized he was behaving like a practical Yemeni man. Of course, for him, cats were just cats.

Later, he confided, "When I go to America, I'll get a new wife."

"What about the wife you have now?" I asked. "Won't she feel sad—maybe angry or abandoned?"

"When I told her I'm getting an American wife, she cried," he said. "Maybe she'll be happy or unhappy, but she has to get used to the idea."

18

FOULE, BREAD, AND TEA

Vitality shows in not only the ability to persist but the ability to start over.
—F. SCOTT FITZGERALD

For once, the electricity did not go off during class. The tape player worked. Mohammed waited outside the classroom to walk me to the hotel. "You can study with the class," I said, handing Mohammed a textbook. "Dr. Mustafa agreed."

"Can we walk to Marib?" I then asked. "I want to use a computer at the Internet café."

Mohammed looked at me as if I had lost my mind. "No, I can't see down any of the *wadis* [the gravely dry stream beds] after dark. Anything might happen. Even soldiers don't go to Marib at night unless we go in groups."

"Well, Marib doesn't seem that scary," I replied.

"What's 'scary' mean?" he asked as we walked.

The next morning, Mohammed banged on my door, holding three loaves of kidam in his hand. "I signed a letter. I'll be responsible for you," Mohammed said grinning. "We can walk to Marib in the evenings if we're back at the hotel by nine o'clock."

"You did that for me?" I asked.

"Well, you'll help me study English," he replied.

"Let's go out to dinner," I suggested.

At seven that evening, Mohammed and I walked the road to Marib. With each passing car, Mohammed tensed and reached for his rifle. The wadis snaked into dark shadows. His eyes scanned the landscape, fully alert. Obviously, walking with me in the evening was not much fun for Mohammed.

Trying to make conversation, I said how thrilled I was to be in Marib.

"Why?" he asked and stopped to face me.

"It's a romantic place lost in time," I replied. "We could be walking in Queen Bilqis's footprints. Did you know Prophet Jesus lectured in Sana'a?"

"Are you married?" he asked.

His question was not in keeping with the conversation, but I answered, "Three times," feeling the air light on my face. He slowed his walk, waiting for me to continue. "Once out of high school, but it didn't last. Then, I married a man with three children—two sons and a daughter. He died. Again, I married in China a man who had a son, but we divorced." Saying the words was like discussing someone else's life—a woman I barely knew—a stranger.

The open-front, three-sided restaurant he suggested that was situated on the main highway between a greasy tire repair shop and paint store looked un-inviting. Several wooden tables with chipped white Formica tops were perched at odd angles on the beaten-earth floor. Shaky wooden benches sat on either side of the tables. Mohammed and I sat opposite each other—he faced front. "Do women ever eat in restaurants?" I asked.

"Not in Marib," he answered and then changed his mind. "Sometimes there are women traveling with men on buses that stop at the restaurant by the bus station."

Mohammed told me to wash my hands. We stood and walked to a sink. I dipped my fingers into a mound of laundry detergent and waited as a trickle of water escaped from the broken tap. Mohammed stood behind me. Two men approach the sink, but Mohammed told them to wait.

The restaurant served *foule* (spicy bean stew), large rounds of flat bread, and tea. There was no need for menus. "Stay," Mohammed said and left to place the order. When he returned, I explained that "stay" was a command for dogs to remain in place. We could not use "stay" with people—it was not polite.

A boy smoothed two sheets of the *Straits Times* (an English-language Singapore newspaper) on the tabletop. Next, he plopped the piping-hot, scorched flat bread on top. Mohammed told me to remove my veil, so I did. The waiter brought foule on a dented aluminum plate, and we used torn pieces of bread to scoop the spicy beans. When eating, I knew to use my right hand, but Mohammed used both hands to tear bread. I knew to eat and not talk.

We repeated the hand-washing ritual after the meal, and the waiter brought glasses of sweetened milk tea flavored with crushed cardamom seeds.

I retied the veil and drank tea by ducking it under the black fabric. Moham-med signaled that he was ready to leave. I passed him my wallet.

While I sat at the table waiting for him to pay, I noticed a man standing at the washbasin. He opened the trickling tap and cleaned his teeth with his in-dex finger, spit, splashed water on his face, looked around, grabbed someone's jacket hanging on a nearby hook, and wiped his hands and face on its sleeve.

Mohammed said I could use the computer at the Internet café for one hour. He sat in a chair next to me and jiggled his stainless-steel watchband held together with plastic tape. "Would you like to walk around while I finish typing?" I asked, sensing his anxiousness. He shook his head and farted.

Walking back to the hotel, near the Bank of Yemen, Mohammed, who was not dressed in a military uniform, showed his identity card to soldiers guard-ing the intersection—the military card allowed him to carry a rifle. Weapons are allegedly illegal in Marib, but what is legal or illegal depends on who you know. Men in Marib walk the streets, handguns strapped next to jambiyas and mobile phones and with rifles casually tossed over shoulders. "Anyone with money can buy a gun permit," Mohammed explained.

Our walk to the hotel was uneventful—no one kidnapped us. The starry, starry sky lighted the way. "Thanks," I said to Mohammed, "dinner was fun."

"What does 'fun' mean?" he asked. I explained the best I could. "We're the same," he replied.

19

BLACK GOAT-HAIR TENT

If you stop every time a dog barks, your road will never end.
—ARAB PROVERB

Sa'id Mohammed, a young Bedouin with long, wavy, chestnut-brown hair, was introduced to me at a friend's house in Sana'a. He worked for Hunt Oil Company in Marib as an armed guard. Oil companies hired local Bedouin to placate local tribes so that they would not blow up the pipelines, or at least not blow them up so often. However, buying the loyalty of tribesmen in the region did not always work. Disgruntled people occasionally targeted pipelines, and recently the local Bedouin hired to protect the oil properties needed bodyguards themselves.

After three months in Marib, I telephoned Sa'id Mohammed because he had earlier invited me to visit his family in the desert; maybe he would know how to contact Mohammed al-Baraki.

Unhappy with the idea, Mohammed gave me twenty reasons why I should not and could not go. I pleaded. He thought it was dangerous because he did not know Sa'id Mohammed's tribe or tribal connections. I understood his concerns, but I pushed, and hesitantly, he said, "Yes."

Sa'id Mohammed and his brother picked us up at the hotel in a brand new indigo-colored Suzuki. Mohammed wrote the car's license number on a scrap of paper and passed it to the military guard as we exited the hotel gate. We sat in the backseat of the car, and for the first time, I noticed a handgun strapped to Mohammed's belt. He hid the rifle under his long white thobe until we passed through Marib's checkpoint. I was invisible, covered from head to toe to fingertip in black.

The Suzuki stopped on a deserted stretch of dirt track to let air out of the tires, and we continued over swelling sand dunes, traveling eastward. Without signposts, Sa'id Mohammed's brother navigated the undulating, unmarked

sands, guided by ancestors who traveled the desert long ago. The only difference was that he was driving a car, not riding a donkey or camel. His ancestors
passed wisdom to him, which he draws upon for survival. My ancestors passed
knowledge to me, but I cannot say what it is. For my lack of knowing, I feel
sorry.

While we drove, Sa'id Mohammed explained that his brother had two
wives—one in her early thirties with eight children, and a young wife he recently
married. He sounded serious when he asked if I wanted to be his brother's
third wife. I shook my head and hoped he was joking.

To drive so long and see nothing but sand and more sand and then to encounter a settlement in the middle of the desert was startling. For an instant,
it looked like a mirage. We stopped. Black goat-hair tents and low mud-brick
houses blended into the desert landscape. Scattered makeshift pens constructed by weaving bits of wire, palm-fronds, and thorn bushes together housed
sheep and goats. Silhouettes on the distant dunes resembled one-dimensional
brown felt camels, the kind you see for sale at Christmastime.

Sa'id Mohammed asked me to wait in the car while he escorted Mohammed to a safe place. Watching Mohammed's stiff gait, I knew he was uneasy.
Since Mohammed was an outsider, his presence would bring questions, and
if anyone guessed that he was guarding an American . . . well, there would be
trouble. Sa'id Mohammed's family guaranteed my safety. I was a guest, they
would protect me. Keeping Mohammed hidden was sensible and protected
him too.

When Sa'id Mohammed returned to the car, I followed his footsteps into
a large, black goat-hair tent. Thirty or more women and numerous children
were seated inside the tent on brown goat-hair rugs. Sa'id Mohammed's
mother wore a dark-print, long-sleeved cotton dress. Around her head, a wide
band of dark satin peaked in front. She wore it like a crown. Blurred blue lines
and dots—tattoos—ran from her brown, creased forehead to her nose and
from her lower lip to her chin. Her right leg was wrapped in cloth bandages
and suspended in the air, held by two ropes that were tied to the tent's central
pole. She lay flat on her back. She had been in this position for weeks. The
women seated nearby massaged her arms and back and plumped blankets and
pillows to keep her comfortable. She praised God without complaint. Bending
to kiss her hand made me aware of an expectation in the West where people

require comfort and convenience. If either is withheld, we can become demanding and resentful.

Seated beside Sa'id Mohammed's elder sister, I thanked her for the privilege of meeting the family. Eight small glasses of amber-colored tea appeared on a metal tray, which was passed through the tent opening by an unseen hand. There were many more people than glasses of tea. A veiled woman handed me a scalding glass. Finding it impossible to hold, I sat it in front of me on the goat-hair rug. When the first people finished drinking, the glasses were apparently rinsed and reused. Each time, I was served tea.

Women and teenage girls wore colorful, long dresses beneath the open-front, long black *abayas*. The adult women's faces stayed hidden behind black rectangular velvet veils that hung to mid-chest. Each one was decorated with individual designs using antique glass-beads. Sweet-smelling incense smoldering in a small metal censer was passed around the tent counterclockwise, and we took turns standing over the censer, which allowed perfumed smoke to scent our skirts.

When it was my turn to stand over the censer, dark, kohl-rimmed eyes peered intently from behind shifting masks. Kohl is made from various compounds such as soot from burning amber, aloe wood, and frankincense mixed with oils. It was, and still is, made from antimony, which is toxic, but the chemical prevented bacterial eye infections and for that reason proved useful. Kohl adds a mysterious glamour and helps control the sun's glare in the desert. Men, women, children, and babies all use kohl around their eyes.

When veils shifted, I saw blue tattooed designs on chins. Two young women sat off to the side, breastfeeding thin babies. Sa'id Mohammed introduced me to his brother's second wife, an unveiled girl of thirteen dressed in a pink satin party dress, her long, hennaed hair in ringlets with a yellow, see-though, sequined wedding scarf embroidered with yellow and orange flowers tossed over her head. She was beautiful.

Young unmarried girls usually did not wear face covers or have tattoos. Very young girls wore *gargush*, pointy bonnets that tied under their chins. The hoods act as protection from jinn. Amulets attached to bonnets aid in protecting girls from the evil eye. The young boys dressed in thobes acted serious and aloof—small replicas of their fathers. None of them smiled.

While drinking tea, Sa'id Mohammed introduced me to the girls by citing male relationships, but not by name—no adult women's names were ever spoken. Mothers are known by their children's names, preferably a boy's name, such as "*Um Ahmed*," the mother of Ahmed. Not having shared experiences and, of course, misunderstanding each other made the job of communicating across the cultural divide interesting but not impossible. Laughter and sign language filled the gaps.

The Bedouin women were curious about my life in America. Was I a Muslim? If not, when would I become one? How many goats did I own? If my house in Hawaii did not have a fence, how do I keep goats from eating my garden or running away? How old was my father? How many children did he have—meaning sons? Daughters are not typically counted but mentioned. How many sons did I have?

My turn. I asked about the ever-present cowry shells. Gargush were frequently studded with shells. A rectangular mirror suspended in the center of the tent was covered by a flap of leather edged with shells. A large basket with a leather lid shaped like a witch's hat also was decorated with cowry shells. Even the cradle made of leather attached to a wooden tripod—but with no baby inside—had straps ornamented with shells. I wanted to ask if the shells were symbols of wealth, merely decorative, or used as amulets to ward off evil spirits, but I did not have the vocabulary for these questions.

Cowry shells had traveled from faraway places by way of trade with Africa or the Maldives, and in African countries, the shells were used as money. In Yemen, in this remote hamlet, in the middle of the desert the shells are abundant. I could only guess that they represented more than simple decorations. They may have been brought by Arab traders thousands of years ago. What they showed is how interconnected we were—and still are.

The afternoon ended, and before saying good-bye, the school-aged girls asked if I would listen while they said their numbers in English. Although the numbers were out of sequence, I did not correct them. The boys finally spoke and asked me to listen while they recited the ABCs. They giggled so hard that the alphabet was impossible to hear.

I thanked the children and kissed the women. I left a tin of Danish shortbread cookies for Sa'id Mohammed's mother, and I gave Sa'id Mohammed an English textbook and dictionary. "Can you buy Scotch?" he asked as we walked to the car.

At first, I thought he might be joking but remembered when we met in Sana'a that he was drinking. I told him, "No."

Mohammed slumped in the backseat of the car and seemed annoyed. "Mohammed, that was great," I said as Sa'id Mohammed's brother started the engine. The late afternoon sun cast shadows on the golden dunes. My love for the desert is strong and makes me think of something lost and not yet found.

"Not for me," Mohammed replied, turning away and looking out the car window.

"The women asked how I keep goats from eating my garden in America," I said laughing. "Isn't that precious?"

"I wondered too," he replied, sinking deeper into the seat.

"You did?"

The car stopped at the hotel gate, and Mohammed got out without saying a word, and we continued to the reception area, where I got out. "Thank you so much," I gushed. "This was a special day." Although I was tempted to wrap my arms around Sa'id Mohammed, I shook his hand. I waved wildly, watching the car disappear and reappear between trees planted along the hotel driveway.

In a lighthearted mood, I walked to the reception desk for my room key. Surprised to see a Western man in the lobby, I wanted to speak with him, but first I asked the receptionist for my key. When he realized I spoke English, he asked, "Why are you dressed like an oppressed Yemeni woman?" I explained that it was easier to cover up in Marib. "You look strict," he said. I suppose covered in black I did look strict, but that was the point.

"I'm from Austria and teach German in Sana'a," he added, "and I would never wear . . . " He made wrapping motions around his middle. "A skirt."

"A futa," I replied.

"Or a jambiya," he said. "If Japanese come to Austria and wore our clothes, they would look ridiculous."

"Marib is different from Sana'a," I answered, thinking back on my time in the desert with Sa'id Mohammed's family. "In Marib, women cover because of modesty and respect for tradition. Of course, it's complicated."

"Well, if I'm not accepted for myself," he said, "I won't go out of my way to please *them*. They'll like me for myself or not at all."

Although I understood his logic and agreed in principle, I tried again. "Marib is extremely traditional. On the street, I wear a baltu and cover my hair. It is easier. Westerners hold broader world views because we travel and have access to information. In less than a hundred years, we have gone from the horse and buggy to automobiles to jets—change is normal and expected for us. How can someone living in the desert herding camels and goats understand our world? Some Yemenis are not aware of anything beyond the village. Many would be shocked to see Sana'a. Even my educated students asked me if I wear a baltu and headscarf in Hawaii. Do I cover my face? For many Yemenis, there is no concept that life should be different outside Yemen."

He frowned shaking his head, "Why do you cover your face?"

"Today, I visited a Bedouin family—" and was going to give the example of the goats eating my garden in Hawaii.

He stopped listening mid-sentence and walked away.

20

CONFRONTING CONSPIRACY

Those who danced were thought to be quite insane by those
who could not hear the music.
—ANGELA MONET

Near the end of each month, Mohammed borrowed my mobile telephone to call his family because he was out of telephone units. He saved only a small portion of his salary for personal needs and sent the rest to his family using the efficient taxi delivery service. Yemenis depended on this delivery system for sending money and goods throughout Yemen.

Since my telephone was out of units on Saturday, I followed Mohammed to the Sabafon office and sat in a chair by the door. He took money from my wallet, paid for the phone card, returned the wallet to my purse, and zippered it. "Can we walk to the suq? I'd like to buy fruit," I said softly when we were outside on the concrete steps. "Do you have time?"

Without answering, Mohammed turned toward Marib, and I followed. At noon, the suq was nearly empty of customers because it was the hottest time of the day. Mangos the size of toy footballs baked in boxes. Pear-shaped tomatoes looked like they might explode. "One half-kilo of grapes," I said to Mohammed. He took my wallet and paid for the purchase.

A man approached me and tried to hand me money. "What's that man doing?" I whispered to Mohammed. "Why is he giving me fifty rials?" Although I tried to give the money back, the man insisted.

"He thinks you're an Egyptian beggar," Mohammed explained, taking the money from my hand.

"Why does he think that?" I asked.

"Women don't come to the suq unless they're begging," he replied, "and I told him you're from Egypt.

88

"I didn't hear you speak to him," I whispered. "Have you told anyone else I'm from Egypt?"

"Usually, I say you're Syrian."

As we exited the suq, Mohammed stopped beside a blue metal oil drum with an orange plastic bucket on top—it was a makeshift limeade stand. He handed the man the fifty-rial note and received two glasses of juice and thirty rials in change, which he kept. My chipped mug had a broken handle, and before putting the liquid to my lips, I silently prayed I would not get sick drinking the water. "What's wrong?" Mohammed asked, wary of my hesitation.

"Nothing," I replied, drinking the limeade.

On the walk to the hotel, Mohammed asked what I was really doing in Marib. "What do you mean?" I asked. "Really doing?"

"Abdullah Shaykh told the secret police you are a spy," he answered.

"A spy?" I stammered. "Who would I be spying on and why?"

"He said that you're spying on the people in Marib and there's a folder at the Public Security office with all the information. That's why you didn't want him as a driver."

"Do you think I'm a spy?" I asked.

"I wonder why you're in Marib," he replied. "Everyone wonders."

"I'm in Marib because I wanted to teach English to the Bedouin," I said. Apparently, people believed that since I willingly lived in Marib—a place they would run from if they could—I must be a spy. Crossing the desert by camel had started a strange chain of events.

"What does the report say?" I asked, feeling paranoid.

"I can't tell you," he replied. "But Dr. Mustafa told the director of the secret police you're not a spy."

"What have you told them?" I asked.

"Nothing," he answered and picked up his pace, looking toward the tops of barren mountains in the distance.

"Whatever you say—tell the truth," I said to his back and stumbled over a pile of broken sacks of concrete in the street. The plastic bags of fruit I was carrying sprawled on the pavement. "Don't lie to make yourself look good."

"Are you okay?" Mohammed asked, seeing me struggle to get up.

"No," I wanted to shout. I picked up the bags and noticed a puddle of blood in the toe of my dusty sandal. I wrapped a tissue around my big toe. We walked in silence.

Conspiracy theories are not new to Yemen. In *Qataban and Sheba*, Wendell Phillips told of his harrowing experiences in Marib during the early 1950s when he and his team cleared away sands while excavating Mahram Bilqis, the oval temple ruled by the Queen of Sheba that is mentioned in the Bible and the Koran. The team barely escaped with their lives, with no thanks to Imam Ahmad, the Yemeni ruler mistrustful of outsiders, and the suspicious people of Marib. Reading travel adventure books in the AIYS library, I knew foreign "spies" were imprisoned and others not heard from again.

We passed one- and two-story cinder-block buildings containing shops with blue metal doors. The color blue repels evil spirits—although if asked, people would argue that they are religious and not superstitious. Clinics and hospitals hovered on side streets. Small shops, one after the other, sold identical merchandise—mostly made in China. Mohammed stopped to look at women's sleepwear. When I asked why he was interested in gauzy nightgowns, he told me he was shopping for his older sister.

At the hotel, Mohammed took the key from my purse and opened my door. "Make sure it's locked from the inside," he reminded. "I'll be in my bedroom." His bedroom was not a room. It was a metal bedframe with a blanket mattress laid out under the sun, moon, and stars.

After I squeezed the bruised fruit into the refrigerator, I sat down to write but thought, "Nightly, Mohammed called the police and reported on the tourists staying at the hotel and when he was in Marib dialed 119 free from telephone booths, saying he was calling a friend. What did he report?"

Zhara lay curled up in her basket and opened her eyes. She stretched. In Yemen, no one trusted me—and I was beginning not to trust myself. I could not write. With words, I am okay. Without words, I am nothing. Zhara hopped out of her basket and sat on the desk. "Thanks kitty," I said when she gently touched noses with me. I thought of a quote by Colette: "Our perfect companions never have fewer than four feet."

A gust of wind rattled the window screens, and before I could shut the bathroom window, the white floor tiles were gritty with sand. Goats trying to escape the sandstorm banged their bodies against the door. Sand soon obliterated the sky, and an early darkness fell. Tumbleweeds rolled. Trees moaned and limbs snapped. Everything turned brown.

With all the noise, it was a wonder I heard Mohammed. "Your flashlight," he shouted, banging on the door and pushing goats aside. A scarf covered his face in such a way that only his sandpapered, bloodshot eyes showed. Puddles of goat pee wetted piles of sand collecting on the walkway. "Don't come out," Mohammed shouted.

For hours, the wind howled. Sand seeped through gaps around the windows and door. Bandaging the openings with masking tape did not help. "Maybe this could last for days," I thought, and with this, the wind settled. I shook the sheets, blankets, and carpets in the bathroom and swept the floor. There was enough sand to fill Zhara's litter box.

PART V

LEARNING AND LISTENING

21

QUEEN OF SHEBA'S TEMPLE

Merely looking at the world around us is
immensely different from seeing it.
—Frederick Franck

Depending on tribal conflicts, kidnappings, and sandstorms, the American Foundation for the Study of Man (AFSM) visited Marib twice a year, in the spring and in the autumn. The organization was eager to unearth proof of the Queen of Sheba's existence and carry on the excavation work established by the late Wendell Phillips, who had been chased out of Yemen. Merilyn Phillips Hodgson, an American and sister to Wendell Phillips, faithfully continued her brother's research.

Merilyn Phillips Hodgson and I met in 2001 at AIYS when she stepped through the wooden gate fashionably dressed in a green-and–yellow, long-sleeved shirt and canary-yellow slacks, as if completing a *Vogue* fashion shoot. Later I learned she had been a model. The small gold cross she wore on a thin gold chain around her tanned neck caught my eye. Her presence and perfectly applied make-up and blonde hair with not a strand out of place made her standout in Sana'a. She was an interesting woman. Our paths first crossed in Sana'a with just a hello, but we were fated to met again in Marib.

Land Cruisers arrived from Sana'a with the AFSM team, and they would stay in the annex. The place buzzed with activity. Zhara and I peered through the half-open bathroom window, watching the show unfold. Luggage and boxes were stacked on the lawn for workers to carry to rooms. Room assignments were shouted in Arabic. The team was made up of mostly men, but two Western women passed the window. Noise and laughter missing from life resumed. "This is going to be fun," I said to Zhara, who was now standing on my feet.

From the bathroom window, I caught a glimpse of Mohammed, an epigrapher from a university in Germany. We had met two summers before at AIYS. He unloaded equipment from the back of a Land Cruiser. Mohammed was originally from Palestine and an expert in reading ancient scripts. I would surely know other members of the team. The thought of meeting interesting people and speaking English was exhilarating. It was as if the visitors had come to see me.

On my way to class, I said hello to Mohammed. Surprised that a veiled woman spoke to him, he replied and immediately went back to unpacking the equipment. It took me a moment to realize that he did not recognize me. I lifted my veil and smiled. "What are you doing in Marib?" he asked, even more surprised that I was behind the veil.

"It's a long story," I answered. "I'm teaching in thirty minutes and have to go. We'll catch up later."

Waiting at the gate to walk me to class, my bodyguard Mohammed seemed edgy. "It's great to have so many people staying in the annex," I said excitedly. "Maybe they'll have parties and fill the fountain with champagne."

"Foreigners cause troubles," he replied.

"How long will they stay?" I asked, curious to find out how much time I had with people who would surely become my friends.

"Usually two months," he answered. "Abdullah Shaykh makes the most money, since he is in charge of organizing the military. He asked me to work for him. But I'm guarding you."

"Should I apologize?" I wondered after hearing how money had slipped through Mohammed's hands.

"A blunt-featured Yemeni man with crowded teeth wearing a shiny, navy-blue Western business suit knocked on my door, but I didn't understand what he wanted," I said. "Even though he spoke English."

"Don't get involved," Mohammed warned, his face unsmiling.

"I'm not involved," I replied. We walked to class.

Only a few lights flickered behind half-closed drapes in annex rooms when I returned from teaching. Just as I spread the peanut butter on flat bread, a knock at the door. "Yes," I said.

Hisham waited outside my door. "You'll have to leave the room," he said, without explanation.

"Why?" I asked, thinking something must be wrong with the electricity or water.

"Dr. Othman wants the room—it's his room," he replied.

"What do you mean he wants his room? I've rented room 408 and signed a contract."

"He always stays in this room," Hisham answered, astonished by my outburst.

"Well not this time," I replied, quickly closing the door so Zhara would not escape. "Zhara and I are not sharing our room with a man."

Before I finished eating my sandwich, there was another knock. "Yes," I said, but this time I made sure Zhara was locked inside the bathroom.

Hisham stood between two sheepish-looking hotel workers. "They'll help you move," he said.

"I'm not going anywhere," I answered.

"You'll have a nice room in the hotel—better than the annex."

"I'm fine, and Zhara likes the garden," I said. "We're not moving." Zhara heard her name and clawed at the bathroom door, and it opened. She hissed and bared her teeth, looking ferocious with her fur on-end. "Zhara doesn't want to move." Zhara did her dance-like routine by pivoting and jumping up and down in front of the door, daring them to enter. I knew it would take a long time for her to calm down. If I tried to move her aside, she would attack me. I asked the hotel worker to shut the door. He did.

An hour later, the room telephone rang. "Hello," I answered. On the line was a soft-spoken male voice. He introduced himself as the general manager of the Universal Hotel chain, informed me that Dr. Othman always stayed in room 408 while in Marib, and asked if I could be so polite to accommodate Dr. Othman, who was a very special guest at the Bilquis Hotel—a noted Yemeni archeologist who studied in America.

"No," I replied courteously.

After hanging-up with the soft-spoken man, I called Dr. Mustafa and explained what was going on. Within thirty minutes, four Bedouin carrying Kalashnikovs dressed in dusty thobes and bullet-filled bandoleers knocked at my door to let me know that no one would bother me. For three days, they camped in the garden, making sure no one entered my room. Ahmed drove Mohammed and me to and from class.

Mohammed assured me no one would disturb me. This was not true, because on the fourth day when the Bedouin left, Hisham returned. "You'll have to move—just two months or maybe less—or I'll lose my job," he pleaded. "Dr. Othman is serious. He wants the room, and he gets what he wants."

The hotel staff, other than Hisham, treated me with respect for my determination but could not show support for fear of losing their jobs.

After class, Mohammed walked with me to the photocopy shop before we returned to the hotel. Ahmed passed us on the road driving Dr. Mustafa's car. He stopped to speak with Mohammed.

"What did he say?" I asked Mohammed as the car sped away.

"No one will bother you about the room," Mohammed replied. "It's settled."

"How did it get settled?" I asked.

"Don't ask," he replied.

Later I found out that Ahmed and the four Bedouin visited Hisham, and whatever they discussed in the privacy of his room was more convincing to him than Dr. Othman's insistence.

Dr. Othman had expected to get his way, and when he did not, he became spiteful. Although he did not speak to me directly, he instructed the hotel workers to tell me to keep my cat in the room or something would happen to her. Zhara stayed inside.

Clay pots on my window ledge with colorful blooms annoyed Dr. Othman. He did not like the sunflowers growing in the flower bed near my door. "They must be moved," he said—not to me but to the gardener, Abdulkarim. The gardener dug up the sunflowers, then loaded the sunflowers and larger pots in the wheelbarrow. I carried the smaller pots to the hotel garden and sat them under a tree. "The goats will eat the plants," Abdulkarim said, setting the uprooted sunflowers and big pots on the ground. I nodded, knowing what he said to be true. The goats would find them delicious. Later that day, he brought me a plastic water bottle filled with warm goat's milk. Perhaps he thought it was a fair exchange: flowers for milk.

Dr. Othman would not acknowledge me if we met on the walkway. However, one afternoon while I collected sand for Zhara's litter box, he came from behind and startled me by asking if I was a Communist. "What?" I turned my head to look up at him, surprised by the remark.

"You lived in China," he said. "Everyone in China's a Communist."

"Well, you lived in America," I said.

"Yes," he replied. "I lived there twelve years—so what!"

"With your logic, you must be a Christian or Jew, because that's who lives in America," I said, waiting for his response. He stomped off.

That evening, Abdullah Shaykh knocked at my door. "This is an official visit," he said, with a glassy-eyed, unofficial stare, qat bulging in his cheek and bits of green leaves on his teeth. With an air of command, he explained that I could not walk around the annex because the team had unearthed valuable antiquities and stored them in a locked room. "You can only walk from your door to the road."

While it is true that many Yemeni treasures "disappeared" because they were sold to the highest bidder—usually by officials—I was not in Yemen for antiquities. First a spy and now a thief.

There were many young archeologists studying under Dr. Othman and they dared not speak to me, fearful of losing positions at the university. However, there was one exception: a mid-thirties, light-haired Yemeni archeologist who had already graduated. He repeatedly knocked on my door, offered qat, and wanted to come inside my room. His room was directly opposite mine, and each time I stepped outside the door, I hoped to avoid him, but that was not to be. "Are you free this afternoon?" he asked suggestively. "You have a beautiful body." This went on for two weeks and stopped the day he knocked on my door when Ahmed was in my room getting help with his homework assignment.

"Who is it?" I said and opened the door. "No, I am busy with a student, and I am not free to chew qat with you any time," I said. "Please go away."

"You're not giving me a chance," he replied. Hearing a man's voice, Ahmed grabbed his rifle. The archeologist's face froze as he peered down the barrel of the gun. Ahmed marched the frightened archeologist straight to the assistant manager's office. Hisham and the American project director discussed the archeologist's unacceptable behavior, and he admitted to doing wrong and lost his job.

After he left, the short-stay international advisors occupied the room opposite mine. We met coming and going, and they asked if I wanted to see the locked-up "finds." I answered, "No." My lack of curiosity must have appeared odd, but I did not want to explain that the Yemeni authorities thought I was a criminal.

Merilyn and I frequently met on the annex walkway during the mornings. She dressed in smart casual attire on her way to the site to do her fair share of the work. In the evenings, I would see her again going to the hotel restaurant dressed in high fashion and high heels. The tuna sandwiches she ordered did not fit with the glamorous outfits she wore. Of course, she was not bullied by Dr. Othman or afraid to speak with me. However, I assumed she did not completely understand why I refused to relinquish my room. We avoided the topic.

Over her years of coming to Yemen, Merilyn adopted Yemeni cats and took them home with her to New York. She loved cats and asked countless times when she could meet Zhara. I made excuses. One evening, she knocked at my door.

Zhara's wild behavior is predictable. After the first burst of energy, hissing and standing on hind legs, front paws flailing the air, she rolls over on her back and looks enticing with limp, furry-padded feet in the air and eyes half-closed. During the next phase, Zhara gets up, moves slowly, and deliberately rubs against legs, fooling the person into believing she likes them and wants to be petted when she really wants to scratch them.

"Zhara is not like other cats," I cautioned. Even though I stressed the importance of not touching her and keeping hands above the waist, Merilyn did not heed my warning and, before I could stop her, laid on the carpet. "Cats like me," she said, initially smiling. Zhara jumped on her face.

What I believed would be a great opportunity turned out to be not even good. For nearly two months, I kept Zhara locked in the room. The potted plants stayed hidden, and of course, the goats ate the flowers. I never saw the treasures. I did not make one new friend.

22

ALI'S INVITATION

The universe will reward you for taking risks on its behalf.
—SHAKTI GAWAIN

Ali, Asma's father, was like many Bedouin. He understood the importance of education even though he was illiterate. His willingness to bring his daughter to and from class maintained her chaste reputation. Most Marib families would not allow daughters to attend class for fear of social scandal. Our class was especially suspect, with men and women in the same room. Widespread gossip damaged reputations even when rumors were unfounded. Women and girls are obligated to uphold men's honor so her behavior does not reflect adversely on the men in the family.

Although the old, rusted, blue truck with bowed wheels Ali drove did not look like it would last another mile, Asma was on time for class. At first, Ali escorted his daughter into the classroom and sat in a chair at the back, making sure no man made heedless advances. After a few weeks, he walked Asma upstairs and waited until she was with her female classmates, then returned downstairs. I saw him seated in the truck when I looked out the window. Twice, I remembered him driving away, but he returned before class finished.

One Wednesday, the final day of class for that week, Asma said her father wanted to speak with me. Asma translated. Ali invited me to lunch on Friday. "I would love to," I said, smiling at Ali's handsome, gray-bearded face, "but I have to ask Mohammed. What's your phone number?"

Asma wrote her telephone number on notebook paper. She folded it and placed it my hand. "Don't tell anyone," she cautioned.

I thought she meant do not give her number out. "I won't," I replied.

"Students are not to invite you to their homes," Mohammed said through gritted teeth while I erased the board. When I turned to look, he had gone.

"Why can't students invite me?" I asked when I caught up with him on the outside steps.

"Dr. Mustafa told them not to invite you," he answered. "It will cause trouble."

"Eating lunch?"

"You're not safe in someone's house," he said as we walked along the concrete driveway of the governor's compound to the main gate. His face was grim.

"It's Ali's family," I said not understanding how going to lunch could cause such concern. Then it occurred to me that Ali was taking a big risk, which none of my other students had done. Dr. Mustafa had a wife—maybe more than one—and children, which I had seen when Ahmed brought them to swim at the hotel pool. Before classes began, students from Marib and out-lying desert communities invited me to meet families, but future invitations never came.

Coming to Marib, I expected to be overwhelmed with Bedouin hospitality, to meet families and be welcomed to women's gatherings. Bedouin believed people in the desert were guests of God, like themselves, and were owed respectful treatment. But my only invitation came from Sa'id Mohammed, who had nothing to do with Dr. Mustafa or teaching.

After living in Marib, I thought people might not want to invite an American into their homes because it would cause problems. Maybe they believed, like Abdullah Shaykh, I was an undercover agent and would report them. However, now I knew that Dr. Mustafa forbid people to invite me. What kind of place was Marib?

"Dr. Mustafa wants you safe," Mohammed said, interrupting my thoughts.

"He's worried about himself, and so are you," I said impatiently and turned the opposite direction toward Marib. Mohammed followed. I walked faster. For the first time, Mohammed followed me.

Mohammed did not like me to shop in the glass-fronted stores on the main street because he said it was dangerous. I dashed inside and looked at nail polish. "What are you doing?" he asked when I exited the store. "I've missed my dinner."

Feeling like a willful child, I apologized. "Sorry." I followed Mohammed to the hotel. At a small grocery, he stopped to buy packaged cakes and juice for dinner. "I'm sorry you missed dinner," I said and passed him my wallet so he could pay. "Please let me go to Ali's house for lunch on Friday. I'm sure they'll serve great food," hoping to appeal to his stomach, since he would have to come along as my murafik. "You don't have to tell Dr. Mustafa. Please, just once."

"Twice." He turned to face me as bits of cake shot from his mouth. "Dr. Mustafa doesn't know you visited Sa'id Mohammed in the desert," he answered and continued jamming hunks of cake in his mouth.

"I'm not sorry," I shouted as loud thunder drowned out my words and chased lightning across the sky. We ran to the hotel, drenched in the downpour.

On Friday morning, exactly at eight o'clock, Mohammed knocked on my door. "Ali's at the gate," he said. Eight o'clock seemed early for lunch. I dressed quickly and walked to the front gate. Mohammed had on a white thobe, a navy blue sport coat, and a black-and-white checked scarf that was draped over his shoulders. He sat in the front seat of the beat-up blue truck, next to Ali. Ali wore a light gray thobe, dark gray suit jacket, and white scarf smartly tied around his head. His beard was tinted orange with henna at the sides near his cheeks.

We exchanged the traditional Muslim greeting *salaam alaykums* (peace be upon you), and I squeezed in beside Mohammed. Ali reached over both of us and latched a wire that secured the door to the car's frame. He maneuvered the truck to the gate and waited for the guard to unlock one of the heavy wooden doors so we could leave. Ali and Mohammed burst out laughing when the guard said something and pointed to the bowed wheels. Catching a few words, I knew it was about riding in a broken truck.

Mohammed was concerned that the soldiers at the main checkpoint would see his Kalashnikov, so he hid it under his thobe. He would be in big trouble if Dr. Mustafa found out we were disobeying his order. Although I did not like causing trouble, I also did not want to stay locked in my room.

Within fifteen minutes, Ali left the paved road and turned onto a side dirt road with well-tended farms and orchards on either side. We were immediately in the countryside. He turned right, headed up a steep incline, and arrived on top of the New Marib Dam, a vast construction connecting two mountains. The dam was a gift to the people of Yemen from the ruler of Abu Dhabi, Shaykh Zayed bin Sultan Al Nahyan, who traced his ancestors to Marib. His family, like many others, exited Yemen sometime after the sixth century CE.

The collapse of the Marib Dam is said to have caused the great exodus and downfall of South Arabian kingdoms, but it is only partly the reason why the people fled Yemen. While the destruction of the dam surely brought about diasporas, another event caused significant economic changes for city-states along the trade routes. With Rome's acceptance of Christianity in the third-century CE, they no longer needed such large quantities of incense for rituals. Camel caravans dwindled, and cities along the incense routes with astonishing pasts, like Marib, all but disappeared.

Regardless of Al Nahyan's family's reasons for leaving Yemen, his generous gift now irrigated large swaths of land, greening the desert as it did during the Queen of Sheba's time. Conflicts then as well as now existed over ownership of water rights, and Ali stopped the truck to tell a story. Mohammed translated:

Once upon a time, two Sabaean kings, both landowners in Marib, shared an irrigation canal. One day the old king made many trips to the canal and then to his garden, pouring buckets of water over plants. The young king watched. Each time the old king fetched another bucket of water, the young king became furious. "You're using all the water!" he shouted.

"I'm using only my half," the old king replied and kept on watering his plants.

"When I need water, there won't be any left!" the younger king complained. "Let's divide the canal in half." He tied a cord across the middle of the canal. "There" he said pointing to the water, "that side is yours and this is mine." They shook hands.

During the night, the young king woke to check on the water in his side of the canal. He lowered a bucket into the old king's side and poured the water into his half. "I'm going to have more water than the old king," he chuckled to himself.

The next morning the young king got up very early to make sure his side of the canal still contained more water. His face flushed with anger because both sides looked the same!

The young king confronted the old king. "I know your trick—you can't fool me!" he shouted. "You got up during the night and poured my water into your side!"

The old king was a clever man and did not like to quarrel. "How many buckets of water do you think I took?" he questioned.

"About fifty," the young king answered.

"Okay, you can take fifty buckets of water from my side of the canal and pour them into yours," he replied.

Smiling, the young king ran off to the canal, knowing he was the winner.

"We're still fighting about water after all these years," Ali laughed. "But now we're not as clever as the old king—we kill each other."

We drove to Old Marib and looked at the tiny-windowed, collapsing mud houses but did not stop. "Do families still live here?" I asked, seeing a pack of dogs.

"Most people moved away," Ali replied. "But it's not deserted." While he spoke, a herd of goats scrambled over a rocky hill, followed by a young shepherd. Dressed in a black cloak and blue head covering, she waved her stick in the air as a greeting.

Ali drove on the bumpy dirt shoulder. We bounced along, nearly hitting our heads on the truck's roof. The thick-walled mud-brick houses in the village with spires and cones on rooftops resembled gingerbread houses decorated with white icing. "How much would it cost to build a mud house like that one?" I said, pointing to a two-story house, but Ali did not understand my question, and Mohammed would not translate.

"They're expensive," Mohammed replied dismissively.

"What does expensive mean?" I asked.

Ali returned to the paved road and sped past a Bedouin camp of at least a hundred families living in packing crates covered with blue plastic tarps and tents of rags. "Tourists are not supposed to see this," I thought, turning around for a better look. The poverty is due to government greed and the unfair distribution of revenues from oil. It is a wonder more oil pipelines are not blown up.

Near Marib, Ali turned off the main road and followed a narrow winding dirt path with fragrant citrus orchards on either side. He stopped the truck in front of a one-story, rectangular, gray cinder-block house. I was disappointed that he did not live in a mud house. After he unlocked a blue metal gate, we entered a narrow, dark, concrete passageway. At the end of the passageway, Ali unlocked a blue metal door, which I thought led to his home, but no. I stared into an enclosed pen housing six goats and one beautiful cow.

Ali instructed Mohammed to sit on a carpet under a blue tarp, and I followed Ali inside the house. He knocked but did not enter the door at the end of the hallway. A woman greeted me, and I stepped into a room full of women and girls of all ages dressed in fancy party clothes seated on mattresses that lined three walls. Astounded by the number of women squeezed into the room, I removed my shoes slowly and looked around. Another woman guided me to a mattress, and I sat beside a pretty woman in her mid-forties who wore a flowing, long–sleeved, green velvet dress with sparkling golden bangles that jangled on her arm. A young woman with shoulder-length dark brown hair dressed in turquoise lace handed me a glass of purple juice. No one else was drinking. Feeling awkward, I sipped the juice to have something to do.

Since all the women in the room were unveiled and heads uncovered, I did not know which one was Asma. She was not dressed in black, so I could not identify her. I could have recognized her shoes, but the women in the room were barefoot. I could not tell by looking at her hands because in class she wore black gloves. Of course, my students knew what I looked like, but I never saw them without cloaks, headscarves, gloves, and veils. The young woman dressed in turquoise lace might be Asma. I studied her eyes, and when she introduced me as her teacher, I was sure.

Moving around the room clockwise, Asma presented me, and I shook hands with the girls and kissed the women. Most visitors were neighbors that had come to see the foreign teacher and listened politely while I bungled the language. When I kissed the last woman, they stood as if prompted by an unheard bell and said good-bye.

Asma's mother and older sisters excused themselves to prepare food. We went to a more intimate sitting room where her younger sister sat by the window, altering a dress made of shiny material embroidered with gold thread. "The fabric is from Saudi Arabia," she said, and I wrote the Arabic word for "sew" and "fabric" in my notebook. Another sister opened a picture book, and together we named animals and flowers in English and Arabic.

When Asma and I spoke English, her sisters leaned close with such concentration that I felt their warm breath on my face. I told Asma I wanted to be independent and walk by myself. She taught me the Arabic word for "myself" and helped me use it in sentences.

Pushing the wooden shutters open, I looked through an open window with vertical iron bars but no glass or screen. It was like peering at an artist's canvas of green fields and tree-lined orchards from a place of protection. Calmness washed over me, and I thought of asking Asma if I could stay with her family so I would not have to return to the hotel "prison." Voices from the kitchen floated down the hallway, and we followed the sounds and joined women in the kitchen. They were busy slicing, dicing, kneading, stirring, and baking. Pots bubbled atop a three-burner propane stove, which sat on a rectangular stone slab on the floor carved with an ancient inscription. A big, round, drum-like metal container squatting in the middle of the kitchen was the oven.

Asma created paper-thin layers of dough on a wooden board by tapping lightly with the tips of her fingers to make *bint as-sahin* ("daughter of the plate"), a flaky pastry. She worked each piece of dough until it was about the size of a large pizza, then fitted the thin dough into a large, round, metal pan and poured in a small amount of melted butter. On top went another layer of dough and another and then another wash of butter. With a metal rod, she whipped melting butter in a small can and poured it over the top of the dough. More layers of thin dough and melted butter, and on the very top, she sprinkled *haba soda* (black seeds).

Asma began a second pan of bint as-sahin. An older sister oversaw bread baking. She divided dough into fist-sized balls. A sister seated on the floor flapped the dough between her hands until the disks grew bigger and bigger. Another sister slapped the flattened dough onto a big, fat pillow with a straw handle on the opposite side. Then she smacked the dough side of the pillow against the inner wall of the hot oven, where the dough stuck. When the bread finished baking, she pried it loose from the metal wall and sailed it through the air, where most of it landed on a big platter—some missed and landed on the floor. The walls of the oven she brushed with a stiff-bristle brush and then pressed more dough against its hot sides. The bint as-sahin pans were placed in the top of the oven to bake.

Asma's mother, who had chopped a dozen tomatoes into a bowl, gave me an upside-down metal loaf pan to sit on. Watching the drama unfold, I realized that this goes on every Friday. It was probably less elaborate during the week. Today, I was included in a way of life in households across Yemen. Feeling privileged to be part of the kitchen life, I caught the flying bread and laughed with the women.

Asma moved to the stove and tossed the bowl of chopped tomatoes into a bubbling pot. She added spices from unmarked metal cans with fingertips and tasted the results with a big spoon. Lifting the lid from another pot, she stirred and tasted, seemingly satisfied. Turning a valve, the gas flames grew higher, and the pot nearly boiled over, but Asma maintained control.

Ali called my name from the hallway, but before I left the kitchen, I retied my headscarf. I followed Ali to the living room, where Mohammed sat on a low mattress. "I'm having so much fun!" I said excitedly and went on and on about baking bread, but he was not interested. Maybe bored, maybe annoyed.

"We're going to the mosque for al-Juma prayers," he said in a flat voice. "But at one o'clock be ready to leave."

It did not make sense to leave before lunch, but I did not argue and said, "Okay." Today, Mohammed would not ruin my joy.

With the men at the mosque, the girls and women showered and dressed in their finest for Friday's lunch. They were to use the bathroom in order of age, the oldest first. I listened to playful bickering because a teenager had showered before her older sister and taken too long.

In my long, black, silk skirt and white, long-sleeved blouse, I felt underdressed. Asma's mother had showered, and her hair was damp. She wore a cobalt-blue, satin ball gown. We sat on a low mattress in a large airy room close to the kitchen and watched a color TV tuned to Saudi Arabia, where thousands of people circled the Ka'bah. "Are you Muslim?" she asked, keeping her eyes glued to the television screen.

"I believe in one God," I answered.

"Then you'll be a Muslim," she replied.

"Inshallah," I added and looked at my watch. It was 2:30 p.m. I was sure Ali and Mohammed had returned from the mosque. Asma's older brother called from the hallway for his wife. He must not enter the women's quarters because I—an unrelated female—am present. He returned the uneaten food to the kitchen after the men had finished eating. Men eat first.

Sisters one-by-one emerged from the bathroom dressed in fancy clothes with towels draped around wet hair. They disappeared down the long hallway.

The older sister spread a thin, plastic, blue-flowered tablecloth on the floor. Asma carried steaming bowls of vegetables and meat. Another sister sat an enormous bowl of rice on the plastic cloth. Fried fish arrived on a giant platter. Salads and bread appeared. Asma carried her work of art, the bint as-sahin, and poured amber-colored honey over its top. "*Bismillah*, In the name of God," we said in unison and began the meal.

Asma looked like a princess dressed in a coffee-colored, crocheted, long-sleeved top and long, lavender, satin skirt, her shiny hair parted in the middle. She adjusted her legs, exposing white cotton *sirwal* (pantaloons) with lace on the cuffs. Women do not talk while eating. Right hands moved quickly and scooped handfuls of food into mouths. There were no plates. Asma passed me a piece of fish. Another sister placed a bowl of cut tomatoes, cucumbers, and red onions in front of me. Food dropped on my skirt when I put my hand to my mouth. Eating with my hands was difficult and slow.

The bint as-sahin vanished before I managed a second helping. The women are serious eaters. One sister stacked the dishes, another cleared away the remaining food, and a third packed up the plastic cloth. Lunch ended.

After tea, it was time to leave—eat and run. Ali and Mohammed were waiting in the truck, but it took me time to say good-bye. On the way to the hotel, Mohammed asked Ali to stop at the qat suq. Ali and I had a few moments alone, and he told me he and his wife were happy that Asma studied English. "She's had a difficult life," he said, and I could tell he wanted to explain, but Mohammed returned with his bag of qat, and our conversation ended.

23

EATING ARSENIC

Experience is the teacher of all things.
—JULIUS CAESAR

Before walking in the garden the next morning, I put on sunscreen and studied the lines on my face in the bathroom mirror. Slathering on cream, I noticed my prune-like earlobes sagging from the weight of gold hoops. *I was shriveling.* The face cream disappeared into skin, and for a moment, the wrinkles vanished. I looked again, and like magic and rabbits, lines multiplied.

While walking inside the walled hotel grounds, I saw Abdulkarim, the gardener, pruning trees. From the very first day we met, he tried to convince me to become a Muslim. Without words—just his outstretched hand—he pointed to the hotel's garden, an area with sprinklers: alive with trees, shrubs, and flowering plants. Then his hand ever so slowly changed direction, and he pointed to desert—dried up and barren. This place or that, he silently gestured.

"Inshallah, God willing," I replied and stopped to pet the goats.

"Goats are for feeding and eating," he shouted. "Not petting."

Ramadan—the holy month—would arrive with the sighting of the new moon, and everyone in Marib had guessed its anticipated date. Ramadan, the ninth month on the Islamic lunar calendar, is a time set aside for praying, fasting, and spiritual searching, with nothing touching lips from sunup to sundown: no water, no food, no cigarettes, no one's lips, and no qat. Fasting allows understanding of the lives of those less fortunate. Time spent reading the Koran is to commemorate God's revelations to Prophet Muhammad. Only good thoughts can be expressed for thirty days. It is a privilege, not a hardship.

People were curious to know if I would fast: the grocer, baker, gardener, military, students, and shopkeepers. A young, pinched-faced, stoop-shouldered hotel worker told me it didn't matter if I fasted. "You're not a Muslim, you don't pray five times a day." I wanted to ask how he could be certain of my religious beliefs or my prayer habits. He was alone in suggesting I should not fast. The others encouraged me to be part of the month-long celebration, to share with millions of people around the world enacting the ritual.

For many Yemenis, the holy month was upside-down—night is day and day is night. They party the night away: staying up, chewing qat, just before dawn eating the last meal, saying prayers, and then sleeping until noon. Then more prayers, sleep, more prayers, rest, more prayers, the breaking of the fast after sundown, and partying.

Just before Ramadan, Amal, my student, waited until the other students were in the hallway and gave me a note written on lined notepaper: "My dear teacher, because I love you, I wish you to become a Muslim and be a part of our family." She had thought long and hard about the sentence. "Thank you," I said and folded the paper and put it in my purse.

"Last night, on the television," she said, taking a breath, "they showed an American woman submitting to Islam." Amal saw me in the woman's place. "The British ambassador's wife became Muslim!" she added. What she said was true: the ambassador's wife had converted.

Something was in the air, because a few nights later Mohammed asked to have a private talk with me. He came to my room after dinner and sat stiffly on the straight-backed chair. "You're a nice woman," he said, as if he had rehearsed. "If you are not a Muslim, you cannot go to the garden of Islamic Heaven. It is a beautiful place where young girls serve platters of delicious food and no one is hungry. Streams flow with wine and you can drink as much as you like. Nobody ages or is sick. There are beautiful girls. If you do not become a Muslim, I cannot see you—because it is only for Muslims. The other place is fiery."

"Being a Muslim would bring changes," I replied. "I would behave differently. Men could not see me alone—and you could not come to my room. In fact, I might stop talking to men outside my family." So far, Mohammed has not brought up the subject of me becoming a Muslim. I forgot to ask why young females served only the boys and men platters of delicious food. Who served the girls and women?

Islamic threads were woven tightly into the tapestry of everyday Yemeni life, and it would be impossible to untangle them. Of course, not everyone in

Yemen is extremely devout, but most display religious conservatism. Living in Yemen, I thought about being a Muslim, but I had not acted on it yet. During Ramadan, I had planned to fast.

"Maybe I would convert to Islam on my deathbed," I thought, shuffling back and forth between the bed and toilet. Two days of diarrhea and vomiting left me physically and emotionally weak. I telephoned Mohammed, but his mobile phone was off because three nights before the sighting of the new moon had declared the opening of Ramadan. Mohammed, along with friends in the guardhouse, chewed qat all night, and they slept all day. Too exhausted to get dressed and walk to the front gate because of fasting and illness, I sat on the bed, feeling sorry for myself.

That evening after the canon sounded to announce that we could eat and drink, Mohammed knocked on my door, bringing food to break the fast. "I saw your missed call," he said, staring skyward to avoid looking at me dressed in a long–sleeved, high-necked nightgown. "What's wrong?"

"I'm ill," I replied.

"Can you walk to Marib?" he asked.

"Impossible," I thought, but heard myself say, "I'll try."

"You look sick," he said, keeping his eyes focused above my neck.

There are numerous clinics in Marib, and Mohammed stopped in front of a nondescript, one-story, cinder-block building with a red cross painted on a blue metal door. The bare concrete inner walls matched the gray concrete floor. I waited in the women's section with four empty beds covered with stained, yellow plastic, the beds positioned so that men passing the door could not see inside. "A woman would have to be near death to lay here," I thought and sat on a metal folding chair.

Two Bedouin women and a boy joined me in the women's waiting room. The woman spoke to me in Arabic, assuming I was Yemeni. Dressed from head to toe in black, they would not have guessed otherwise. I wore a traditional Bedouin face veil connected to the headpiece by a thin black string that rests on the forehead. It left only my sunken eyes exposed and concealed my lower face. I answered the woman and went back to staring out the slats of the wooden shutters wondering why Mohammed had chosen this clinic.

On the opposite side of the street, neon lights blinked on and off on a modern-looking hospital and pharmacy. Worried that some unknown men might see his women, for whom he was responsible, the boy closed the shutters, blocking out light and air. We sat in the dark, stuffy room.

Mohammed slapped the women's waiting room wall with the flat of his hand without looking inside. I followed him down a corridor. A doctor—I assumed so because he wore a white coat—was seated behind a desk and asked questions in English and wrote the answers in a notebook in Arabic. He prescribed an injection and vitamins. Before leaving the room, the doctor told me to remove my baltu. Although I was veiled and fully dressed, I held the baltu to my chest out of modesty. The doctor returned. Just before stabbing the needle in my arm, he wiped the exposed skin with a cotton swab and said, "Bismillah." "This should work," I thought.

On the following Friday, I was sicker, and the clinic would not open until after *Maghrib* (sunset prayer). Mohammed and I waited on the broken sidewalk in front of the clinic. I leaned against the building for support until someone showed up with a key. When the doctor arrived, he asked for blood and stool samples. Blood was easy—he stuck a needle in my wrist—but the stool sample had to wait. The next evening, Mohammed and I delivered the stool sample.

"Giardia lamblia," the doctor diagnosed and prescribed two tablets of 250 mg of Metronidazole three times a day for five days. After five days, the diarrhea had not stopped—in fact, it had barely slowed. During this time, Mohammed and Daood brought food each evening to break the fast, even though I could not eat any of it. After dark, I carried the food dishes outside and fed the stray cats.

Mohammed and I went to the clinic several times a week. By mid-Ramadan, it seemed everyone in Marib was sick. The waiting rooms overflowed. When it was my turn, the exhausted-looking doctor teetered on the edge of a broken metal folding chair. The most recent blood test told him I did not have malaria. He asked for another stool sample, but it should be fresh, not over thirty minutes. "Just walking to the clinic takes thirty minutes," I explained.

I told Mohammed what the doctor wanted. "Call when you have diarrhea," Mohammed said listlessly, and I followed him to the hotel.

One day passed—no diarrhea. "Maybe I am okay," I thought. The second day, diarrhea came in waves. I called Mohammed, but he did not answer his phone. Anyway, the clinic would not open until evening. After Maghrib, I called Mohammed's telephone. "I have to go to the clinic," I said, not having to explain the details.

We crossed the desert—a ten-minute shortcut—not walking on the road. My baltu caught on a thorn bush. I tripped and fell on the ground. Mohammed reflexively reached for me but then stopped. He knew I was weak from illness, and since I was not Yemeni, maybe it was okay to help. But before grabbing my arm and helping me to my feet, he looked around. Since no one was watching, he hoisted me up.

Once in Sana'a, I watched a woman fall in the street while getting off the bus. Men wanted to help her—I could tell from body language—but long-held traditions held them back. The woman eventually picked herself up before the bus ran her over.

Inside the clinic, without words, a male nurse tapped his index finger on the Formica counter where I was to leave the black plastic film container holding the stool sample. "Why didn't you use a match box?" Mohammed asked. Before I could answer, the male nurse pointed to the women's waiting room. I obeyed.

This time, the doctor wrote a new prescription, "Take all four tablets at once," he said. Then he asked a curious question: did Mohammed and I have a contract? I did not understand or know how to reply.

When I told Mohammed what the doctor had asked, he was outraged. "You won't see him again," he shouted. I certainly hoped that was true. We walked to the pharmacy. I pushed the prescription paper through a hole in the glass window. The pharmacist gave me the medicine. I paid. The name on the medicine package did not match the name on the prescription. "You could kill someone," I yelled, handing the medicine back and demanding my money.

I turned to Mohammed. "Do something," I said. "He should be reported."

"It's Ramadan, a time of forgiveness, and the pharmacist probably hasn't had enough sleep," Mohammed mumbled.

"People who can't read think this guy is giving them the correct medicine. They depend on him!" Mohammed, embarrassed by my outburst and since it was Ramadan doubly horrified that I, a woman, made a scene on the street, led me away.

At the modern-hospital pharmacy across the street, I compared the name and dosage on the package to the name written on the prescription. They matched. The pharmacist reminded me to take all four tablets at once.

In my room, I gagged trying to swallow the large, black tablets. Finally, I cut them in quarters. Zhara was asleep on the bed, and I curled up next to her. The bedside lamp was still on when I woke later that evening, and I had no idea how long I slept. A crushing weight pinned me to the bed. I felt like vomiting. "I must be dreaming," I thought.

Hearing pounding on the door, my head stayed firmly on the pillow. "What do you want?" I asked.

"Are you okay?" a man's voice questioned.

"No, but I want to be alone," I said. I fell into a drugged-like sleep.

"Open the door," a man shouted, banging on the window screen.

"Who are you?" I asked.

"Mohammed," he answered. "Open the door!"

"I'm not well," I answered. "Go away."

"I won't go until you open the door," he shouted.

I made my way slowly to the door using the furniture for balance.

"Why are you wearing your baltu?" Mohammed asked, seeing me in the doorway. Apparently, I had slept in it. I sat on the bed, and Mohammed fed me spoonfuls of yogurt. "You've slept two days," he said. "I've called for a car."

While we waited for the car, he poured water into Zhara's bowl and put tuna in her food dish. "Where's my scarf?" I asked. Mohammed found the scarf on the desk next to the empty medicine package and helped me bandage it around my matted hair. I looked like death when I glanced in the mirror.

A driver took us to the clinic. The only place left to sit was on the bed in the women's waiting room. Finally, I saw the doctor. "Arsenic," I screamed, accusing him of trying to kill me. "I've taken arsenic to cure diarrhea. The medicine made me so sick that I thought I'd die—I wanted to die."

"Do you have diarrhea?" he asked.

"No," I answered.

24

THE LOOKING GLASS

The stories we tell ourselves about our own lives
eventually become our lives.
—DAN BAKER

Eid al-Fitr followed Ramadan, a time of celebration after thirty days of fasting. "During Eid, the garden will be filled with girls," the hotel worker—the pinched-faced man who told me fasting for me did not matter since I was not a Muslim—said loudly enough for everyone in the lobby to hear. The men giggled as their eyes glazed over as they thought about the likelihood of catching sight of females. "Yes, all covered in black," I thought. The sheer possibility that girls and women would be in the garden was enough to make grown men quiver.

Yemeni girls and women conceivably know what effect they have on men. Females do not live isolated lives completely separated from fathers, uncles, brothers, and male cousins who must reveal an indication of their fondness for the opposite sex.

Flirting between Yemeni males and females is rarely obvious. Men attracted to black-cloaked women passing in the street might turn to catch a glimpse. Veils are alluring when hiding faces but not expressive eyes. In Sana'a, some bold, young women covered in black pass tables of young men drinking tea and may slip a note to one of the men—maybe her name and phone number. Girls and women act flirtatious, but if confronted, they would deny the behavior because it would mean they disregarded tribal custom, social order, and religious principle. Peers—other females—keep tight rein on girls and women who attempt to step out of traditional boundaries.

Veils in Yemen are symbolic of feminine spirituality: they hide her face, while cloaks conceal her female form, but neither silences her voice, which is considered enticing. Women's voices should be quiet. Burdened with keeping men pure by dressing modestly, behaving shyly, and speaking softly, women are responsible. In Yemen, it is the duty of girls and women to remain invisible so that men are not tempted.

"What about men being accountable for their actions?" I asked Mohammed. He replied with a shake of his head as unspoken words signaled that I was beyond comprehending what was obvious.

Mohammed would travel to Taiz for Eid to celebrate with his family. He wanted to borrow my camera. We walked to the photo studio at the main intersection to buy film. "Look," Mohammed said, dreamy-eyed, pointing to an enlarged poster-sized photograph of a girl. The studio walls were covered with portraits of boys and girls, but mostly five- and six-year-old girls posed alluringly and dressed in off-the-shoulder party dresses or tribal costumes and adorned with heavy make-up and jewelry.

"That's Amir's daughter," Mohammed said, staring, hypnotized, practically drooling. At puberty, girls put on veils and remain hidden from outsiders' eyes. Childhood is the only time they are visible.

"Mohammed," I said, "that's a little girl." He was not the only man who behaved this way. Men in the photo shop gazed at the photographs, completely enchanted. I reminded myself that Western media exploited and degraded females—even young girls in beauty pageants—but at the same time we preached equality of the sexes and freedom from abuse.

Although I did not think of myself as a precious jewel, as Yemeni women are encouraged to believe—part of the reason why they are protected from men's eyes—I continued to veil. Veiling did not make me feel prized, but sometimes I felt comforted as the observer and not the observed. Mohammed assured me veiling for foreign women was against Yemeni law because it made us anonymous. "All, the more reason to veil," I thought. "Maybe I could get away with something."

"I'm going to Sirwah," I said excitedly to Mohammed the next day. "The doctor from Sana'a invited me." Mohammed squatted beside the guardhouse washing clothes in a blue plastic washbasin. This was most unusual, because he usually tricked one of the simple-minded soldiers into doing his laundry.

During my time in Yemen, Sirwah remained a forbidden site. Even Abdulmalik, who took me to prohibited places, would not chance traveling to

Sirwah. It is the original home of the Sabaeans, but because of lack of water and land to sustain a rising population, the capital moved to Marib probably about the time Marib Dam was constructed.

"The car leaves in an hour," I added, since Mohammed had not answered or looked up from his laundry.

"Did you call Dr. Mustafa?" he asked and emptied the sudsy washbasin near my feet.

"No, but I will," I replied.

Driving to Sirwah, I sat in the backseat of the Land Cruiser, my face hidden behind a veil and my hands covered with black gloves. Mohammed and two armed military guards rode in the back. The doctor and his assistant from the health department in Sana'a sat in front, next to the driver. Easy at the military checkpoints, the guards waved us through.

Although the doctors were on official business to meet the director of Sirwah's hospital, later—for fun—we would visit Sirwah Temple. Dramatic scenery between Marib and Sirwah changed from rolling volcanic desert to swelling lavender and purple hump-shaped mountains. Veins of exposed lava traveled on the ground and resembled jagged black ribbons marking the corrugated landscape.

Sirwah looked like a small village at first glance, with its scattered one- and two-story, brown, mud-brick and gray cinder-block houses that dotted the desert. Several stores with blue metal doors swung wide open were clumped along the U-shaped paved road in the center of town. The driver turned off onto a dirt road that led to the hospital, which was surrounded by high concrete brick walls and a locked gate. The car passed through the gate and stopped in front of a one-story green building that could be mistaken for a house.

At the hospital's entrance were thirty or more women holding infants. Women dressed modestly, but none wore all black. Mothers seated on cement window ledges nursed infants wrapped in colorful blankets. Some women stood in line, holding babies, and waited to speak with the female health-care worker dressed in white. A scale for weighing babies and a ledger sat on a long green conference table.

The atmosphere seemed relaxed until we entered. Seeing the doctor from Sana'a, the health-care worker stopped writing in the ledger. "This is impossible," she whispered, on the verge of tears. "The scale's broken—I can't weigh the babies. There's no medicine for diarrhea."

The Sana'a doctor listened but made no reply and walked away. The doctor took my arm and escorted me along a corridor until we came to double doors, which opened to an abandoned operating theater. Scattered on the dusty, tiled floor were bunches of dried qat leaves, plastic bags, and empty water bottles. "How can you get my daughters to America?" he asked. Then I understood why he offered the invitation to Sirwah. Although he was not the first person to ask to go to America, I have yet to come up with a suitable reply. The doctor dropped my arm after hearing footsteps approaching in the hallway and whispered, "I know you'll help."

The hospital lacked everything except patients. Dr. Salim, the resident doctor, looked ready to cry. "Electricity is not dependable," he explained and pointed to a generator half covered by sand outside his office window. "It only worked two months."

"Can't someone fix it?" I asked, seeing that it would disappear beneath the sand.

"I've asked for parts from Sana'a," he answered in British-accented English, "three months ago." Frustration at not being able to offer his patients even basic health care showed on his tense-looking face. The hospital needed a scale for weighing babies. They were also in need of a water filter, since Sirwah's water was salty and changed lab results and discolored glass slides. Dr. Salim required emergency drugs, such as antidotes for snake bites and scorpion stings. He needed a simple microscope and repair parts for the broken generator. He had given up asking for X-ray equipment. I wrote the list in my notebook.

While Dr. Salim attended to patients, the doctor from Sana'a and I stayed in the room. Surprisingly, the Bedouin women were not shy during the examinations. Face veils stayed in place as women peeled away layers of clothing, exposing chests, midriffs, stomachs, arms, and legs. After each diagnosis, the doctor from Sana'a and Dr. Salim conferred. "These are Bedouin," the doctor said to me in English, looking annoyed, "he treats them too nice."

Dr. Hanafi from Sana'a, who worked with Cheri, entered the hospital and escorted a group of Yemeni doctors and two executives from Washington, D.C. Of course, Dr. Hanafi did not recognize me covered in black. He would have no reason to think I would be in Sirwah. Dr. Hanafi had given me plants for the garden, a corkscrew to open the wine, and advice and canned milk for Zhara.

The doctors and officials were ushered into a conference room—I was included—and sat next to Dr. Hanafi. Mohammed stood by the door but seemed extra alert clutching his rifle. The director of Sirwah's hospital, Naji, arrived and welcomed the executives and doctors, but seeing me, he backed out the door. The meeting stopped. He returned surrounded by six armed bodyguards. Warm bottles of strawberry soda were passed out to people in the room, but I declined.

Mohammed stood behind Dr. Hanafi's chair and whispered to him. Dr. Hanafi turned to me and quickly looked away. When we stood to leave, Dr. Hanafi touched my arm. "Take off the veil," he whispered without looking in my direction.

"Why?" I asked.

"Naji thinks you're Shaykh Rabeesh's wife, his sworn enemy," Dr. Hanafi replied. "You have to show your face—he thinks you came here to kill him."

"I won't take it off," I answered.

"This is serious," he whispered.

Mohammed had explained to Naji that I was an American teaching English in Marib, in fact, his teacher. Naji was not convinced of my nationality or intentions.

"I told Naji to call Dr. Mustafa," Mohammed said as we got in the car to drive to the temple.

"Sorry, I forgot to call Dr. Mustafa," I replied. "He doesn't know we're in Sirwah or not yet."

A toothless, wizened groundskeeper guarding the temple grounds unlocked the wire gate, and we stepped into a fantastic world. A German archeologist and his team showed us around the ancient site and answered questions. Hundreds of ibex (*wa'al* in Arabic) figures exquisitely carved from stone once decorated the top perimeter of the temple. Over the centuries, statues tumbled to the ground and now guarded the inner courtyard. I rubbed my hand over the smooth stone carvings.

In profile, the ibex looked like a unicorn, but the archeologist said the ibex in Sabaean times represented the moon god and its curved horn—a crescent moon or the moon in its first quarter. The ibex was venerated by ancient South Arabians, and its image was used for decorations and commonly carved from alabaster. I remembered seeing ibex statues at the National Museum in Sana'a. The crescent moon is a key symbol in Islam.

We crawled on our hands and knees through an underground passageway, which was scary, because if Mohammed's gun fired, the tunnel would collapse, making it our tomb. This unpleasant thought stayed with me, and I could not shake the feeling until we emerged above ground on the other side of the temple. "I never want to do that again," I said to Mohammed, brushing dirt from my clothes.

Massive steles with ancient inscriptions leaned against giant pillars in the center of the temple complex near where we exited the tunnel. "Naji must believe I'm the Shaykh's wife," I said to Mohammed. "He's glaring at me."

"Stay close," Mohammed replied.

An "eye for an eye" is how scores are settled. Things have not changed in thousands of years. Sirwah is the looking glass that reflects how little we have learned.

25

WORDS OF CONDOLENCE

All sorrows can be borne if you put them into a story
or tell a story about them.
—Isak Dinesen

Outside my window on Thursday, men gathered under a hastily erected tent for a qat session to honor the passing of Abdullah Shaykh.

On Wednesday, Abdullah Shaykh had driven one of the military trucks that escorted the Dutch ambassador to Sayun. The police truck flipped, and he along with two soldiers were killed upon impact. Mohammed told me the news before leaving for the military hospital to donate blood for the injured men. Abdullah Shaykh's unexpected death was the topic of conversation. Insincere men who disliked him in life now praised him in death.

His one-story, cinder-block house located just outside the entrance to the hotel was busy with women coming and going. "What can I do?" I asked Mohammed. Showing respect to his wife and family seemed right.

"You can take his family a cake," he suggested.

Mohammed walked with me to Hant Supermarket, and I asked questions about Muslim funerals. "Men wash the man's body, being careful not to look or touch his private parts," he said in a solemn voice.

"And if it's a woman?" I asked. "Women wash the body?" He nodded.

"The body is wrapped in many meters of plain white cloth." We had seen the muslin fabric folded and stacked in the suq. "Usually before sundown— within twenty-four hours—the body is placed in the ground on the right side, head faced toward Mecca," he replied.

"What should I do," I asked, "when I take the cake to his family? They will be crying and sad."

"A good Muslim knows that death is God's will," he replied. "Life and death are in God's hands, and He appoints a time for each person to pass from

121

one existence into another." He quoted words from the Koran in Arabic but did not explain the meaning. "Women can't go to the cemetery because they are weak—unable to control emotions."

"Expressing emotions can be good—you shouldn't keep the sadness inside," I said. "If you don't cry the first time, you'll cry for the rest of your life."

"That's your western way. When my wife died," he said, "I was sad, but I didn't cry—I am strong."

"I didn't know you were married." I slowed and looked at him, surprised by his words.

"Yes, I married at sixteen and my wife was thirteen years old; she was my cousin. She coughed and coughed, and blood came from her mouth—there was blood everywhere. We took her to a clinic in the village, but the doctor could do nothing."

"I'm so sorry," I said.

"It's God's will," he replied and resumed walking. I followed.

The selection of cakes at the market was poor. I thought of giving money, but Mohammed said that would be wrong. Returning with a cake, I practiced the Arabic words Mohammed taught me, words of comfort for the widow.

"Good-bye," I said to Mohammed just before we reached the entrance to the hotel. I followed a dirt path to the right, walking on parched, stony ground to the widow's house, practicing the words of condolence in Arabic.

At the backdoor, a young girl invited me inside. Only women were present. I could see them in the room down the hallway. A woman in the kitchen untied her apron, wiped perspiration from her forehead with a corner of the material, and introduced herself as Abdullah Shaykh's widow. We kissed cheeks, and I mixed up the Arabic words of sympathy, but I could tell she understood my meaning. She smiled, thanking me in English. "Please come in," she said.

Her red-ringed eyes held the only outward sign of sorrow. She was very pretty and much younger than I had expected. From talking with Mohammed, I knew women were not supposed to show emotion because that would mean they questioned God's will. Abdullah Shaykh's widow had suffered an unexpected loss, and raising seven children would not be easy.

Although I wanted to say more, I did not have the words of comfort in Arabic. She took the cake from my hands and thanked me. After I left, I suppose she went back to cooking and I back to the hotel. Later, I thought of the widow—she radiated serenity, strengthened by her spiritual beliefs. On my desk sat a copy of *Self* magazine with an article titled "96 Great-Body Tricks of the Stars." Our worlds were far apart—in Marib it is the 99 names of God that are important to know.

From my window, I saw Abdullah Shaykh's eldest son, Nasser Abdullah, seeming more mature than his twenty-one years, chewing qat with the men. He would take his father's place as head of the family. A big responsibility, but from what I knew of him, he would be a great help to his mother. He had inherited his father's good looks and the old Land Cruiser, which later that day I saw him drive, but he had not inherited his father's suspicious nature.

26

CHOOSING THE VEIL

*Learn to get in touch with the silence within yourself and
know that everything in this life has a purpose.*
—ELISABETH KUBLER-ROSS

One evening as Mohammed and I walked on "Street Marib" (as he called
it), a man stepped in Mohammed's path, taunting him with words and gestures. Mohammed continued his purposeful walk without missing a stride,
chest thrust forward, as though the man did not exist. I walked at his heels.
Stunned, the man bounced off Mohammed's chest and landed in an awkward
stance some distance away.

Afterward he stopped to speak with a military man at the intersection.
I thought he was reporting the incident, but Mohammed introduced me to
Malik, his brother-in-law. Gusts of wind swept sand across the road from the
open desert and stung my eyes. I lowered the second face veil. The conversation in Taiz dialect I could not understand, and my mind drifted, lost in
my own world. When I was veiled, my mind turned inward. Being wrapped
in black changed my personality—I had the sensation of shrinking. Perhaps
veiled women gained an inner calmness through meditative solitude of not
being in the world.

Although the overwhelming majority of women in Yemen covered their
faces, wearing a face veil was new for me. Yemeni girls grew up seeing veiled
women. However, the Koran itself does not order women to cover their faces.
During pilgrimages to Mecca in Saudi Arabia, Muslim women perform religious rites with faces and hands exposed. Veiling and wearing gloves are
cultural practices and considered traditional in Yemen's conservative society.

In Sana'a, my face remained exposed, but in Marib it was practical to veil.
Veiled women drove cars and trucks, parked the vehicles, and sent men and

boys to shop for bolts of fabric, shoes, small electrical appliances, rugs, cosmetics, and jewelry. Yemeni women did not walk on Marib streets. My highest count of women in Marib was the day before Ramadan, when seventeen out of a population of approximately seventy-five thousand were visible.

When I veiled and people recognized me by shoes or baltu, they commented, "You're beautiful." At first, I thought they meant since I was completely covered, I looked better. However, that was not the meaning. They were complimenting me, because veiled, I resembled a Yemeni woman whom they thought of as spiritually chaste.

Tribal traditions and religion maintain tight control of Yemeni girls and women. Veils are an outward sign of modesty and protection from unknown men—they keep her pure, and therefore she brings no shame to the men in her family. Girls understand from early childhood that upholding tribal honor by maintaining their virginity is a solemn responsibility. With the loss of female honor, fathers are ridiculed. Brothers are humiliated. Sisters are ostracized.

Mohammed and Malik's conversation ended, and we continued on our way, stopping for juice and cookies at the small grocery store close to the hotel. Since the electricity was off, candlelight flickered in the shop's widow. I sat on the rock, and Mohammed squatted. The moon gave plenty of light. "Is Malik your deceased wife's brother?" I asked and flipped the veil over the back of my head.

"Malik's my cousin," he replied. "My wife lives with my father and her grandmother. She's helping my father because he is ill."

The conversation made no sense. "I thought your wife died," I said.

"My first wife died, but as soon as I get money, I'll marry again," he said, "to Malik's sister, my cousin, that's helping my father."

"So you're engaged?" I asked, knowing it was not my business but intrigued nonetheless.

"She's very open minded, you'll like her," he said. "Her father is mean and wants more money—he keeps raising the bride price. When I call, she always asks about you."

"The silver band you wear—is it an engagement ring?" I questioned.

"No, a tailor gave it to me," he answered.

"A tailor gave you a wedding band?" I asked. "Why?" Seeing an approaching truck, I lowered the veil and remained quiet.

A blue-and-white police truck stopped. Two police got out and unloaded cases of long-life milk, bags of sugar, rice, and flour while the truck driver and the shopkeeper talked. When all the goods were inside the store, the shopkeeper counted out a stack of a thousand rials and gave them to the driver.

"What's going on?" I whispered to Mohammed

"The military sells food," Mohammed said. "It's a way to make money. Wages are low."

27

A Bedouin Tale

We think in words, and these words have the power to limit us or set us free;
they can frighten us or evoke our courage.
—DAN BAKER

Dr. Ahmed (my contact who represented the American Embassy in Sana'a) and Dr. Mustafa asked me to join them in the hotel dining room to discuss my fate. "I'm under house arrest," I said to Dr. Ahmed and hoped that he might be able to explain to Dr. Mustafa that as an American, I did not like to be caged.

"We want your safety," Dr. Ahmed replied.

"I'm safe," I answered.

I turned to Dr. Mustafa. "Please, I don't need a bodyguard during the day," I said for the umpteenth time. "I want to walk to morning classes and the suq in the daytime. No one bothers women. Tribal law protects us. If I go out at night, I will, of course, take Mohammed."

"What if Mohammed follows you?" Dr. Mustafa asked.

"Well, that's not going alone is it?" I said. "I trust God to take care of me. Yemen is an Islamic state and no one trusts God. They trust guns." Dr. Mustafa repeatedly said Marib was safe (even though he would not be without bodyguards), but he was a man, and perhaps men have different rules.

"No murafik," Dr. Mustafa agreed. "Okay, but only during the daytime."

At eleven o'clock, I walked to the hotel gate. "I'm walking to class by myself," I said to Mohammed. "Did Dr. Mustafa call you?"

"Yes," he replied.

It felt good to walk out the arched gate on my own.

"If anything happens to you, I'm responsible," Mohammed shouted. "I'll go to prison or worse."

"It's daytime. I'm walking across the highway," I said.

"What will happen to me?" he shouted.

"Mohammed," I said looking over my shoulder, "Dr. Mustafa said it is okay. During daytime, I can walk by myself!"

"This is Marib!"

"Okay, okay, Dr. Mustafa said stay fifty meters behind me," I caved. "Let me be on my own—humor me."

Clearly, this was unacceptable. "I like walking together," he shouted, running to catch up, the Kalashnikov's strap weighing heavily on his shoulder.

Sand collected in my sandals as we walked a rock-strewn path that led across the desert to a garbage dump littered with rusted cans, plastic bags, and human excrement. "Careful," Mohammed cautioned, stepping over shards of broken glass.

Classes for nurses and midwives were held in the still-under-construction health institute beside the dormitory where Dr. Mustafa first suggested I live. I shuddered seeing the "prison yard" covered with broken concrete and smashed tiles.

Walking in clay-like sand, the hem of my baltu turned white from the chalky powder. Shaking off dust, I followed Mohammed up the cement steps, and we entered the director's office. The nurses had not returned from the hospital, so class would begin late.

A Bedouin with an orange, hennaed beard and wisps of orange-colored hair stuck out of his loosely wrapped turban entered the room. With great attention to politeness, he shook hands with the men and ignored me. However, I caught him taking sideways glances at me from time to time.

Mohammed left the office and returned to the hotel because it was nearly lunchtime. A military truck delivered bread to the hotel, but the hotel cooks prepared the soldiers' meals. He had to be present or miss lunch. I sat outside the director's office on the cement railing.

The students had not arrived by 1:30, so class was cancelled. Seated on the railing, I waited for Mohammed. The bus pulled up in front of the building, and a flock of nursing students, but not mine, got off and like black birds surrounded me. Are you married? Where is your husband? How old are you? Are you a Muslim? Do you know my name? Do you know her name? "Do you think she is beautiful?" a student asked and pointed to her classmate wearing head to toe black. "I'm sure she's beautiful—you're all beautiful," I replied.

Mohammed apologized for being late. "I thought of walking without you," I said. "I lost my chance."

"Thanks for waiting," he answered, and we retraced our steps through the garbage dump. "It's hot," I complained, tugging at the folds of fabric hugging my neck. "There should be a law that men are required to wear black cloaks and headscarves once a week. Then the dress code for women would change."

Mohammed cleared his throat, "What's your point?" he asked.

"Never mind," I replied.

"You had a marriage proposal," he said. "The old man in the director's office came to the hotel and asked if you would be interested."

"Not the bird-like man with an orange beard?" I asked. "What did you tell him?"

"I said you had a car in America and didn't want his truck."

"Are you kidding?"

"No."

At the hotel, I met Dr. Ahmed, and we had coffee before he returned to Sana'a. "Did you walk to class alone?" he asked, pulling out my chair.

"No, Mohammed went with me—we are joined at the hip," I answered. "I'm not free. I hate it."

"You need to understand two governments want your safety," he replied.

"Well they're squeezing the life out of me," I answered. "I'm a prisoner."

"Let me tell you a story," he said. "One I heard yesterday. Perhaps it will convince you that desert people think differently."

Living in a hamlet in the middle of the desert were seven families—all related to each other—who shared the same tribal name. Because they were isolated, cut off from the rest of society, they depended on each other.

The rough and tough, arms-toting men wore long, dust-colored thobes and flaunted curved daggers. Dark leather faces peered out from under scarves wrapped closely around tightly curled hair—turban fashion. They were serious, no-nonsense men.

The women dressed modestly in practical clothing and worked together, tending children and the vegetable gardens in the sun-dried soil.

A nearby well, which supplied water for the families, became the problem. The well was located at the edge of the village near Ahmed's mud-brick house, but it began to dry up.

There was not enough water for the families, and the men began to quarrel. "You're using more than your share," Mohammed said to his brother Ahmed. "The well is near your house and easy for you to dip your bucket into it when we're not looking."

The women paid little attention to the men's bickering and collected small amounts of water for the children and vegetable garden—hardly any for themselves. The women began to shrivel in the hot desert sun.

One day when Mohammed's wife walked to the well, she heard a man's voice complaining. "There she goes again," Ahmed said to his wife, but his wife did not answer.

The men were soon divided, four to three, on who should control the amount of water each family could take from the well. "Someone should stand guard," Salah suggested.

That night Salah stood guard beside the well with his rifle. The sound of footsteps made Salah react; he leveled his rifle and accidently shot his cousin, Sa'id, in the stomach.

The loud gunfire brought the other families to the well. "What have you done?" screamed Sa'id's wife. "You've killed my husband."

Trying to console the widow, the women wrapped her in a blanket and took her inside. Weeping continued throughout the night. Sa'id, was buried the next day.

The angry men shouted and blamed each other. Once the discussion became so heated that they picked up their rifles and aimed them at each other. One rifle accidentally discharged, and Salah's brother lay lifeless on the ground. As tradition dictates, Salah was obligated to avenge his brother's death—and Mohammed and Ahmed lost their lives.

At the end of the day, the women working together dug the graves to bury the last of the men.

28

DISAPPEARING IN MARIB

I know I shall not know.
—T. S. ELIOT

The soles of our sandals made kissing sounds, sticking to the gluey asphalt as Mohammed and I walked to the health department for afternoon class. Students had disappeared, and only three women and three men remained. The English course for the nurses and midwives met just twice a week. With fewer assignments to grade, I had more time. Since I was not writing, I planned to teach English to businesspeople and Bedouin in the community—anyone who was willing to learn.

Directors at private institutes said I could use their classroom facilities in exchange for instructing staff. It was an ideal situation. Classes would begin the following Saturday.

"Why can't I teach?" I asked Dr. Mustafa. "It's my own time."

"You belong to me," he answered. "They can get their own teachers."

"But I'm in Marib," I said. "It's an opportunity for a native speaker instructor to help the community."

"No," he replied shaking his head.

"Cheri told me I could teach in my spare time," I protested.

"Not in Marib!" he answered, his unapologetic eyes fixed on mine.

A dinner of flat bread and cheese triangles tasted like cardboard. "I hate Marib," I thought to myself, drinking a Pepsi. "I cannot write. I cannot teach students willing to learn." The telephone rang. "Hello," I answered crossly.

"Is something wrong?" Daood asked.

"No—yes—everything," I replied.

"A hotel guest wants to speak with you," Daood said. "Her name's Layla." Mohammed had mentioned that an American was staying at the hotel. He

131

knew guests by nationalities, since he filed police reports. He also knew the color of Layla's swimsuit, blue.

Layla waited for me at the reception desk. "Hi," I said and introduced myself. We sat on the hotel steps, still warm from the afternoon sun.

"What brings you to Marib?" I asked.

"A study on infant mortality," she replied. "The survey is for a health agency in Washington, D.C. Eighty thousand children under the age of five die annually in Yemen. That's what's reported—the numbers are probably higher."

"Death rates must be high," I said. "Filthy hospital conditions—no running water, no medicines, and no follow-up care." I remembered one mother's hollow-eyed plea on her knees, cradling a dying baby in her thin arms, begging someone for help not with words (because she was a Yemeni woman and could not speak in public) but with sunken eyes. "No one cares—except about making money."

"Someone told me you're teaching English," she said. "I wanted to meet you. It must be difficult living in Marib. Two days are enough for me."

"It's hard," I replied. "I thought I could make a difference by teaching English, especially to help those who had no opportunity to study outside Marib. When students realized they would not receive money or could not chew qat in class, they quit. One student said English was haram and I should leave Marib because the Koran forbids any language other than Arabic. There are those who want to study, but I cannot teach them. In the quiet of the desert, I hoped to write, but creativity needs inspiration. My muse wanted no part of this prison."

"Why do you stay?"

"I signed a contract and will keep my word," I answered. A moment passed in silence, and we listened to the rustling of wind in the palm trees.

"What's most difficult?" she asked.

"Being locked up," I answered. "Not being trusted."

"Anything else?" she asked.

"Yes, I'm tired of asking permission."

Late afternoon the following day, Mohammed came to my door and announced that an American man was staying at the hotel. John, an educational expert who headed a U.S. government-funded project, came infrequently to

Marib with his Yemeni staff. A few minutes later, my room telephone rang, and John asked me to join them for dinner.

Dressed in a white, long-sleeved, high-necked blouse and a long, chocolate-brown, printed cotton skirt, I felt pretty. My hair had grown, and I wore it in a French braid. Walking to the dining room, I saw Mohammed on his way to the hotel to place his nightly telephone police report.

John waited by the entrance to the dining room. He introduced me to the Yemeni men, and we shook hands. They were surprised that I lived in Marib and assured me they would not consider such a crazy idea—convincing their wives would be impossible. Food came as soon as we were seated, since it had been ordered in advance. I watched Mohammed through the glass that separated the dining room from the lobby as he talked on the telephone. "I'm not allowed outside the hotel without a murafik," I whined to John while eating my salad. "I'm a hostage, and sometimes Mohammed doesn't give his permission for me to go outside the gate."

He listened and cut a piece of cucumber. "Why don't you marry him?" he suggested.

"Marry who?" I asked, shocked by his words.

"Marry Mohammed, the bodyguard," John replied. "If he's a typical Yemeni, you'll never see him again. He'll be off with friends chewing qat." John made me laugh and put me at ease. It stopped my complaining. I looked forward to John's visits, but they were too short and too far between.

Waving good-bye to John the next day, I stopped at the guardhouse to speak with Mohammed. "I have photocopying for class," I said.

"What time?" Mohammed asked.

"Now, please," I answered.

"I can't," he said. "I'm busy. Let's talk over there." Under the droopy pepper trees that lined the dirt path far from the guardhouse he spoke quietly, which was unnecessary since none of the guards understood English.

"I'm busy with personal things," he whispered. "Can I use your phone?"

"Okay, but I'm low on units," I answered.

"I'll go to Sabafon after Asr," he replied.

"Why are you wearing a military uniform?" I asked. "You said you had quit the army to guard me. You told me your military pay stopped."

"I like the uniform," he answered.

After three o'clock, Mohammed, now wearing street clothes, knocked at my door. "Give me the money," he said. "I'll walk to Sabafon and do the photocopying."

"But I want to walk," I replied.

"The men at Sabafon look at you," he said, his eyes open wide. "They say they want to study English, but they're not good."

"Okay, they are not good, but I still want to go."

"Modest women in Marib don't go outside," he insisted. "Do you see women on the street?" I reluctantly gave Mohammed the money, telephone, and test paper.

"Don't look at the test," I said, closing the door.

We walked to class the following afternoon. Mohammed could not yet stop me from teaching.

"Where's Asma?" I asked the female students. "It's not like her to miss class."

"She's getting married," Amal said but stopped when the men entered the classroom.

Asma—I later found out—had been married at age sixteen to a Yemeni man, but after several months the marriage had been annulled. Now betrothed to a wealthy Saudi man who came to Marib seeking a fourth wife, he paid a sizable bride price—even though Asma, in Amal's words, was "used merchandise." It is common for Saudi men to find young wives in Yemen. Families gladly accepted high bride prices that the Saudi men paid, but there were more instances of young girls being abandoned, which created significant social problems in Yemen.

Asma's upcoming wedding prompted a discussion about respectable women among the female students when the men went to pray. "Nobody wants an opened package," Jamila said in a high-pitched squeak. When I asked what they thought of television programs from Egypt featuring unveiled women wearing make-up and tight-fitting clothes, they said the actresses were only half-Muslim. "Which half?" I wondered.

One day I saw Mohammed looking at pornography sites at the Internet café. I knew that he could not be alone in his interest. Mohammed tried to switch screens but was not quick enough. After the Internet café incident, I asked him about prostitution. He said there are prostitutes available but did not volunteer added information. In Sana'a, I noticed boys walking aimlessly on the sidewalks in the evenings with single women. The woman would stay back while the boy spoke to a man or group of men. Perhaps prostitution, I could only guess.

After class, I asked Mohammed to walk with me to Marib because I wanted a painted "pilgrim" trunk for the classroom to lock up books and supplies. The rectangular metal trunks come in various sizes and colors. We stopped at a shop that sold brightly painted trunks. "That one," I said to Mohammed and pointed to a medium-sized green trunk with a painting of the Dome of the Rock on its lid.

"One thousand rials," the storekeeper replied. I turned around, and Mohammed was gone.

I found him standing outside the store on the street. "It's expensive," he said and muttered something about the price. I followed him, thinking we would stop at the next store. "What's wrong with you?" he asked when I halted in my tracks.

"Last week, you said I couldn't buy black gloves and now the storage box. It's my money."

"You're always sad," he sighed. "You'd be happy if you lived with my family."

If I were milking goats and plowing fields without time to think. "Thanks," I said. "I know you're protecting me from shop clerks charging high prices."

"I'm protecting myself," he replied. "The soldiers asked why I'm with you. They say it's not right."

"Is that why you were angry when the doctor asked if we had a contract?" I asked, laughing. "He meant a marriage contract."

"Yes," he replied. "Everyone thinks we should be married to walk together."

"We're together because you're my bodyguard. Didn't you tell them it's a job and you get paid?"

"They can't understand," he said. "You're a woman."

"Yes, a much older woman," I said.

"Prophet Muhammad married a woman fifteen years older than him."

29

My Teachers

The years teach much which the days never know.
—Ralph Waldo Emerson

Since invitations to homes in Marib seemed unlikely, I asked the female students to come to the hotel on Thursday afternoon. "We'll sit by the pool and drink tea," I said, thinking that would be a treat. From alarmed looks behind veils and rigid body language, I could tell it was a poor suggestion.

"We'll come to your room," Amal replied.

After cleaning the room on Thursday, I put a bouquet of pink flowers and basil on the bookcase. I locked Zhara in the bathroom with her bowl of cookies. She would entertain herself by jumping up, trying to remove my bath towel from the wall hook, and when successful, she would make a nest on the floor.

Hearing knocking at exactly four o'clock, I opened the door to find four women. I had three female students. When they began to shed outer layers of black, I was not sure who was who. I immediately recognized Asma.

"You must be Jamila," I said to the woman with a beautiful aquiline nose, like a bird's beak. Her dark skin glowed.

"Of course," she said, annoyed and not realizing that I had never seen her uncovered face before. She removed her headscarf to reveal black, kinky hair tied in a knot at the nape of her neck.

Hesitantly, I asked, "And you?" looking at an uncovered face.

"Don't you know me?" she asked, dark wavy hair plastered against her head after being freed from her scarf. "I'm Amal."

"Yes, of course," I said and recognized her by the extra layer of drape of black material worn like a cape over her shoulders, an added sign of piety for women.

136

The woman with henna-colored red hair done up in a bun introduced herself as Nura, a friend of all three, and a middle-school English teacher in Marib.

"*Ahlan*, welcome," I said. "Please sit down." They sat on the carpeted floor and leaned against the bed. Nura dominated the conversation with questions about grammar. It felt like class. Politely, my students remained silent until I asked about their lives.

A knock at the door sent the women into a frenzy, grabbing scarves and veils. I opened the door an inch. "Mohammed, you know I have guests," I said.

"The guard told me four women came to your room," he said, tight-lipped, his foot firmly wedged in the opening. "Who is she?"

"I'll explain later," I answered. The scowl stayed on his face, but he removed his foot, and I shut the door and apologized to the women for the interruption.

Jamila, now wearing a headscarf, continued. "I'm studying to be a midwife," she said. "I'm the oldest of eleven children, and I want to get married." Prospects looked dim because she was twenty-two years old and in Marib already considered a spinster. "Do you know if Mohammed is married?" she asked.

"Mohammed the murafik?" I questioned and pointed over my shoulder to the door. I was shocked by her directness. "Maybe he's engaged—he wears a silver ring, but I don't think he's married."

"Could you find out?" she asked.

There is no future for Yemeni females except in marriage. "A woman without a husband is like a bird with only one wing," an Arabic proverb warns. After marriage women should bear children—preferably sons. If she does not, the husband has the right to take another wife because his social status relies on the number of sons.

Amal, the youngest at nineteen years old, was from an ultra-conservative religious family. Her father refused marriage proposals because the suitors were insufficiently devout in his eyes. Marrying just anyone would indicate that he had not brought her up properly. Unfortunately, Amal had fallen in love with a man her father could not accept, a doctor from Sana'a who worked at the hospital. Resigned to the fact that she would marry her uncle's son—a man nearly twice her age—she accepted her fate. The others agreed it was the unquestioned interpretation of Islam to do what your father decides. A custom so rooted in tribal tradition it had the force of law and declared that a father, not the parents or girl, chooses his daughter's husband. The old tribal custom maintained that finances and property stayed in the family. To think or do otherwise would be an insult to the centuries-old traditions.

"What if your father might be wrong?" I asked, standing up to make tea.

"You do it anyway," they replied, shocked that I would even suggest a father's fallibility.

Asma had brought a freshly baked bint as-sahin and poured honey from a can over its top. We broke the flaky pastry with our hands. "What if Amal told her father she was in love?" I asked, wiping honey from my fingers with a napkin.

"She can't," they explained. "He would think the worst. Maybe seek revenge."

Allahu Akbar (God is great), the call to prayer, sounded and the women asked if they could use the bathroom to wash. "Zhara's inside," I said worriedly. "If you don't mind, I'll let her out." Zhara, her tail bushy, dashed out the door, but she stopped abruptly upon seeing so many people.

"She's young," Asma said and watched Zhara tear at the leather tassels hanging from Amal's purse. Zhara raced around the room, glad to be out of the bathroom, and settled on the bed.

"Don't pet her," I warned. "She scratches."

"Why don't you pray with us?" Amal asked. "We'll teach you."

"Okay," I answered, slipping off my sandals.

"Your shoe," Amal said, pointing to my upside-down sandal. "The bottom of your shoe can't point to Allah." I repositioned my shoes with their soles on the floor so as not to offend God.

They washed, and I followed their example. Beginning with the right foot, I washed it three times, and then the same with the left foot. Arms washed three times in the same sequence. Rinsed my mouth three times. Rinsed my nose three times. Face three times. Right hand and left hand three times. Hair once—I ran a wet hand over the top of my head. Ears washed once. When we finished the prescribed ablutions, we retied our scarves and lined up facing Mecca. Amal told me to cover my feet with my skirt, which required that I step on the hem. "God doesn't like to see your feet," she said. This was tricky because when I kneeled and stood up again, my feet showed. Zhara watched with half-closed eyes from the bed.

With the last prayer, Nura's telephone rang. She barely uttered a word and burst out crying. "What's wrong?" Asma asked.

Between sobs, we learned that Nura's eleven-year-old sister had fallen. I think that the problem may be broken bones, but it turns out her father is worried that her hymen might be damaged. No membrane, no marriage. Out of angry frustration, he had beaten Nura's mother. "If I don't get home, he'll hurt my sister," Nura said, fastening her baltu.

"I don't understand," I said to Amal while walking to the gate. "Why did he beat the mother?"

"For her carelessness," she replied.

Four black shadows waved good-bye to me at the hotel gate. They returned to their lives. I returned to mine.

"Who were the sweet things in your room?" a hotel worker sidled up to me on the tree-lined path and asked.

"Those women," I answered, "are my teachers."

30

RAFALLAH'S TENT

The problem with the world is that we draw
the circle of our family too small.
—MOTHER TERESA

Mohammed waited by the classroom door, listening as the female students and I made plans to meet the following Thursday. I noticed his fixed gaze like a glinting knife-edge.

"Are you saying I can't have women come to my room?" I nearly shouted at Mohammed, feeling frustrated as we walked down the stairs.

"Only your students," he replied. "No one else is allowed."

"We'll see," I said and stomped down the last few steps.

On Thursday afternoon, I sat on the wooden bench by the hotel gate. Mohammed was not around. I did not want the guards to turn my visitors away. I waited until five o'clock. No one came.

"Did you tell my students not to come to the hotel?" I asked Mohammed the following Saturday. He pretended not to understand as we walked to the Internet café. "My students," I tried again, "did you call them?"

"No," he replied defensively.

The Internet café door was padlocked twice: once with the regular lock and an additional chain and lock because the owner had not paid his electric bill. No one at the teahouse knew when it might open. Heavy-hearted, I followed Mohammed's slow, deliberate steps through the dusty alley. The wind picked up, and sand blew. He wrapped the black-and-white scarf in such a way that it covered the lower half of his face like a mask. I lowered my veil.

Near the intersection, an old jalopy of a Toyota truck stopped. The driver, a high-cheekboned, kohl-rimmed-eyed Bedouin spoke with Mohammed. The Bedouin leaned over and opened the passenger door, and Mohammed got in. I sat next to Mohammed. The driver, Rafallah, lived in a tent opposite the hotel behind the small grocery store, but it was the first time for me to see him. Over the months, he and his family watched us coming and going. Today in Marib, he learned that someone might try to harm the American teacher, and he felt it a duty to protect me—a neighbor.

Rafallah invited us to drink tea in his tent. Surprisingly, Mohammed agreed. A rectangular wire-mesh frame—like a cage—held the tent's outer fabric, and its earth floor was carpeted with striped brown-and-tan goat-hair rugs. Opposite walls lined with low mattresses were covered with red, white, and black woven fabric with pillow backs and bolsters in the same material. The mattresses are used for seating during the daytime and sleeping at night. A tall, wooden, glass-fronted cupboard painted blue held dishes and glasses. A mirror hung on the wall beside the cupboard, its leather flap decorated with cowry shells.

Mohammed looked comfortable—not his usual guarded self. A warm breeze blew through the tent. Rafallah's four young sons joined us, and the boys tried unsuccessfully not to stare. A fifth son, the oldest, carried a metal tray covered with small glasses of hot, sugary tea. Rafallah proudly introduced his sons, and Mohammed translated names.

Rafallah's wife entered the tent, followed by two young daughters. She was slender and tall and looked like a fairy-tale princess stepping out from the pages of an Arabian storybook. Bright with self-assurance, she gracefully approached and shook my hand and kissed my cheeks. Her intelligent, intense eyes sparkled when she spoke. Dressed as if for a special occasion, she wore layers of colorful skirts—I could see the different colors of the skirts when she tucked her bare feet under them as she sat on the mattress. Her dark-blue sirwal pantaloons were edged with embroidered blue and yellow geometric designs.

She asked none of the standard questions. Her pretty daughters sat on either side of her, and surprisingly she introduced them. Mohammed translated. Giving children—especially girls—ugly names is usual practice in Marib. Families believed jinn would notice and harm girls with beautiful names. Both girls had somewhat ugly-sounding names.

I admired her heavy antique silver arm and ankle bracelets, but not too much, or she would have felt obliged to offer them. She wore a long necklace of spool-like amber beads strung around her neck. Although her face remained hidden behind a black velvet veil studded with beads, I knew she was beautiful. I liked her immediately.

Women's lives compared to men have changed and are changing in the developed Arab world to become more like the West, but most Yemeni Bedouin women do not even have the opportunity for education. However, neither do the Yemeni Bedouin men. I wondered how much better women's lives would be if they had education, access to other women, and could make more choices—what some people call freedom. What doors would open and what doors would close? Was the western way right for everyone? We finished our teas and thanked Rafallah, the provider of the family. He invited us to visit again, sincerity reflected in his dark eyes.

"Rafallah's location in front of the museum will be good," I said to Mohammed as we crossed the road that led to the hotel.

"If the museum is ever built," Mohammed replied, laughing.

A tall concrete wall encircled a large area planned for the museum, but the walls had started to crumble. Money given to Yemen by American taxpayers to build the Marib Museum had—like Yemeni antiques—disappeared. The half-moon sign outside the fence advertising U. S. financial aid had so many bullet holes that the words were unreadable. I thought of the American ambassador.

Over the years, artifacts and treasures from Marib stored in the basement of the Sana'a National Museum have collected dust while awaiting construction of the Marib Museum. No one knows what is stored because there is no efficient cataloging system. Cultural relics have been sold to private collectors in Europe, Japan, and America. Trafficking in antiques is widespread and hard to stop, since it involves so much money.

"Do you think the President's Hospital will ever be finished?" I asked, looking in its direction. It was another project built with American money.

"Maybe before the museum," he answered. The President's Hospital in Marib (named for the president of Yemen) had been scheduled to open the year before I arrived in Marib. The last time I had visited the site, it was still under construction, and the front and back windows were riddled with bullet holes from a shoot-out between tribes. Hospital equipment costing millions of dollars, the finest up-to-date computer technology, sat forlorn. Wind blew through the broken windows, and sand dunes formed on opposite walls.

31

BROKEN IMAGES

All things are connected. Whatever befalls the earth befalls the sons of the earth. Man did not weave the web of life. He is merely a strand of it. Whatever he does to the web he does to himself.
—CHIEF SEATTLE

Three Yemeni girls dressed in green cloaks and white headscarves—school uniforms—walked to the hotel's entrance, tying and untying scarves, fitting them just right, fiddling with them as young girls in America would fiddle with their hair on the way to school. They were the daughters of hotel workers who lived on the hotel grounds. Whenever I said hello, the girls scampered away.

"Why are the children frightened of me?" I asked Mohammed.

"They're afraid of Americans," he answered.

"Why?" I asked, amazed by his answer.

Months before I had arrived in Marib, the American military rented the annex at the hotel to house broad-shouldered American military men. Although no one knew exactly why they were in Marib, people speculated it was a secret training mission to do aerial photography, because at the same time unmarked planes appeared in Marib's sky.

During the day, the American military men disappeared into the desert, but at night at the hotel, they drank. Alcohol is illegal in Yemen, an Islamic state, but the embassy probably supplied them with drinks. Travelers coming from abroad can bring limited quantities into the country, and there were "not so secret" places to buy smuggled Djibouti liquor, but generally, alcohol was unavailable. The drunken military men caused extensive damage to the annex rooms and to America's reputation.

Parents warned children to stay away from me because I was an American. They assumed all Americans were alike. Since I had just found out about the

American military presence in Marib, I wondered if my students had heard stories. They had. Apparently, everyone knew except me.

The students in class spoke openly about America in mostly negative terms. Invading Afghanistan and later Iraq, which had no direct connection to September 11, was high on the list of why they did not like or trust Americans. They knew the reason America had not targeted Saudi Arabia even though the hijackers had come from there. When President Bush declared America was engaged in a global "war on terror," they believed America wanted to take over the world. To them, it was evident, watching nightly news that showed butchery and bloodshed of innocents. His declaration made the whole world a battlefield. However, none of them thought America would have the slightest interest in invading Yemen because it had nothing to offer—oil and water in limited supply. For this they felt grateful. They recognized the difference between the "Bush War" and individual Americans and warned me not everyone in Marib felt the same. "Some people hate Americans." I knew that must be true.

After class, Asma's father, Ali, waited near the door. When I passed, he handed me a small folded paper, which I slipped into my bag. Walking home—"home" is what I called the hotel— I opened the paper to find a passport-sized color photograph of Ali, his salt-and-pepper beard neatly combed. He wore a thobe and suit jacket and a white scarf wrapped turban fashion. I held the photo in my hand. Mohammed rambled on about his views of America and those of his classmates. "None of the students like America," he explained. "But they all want to go there."

"And you?" I asked.

"Of course," he answered without hesitation. "It's a dream."

"What would you do in America?" I asked. "Would you study?" Mohammed had been in a degree program but stopped because he ran out of money, which is why he joined the military.

"No, I'd work and make so much money then return to Yemen, famous," he said, grinning. "I'd build a school and mosque in my village." I think he visualized the school and mosque already standing in his village, from the dreamy, faraway expression in his eyes.

"What kind of work would you do?" I asked.

"Any kind," he replied. "Yemenis go to America and come back rich."

Listening to Mohammed, I wondered how well Yemeni workers coped with living in America. Many had low-paying jobs as clerks in markets. Now, after September 11, they were suspect and jailed.

"Ali gave me his photo," I said, holding the color image.

"That's wrong of him," Mohammed said, picking up his pace.

"I think it's nice," I replied, following Mohammed's footsteps.

Two Land Cruisers were parked next to the annex when I returned from class. The tiled fountain in the garden sprayed watery diamonds high into the azure evening sky. It was only turned on when annex guests arrived and quickly turned off so as not to waste precious water. Soft yellow lights peeked from behind drawn curtains that covered windows. People in stylish clothes stood in small groups in the garden, talking and laughing. The annex felt alive.

Nasser operated the water controls and waved to me. "A French tour group," he said. "They will travel tomorrow to Sayun. "I joined the group standing near my bathroom window. Zhara's face pressed against the screen, wanting attention. "Do you live here?" they asked. I explained I did and that it was nice to have neighbors. I let Zhara outside, and she chased imaginary creatures in the fading light. "She's a Marib cat. I found her right here," I said and pointed to the basil plants.

"Can you join us for dinner?" the French tour leader asked. Delighted, I accepted and coaxed Zhara back into the room. We walked to the hotel.

Two long tables pushed together covered with white tablecloths and napkins on the terrace overlooked the pool. The desert evening was balmy and perfect for eating outside. Candles flickered on the tables, giving light and atmosphere. It seemed more like France—without the wine—than Yemen. A bottle of gin, hidden in a towel, circulated under the table. We poured ourselves drinks. Mubarak, a Yemeni French-speaking tour guide, joined us; he pretended not to notice the gin bottle.

Drivers and guides dealing with foreign guests see surprising and perhaps shocking conduct. International women came to Yemen for more than the sights. They come to have sexual adventures, which explained creaking doors during the night when tour groups stayed in the annex. An attractive blonde woman in her mid-thirties refused to eat the food in the hotel dining room. She insisted the tour driver take her to Marib for meals. He obliged. Later, they both returned to her room.

More than one driver boasted that he purchased a new Land Cruiser with money from clients. I believed them. While in Marib, drivers' cell phones rang with calls from women around the world. Excusing themselves, they would step aside and speak Italian, German, Spanish, English, or whatever language was necessary, promising women their hearts.

Innocent flirting also went on between the tour drivers and female tourists. It was all done in self-interest because it meant higher tips for the men. Yemeni "Casanovas" raked in cash. Women gladly paid handsomely to not-so-handsome men.

Military men had part of the action. Mohammed said a European woman assumed he would stay with her the night. He refused. She offered more money. "What did you do?" I asked.

"I told her no," he said. "She didn't talk to me the next day, but I didn't care. That kind probably had disease."

"Does it happen very often?" I asked.

"Tourists sleeping with Yemeni men, yes," he replied.

"No, I meant women asking you?" He did not answer.

Two unmarried women in their mid-forties—one thin and one plump, both named Mary—came to Yemen for a month's holiday to see the sights. Since neither spoke Arabic, they hired a translator/guide as well as a car with a driver. The four set off from Sana'a and spent the first night in Marib, the Marys in separate rooms in the Bilquis Hotel. The men slept in the driver's quarters of the annex.

Early the next morning they drove to Sayun. While crossing the sand dunes that stretched to the Rub al-Khali, the four formed a pleasant friendship. In Shibam, three days later, the driver and Mary decided to marry. He, of course, had a Yemeni wife, but being Muslim, he could have up to four.

The road trip continued for another two weeks, and by the time they arrived in al-Mukalla, on the Arabian Sea, the translator/guide and the other Mary fancied each other and wanted to marry.

Each year Mary and Mary returned to Yemen and spent time with their Yemeni husbands.

PART VI

NEW FRIENDS AND OLD TRADITIONS

32

SANA'A

If we wait for the moment when everything,
absolutely everything is ready, we shall never begin.
—IVAN TURGENEV

"Many words in English are borrowed from Arabic," I explained. The students looked dubious. "'Alcohol,' 'alcove,' 'alfalfa,' 'algebra,' 'azimuth,' 'alkali,' and many more . . . " I asked them to think of additional words, but they remained silent. I added "algodon" (cotton), "alquimia" (alchemy), "azucar" (sugar), and "azafran" (saffron). The word game did not hold the student's attention—they listened for the *adhan*, call to prayer, which announced for them that the lesson had ended. They wanted test results. I had stopped passing out corrected tests before class ended because they frantically tore papers from each other's hands.

"You're only in competition with yourself," I said and watched men run toward the door. Outside they compared scores. Mohammed hung back—his low score showed he had not studied, and he did not want his classmates to know. The women stayed in the classroom and snatched papers from each other's hands.

For the past week, Mohammed looked gloomy. "What's going on?" I asked as we left the classroom. "Do you want to stop for a Pepsi so we can talk?" He shook his head. "See you tomorrow—inshallah, God willing," I said at the hotel gate.

"Inshallah," he replied listlessly.

In a patriarchy, it is easy to focus on women's troubles—hidden behind veils, women are often voiceless. They seem the sufferers, and, of course, they are.

However, boys and men in Yemen lead difficult lives—they are sometimes voiceless as well. At early ages, some young village boys from poor families are

148

taken to cities and work selling tea, polishing shoes, washing cars, or begging. Education is out of the question because school uniforms and books are too expensive. Without education, they have few opportunities for jobs as men. Young men face unemployment rates of up to 40 percent and, lacking financial resources, they stay single until families can afford the costly bride prices.

Both men and women suffer when forced into marriages to secure family alliances and financial prospects. According to Islamic law, a woman must give her consent or the marriage is invalid. In the nuptial contract, she can include any condition she likes, including prohibiting her husband from taking a second wife. However, young uneducated people do not understand or know their rights. Out of a sense of duty or fear, they submit to the will of fathers.

The bride price has become extremely expensive. Girls—sometimes as young as ten years old—are sold into marriage to much older men. There is tribal belief that young wives can be fashioned into obedient wives as stated in a proverb: "Give me a girl of eight and I can give you a guarantee for a good marriage."

In 1992 Yemeni law set the minimum marriage age for girls at fifteen, but in 1998 parliament revised the law and allowed girls to marry earlier as long as they did not "live" with their husbands until reaching sexual maturity. Ultra-conservatives with great influence in north Yemen defended early marriage using Prophet Muhammad's marriage to a nine-year-old girl as an example.

Marriageable ages for girls in rural areas are twelve to thirteen years. Forced to bear children long before their bodies are ready, many girls suffer serious health problems. Yemen has one of the highest maternal mortality rates in the world. One out of every fifty women dies during childbearing age because of multiple pregnancies.

Marriages are usually between first cousins. "Marrying a strange girl [someone outside your family] is drinking water from an earthenware crock, while marriage with a cousin is a drink from a dish," as the proverb states. A girl typically marries her first cousin, the son of her father's brother. When the man cannot afford an expensive bride price, it is common for his sister to be payment and given to one of the bride's brothers. Sisters are brought up to serve brothers and out of a sense of duty willingly become an offering. If one couple divorces, the other couple is likely to divorce, or it will cause a split in the family. Children are property—they stay with the father.

If Mohammed did not produce the final payment of 100,000 rials for the bride price by the end of the month, the wedding would be off. His one sister was already married. His cousin, the betrothed, would then go to the next bidder. Mohammed would lose his intended, the money, and possibly self-respect within his community.

"Can you give me money?" he asked on the second-to-last day of the month.

"No, I can't," I replied. "What will happen?"

"She'll return to her father's house," he said.

"It's a big disappointment," I said. "You must be sad."

"She won't be able to help my father," he replied. "I'm sad for him."

"What about for yourself?" I asked.

He thought for a minute before answering, "A little sad."

"What will happen to the bride price money your family has already paid?" I questioned.

"Maybe my uncle will give what he hasn't spent to my father, inshallah," he replied.

After the noon sermon at the mosque on Fridays, Mohammed chewed qat with friends. I stayed in my room. Writing seemed impossible. I kept a journal called "Lost Desert Pages." In America, my latest children's book would be out, but I sat alone, with no way and no one to celebrate with. I put a CD in the player. "I will celebrate in Sana'a," I thought and turned up the music and picked Zhara up in my arms and danced.

Mohammed's eyebrows rose when I explained I would travel to Sana'a. "I don't think Dr. Mustafa will allow it," he said, lowering his brows.

"He can't stop me," I replied. "Cheri said I could travel."

"Dr. Mustafa signs the papers or you can't go," he answered.

"What if I travel by shared taxi?" I asked. "I'll go veiled."

"The taxi driver won't take you," he replied.

"If he thinks I'm a Yemeni woman, he will," I argued.

"Yemeni women don't travel alone," he said, his eyes opening wide. "The only way is to ask Dr. Mustafa and me," he added.

"Why do I ask you?" I questioned.

"Because you can't leave Marib without me," he said and laughed so hard he snorted. It had not occurred to me that Mohammed would accompany me to Sana'a. I would pay for his travel expenses, hotel, and food. "Okay," I thought, "it is worth it."

Without hesitation, Dr. Mustafa agreed to the trip and signed official traveling documents. Mohammed photocopied a stack of papers to pass to the soldiers at seventeen checkpoints between Marib and Sana'a and again on the return. I reserved a room at AIYS. Tuesday night, I set my alarm to wake the next morning at five o'clock. Daood would stay in my room and kitty-sit. I pasted notes—yellow Post-its—all over the place. "Here are Zhara's bowls," "Fill one bowl with water." "Keep the tuna in the refrigerator after it's opened." "Give her canned milk in the mornings." "Clean her kitty-litter box twice a day."

Wednesday morning at 5:30 a.m., I walked to hotel reception, where I found Daood half-asleep on the floor, one eye on the television screen. "Thank you so much," I said and gave him my room key.

"When will you be back?" he asked.

"Three days—inshallah," I answered. "Will you be okay?"

"Inshallah," he replied.

Mohammed waited at the gate, arms wrapped around his chest, trying to keep warm. Temperatures had dropped dramatically during the night, and we shivered from the early morning cold as we walked to the shared taxi stand. Only two cars passed us on the road, and neither offered rides. I tried to explain why going to Sana'a was important. "My children's book will be published," I said. "It is a big deal in America!"

"How will you celebrate?" he asked. "Drink wine?"

"I hope," I replied. That stopped the conversation. Mohammed associated drinking wine with obnoxious behavior. However, he is looking forward to drinking wine in Islamic heaven poured by young girls.

At the taxi stand, I gave Mohammed 3,000 rials, and he negotiated the price with the taxi driver. We squeezed into the rear seat of the long-distance station-wagon taxi. Mohammed paid for three seats, which meant a man sat beside him—there are four paid seats to a row. Since Mohammed did not return any money, I assumed each seat cost 1,000 rials.

Mohammed wrote his family name twice on the clipboard and showed the driver his military card. Dressed head-to-toe in black, I traveled as a relative. As a Yemeni woman, I could not speak.

A small parcel was on my lap, and Mohammed's Kalashnikov was jammed into my leg. After the driver said "Bismillah," we headed for Sana'a. The car did not stop at any military checkpoints, nor did Mohammed give out copies of the traveling papers. When the men stopped for tea and pee breaks, I stayed in the car.

The shared taxi dropped us in the middle of the city. Although I knew Sana'a well, it seemed intimidating and disorienting. Cars, people, and chaos. I was thankful for Mohammed's help. He flagged a local taxi to take us to AIYS.

Mohammed sat in the front seat. I sat in back. After discussing the merits of qat sold in Marib and Sana'a (both men were from Taiz), they worked out relationships. "Oh, her," he said to the taxi driver. "She's an American." They talked about me as if I were absent. Mohammed explained that I was from Hawaii, like a curious creature. The driver turned his head for a better look. Dressed in black, there was not much to see. Nevertheless the driver glanced in his rearview mirror, trying to get a better look at the oddity until we reached AIYS.

"Please don't do that again," I said to Mohammed when I stepped out of the taxi.

"What?" he asked looking startled.

"Tell taxi drivers about me." I said. "You wouldn't do that to your sister."

"But you're not Yemeni," he replied.

Shakeeb, the AIYS gate guard, greeted us when we stepped through the wooden gate. Mohammed waited with Shakeeb in the guardhouse while I went upstairs. "Hello, hello," I called on each landing, but no answer. I guessed a room on the fourth floor was mine—a key dangled from a lock. After putting my bag in the room, I went downstairs to the third-floor bathroom.

Seeing my reflection in the full-length mirror surprised me—I looked thinner and taller. I removed the black veil and scarf. My hair was plastered flat against my head. I retied the scarf not because my hair looked a mess, which it did, but because I felt exposed without the scarf. For the first time in Sana'a, I covered my hair.

Mohammed's Kalashnikov stayed in the guardhouse—no need for it in Sana'a—and we walked to the Dubai restaurant and ate foule and bread. After breakfast, we went to Fares's Internet café next door.

Reading e-mails was not as satisfying as I had anticipated. Friends did not understand why I lived in Yemen, and explaining seemed impossible. Many believed Yemeni women were downtrodden and oppressed, kept veiled and segregated because of religion. Women and men under Islam have had equal rights, except for inheritance, for more than fourteen hundred years. Of course, Yemen was not that way today, but it was not because of religion; it was the interpretation of religion. Mohammed tapped his foot, waiting impatiently for me to finish typing, because he wanted to buy qat for an afternoon chew with friends. "You can go," I said. "This is Sana'a. I'm safe!" He waited.

After buying a bag of qat sold by a man seated in the trunk of his car parked in front of the Internet café, Mohammed and I looked at *lukandas*, basic hotel rooms with one bedsheet (usually well used) on each bed. "You can't stay here—it's only for Yemenis," Mohammed whispered as I waited at the bottom of the dirty, brown-carpeted stairs.

"Did the manager think I was staying with you?" I asked. Mohammed grinned. Sex between unmarried people is punishable by one hundred lashes and up to a year in prison. Maybe this place rented rooms. Mohammed showed his ID card and paid one thousand rials for the first night. "You have money, why didn't you pay for two nights?" I asked. He shrugged his shoulders.

"Good-bye, Mohammed," I said, shaking his hand in plain view of the hotel manager. "See you Friday afternoon." While walking through Tahrir Square and before arriving at AIYS, my telephone rang. "Hello," I answered.

"Any service?" Mohammed asked.

"Thanks," I replied. "I'm fine."

The kitchen on the fourth floor of AIYS had a telephone. I leafed though my phone book and dialed Kamal's telephone number. We made plans to meet for lunch on Thursday. I could not call Daood to check on Zhara because he would still be asleep.

Kitchen cabinets hung unevenly on whitewashed walls. I opened cabinets and peered inside them. Pots and pans of every description lined the shelves. Mismatched bowls, plates, glasses, and cups sat in a cupboard. Next to the brown, propane-gas stove was a cabinet with half-used sacks of rice, spaghetti, tea, instant coffee, a carton of foil-wrapped cheese triangles, a box of prunes, and foil packets of cappuccino with instructions in six languages.

Lighting the stove was tricky. I turned on the gas and struck a match. Shriveled, black, wooden matches piled high on the sink. I filled the teakettle with filtered water and placed it on the burner. Sitting at the table, I waited for the water to boil and from a narrowly slit window watched sunlight land on the tablecloth, causing silver threads to sparkle.

Potted plants perched on shelves built into the uneven walls made the kitchen look like a greenhouse. Before the water boiled, Mulk, the housekeeper burst into the kitchen. With a flourish, she removed her black outer cloak, revealing a long red-and-green paisley party dress with a girlish sweetheart neckline. She rewrapped her headscarf with such deft movements that my eyes could not follow her hands. Before work she plopped her petite frame opposite me on a bench for a rest. In Sana'ani dialect, which for Mulk included sweeping hand gestures, she explained that climbing the stairs had exhausted her. Opening a brown paper sack, she placed bread on the table. When the water boiled, Mulk jumped up to make two cups of tea.

"Shukran," I said as we broke bread and drank tea together.

Being in Sana'a felt heavenly. I was free to go shopping by myself. On Gamal Street, the main shopping avenue, I window-shopped. Slinky dresses, skintight pants, and hip-hugging skirts made from synthetic fabrics manufactured in China adorned curvy blonde and blue-eyed mannequins. White tulle wedding dresses with bodices and skirts studded with pearls along with rainbow-hued bridesmaid's costumes were displayed in shop windows. More intimate apparel (bras, panties, thongs, slips, gauzy nightgowns in bright colors) was hawked on streets by teenage boys from wheelbarrows. There is much to see, but walking and window-shopping can be dangerous on the cracked, uneven sidewalks. I dodged a boy selling packaged perfume from his wheelbarrow and tripped over a pile of bath towels.

As I passed a store selling cheap made-in-China luggage with misspelled logos, the shopkeeper leaned out the door as I passed. "Saddam Hussein," he shouted, perhaps not knowing other words to get my attention or as insult. Saddam Hussein posters decorated storefronts and the sides of buses. I smiled and waved. "Saddam Hussein," he yelled again and held up his thumb.

Baltu stores looked like black holes. I entered one. And, in a festive mood, bought a black chiffon scarf edged with shiny black sequins. I paid the asking price of 800 rials, not bothering to bargain. The clerk wrapped my purchase in tissue paper and handed it to me in a pink bag.

Shops along Gamal Street are famous for high-karat gold jewelry, and I searched for plain gold bangles. Most of the gold jewelry is too glittery for my taste, but I found plain bangles in 22-karat gold. I asked the shopkeeper to weigh one bangle on his scale—$122. "Thanks," I said and gave it back. Someday, I will replace the gold I sold for the camel trip.

Shopping for gold is a favorite pastime for women during afternoons. The shops are crowded with black-cloaked women huddled together in groups, examining jewelry. This activity appeared to be okay to do for women and without male escorts. Since women cannot remove black clothing, the male shopkeepers modeled the jewelry. "Shukran," I said to a shopkeeper who struck a feminine pose and held a pair of dangling gold earrings to his ears.

At the next store, an excruciatingly thin, tall, unshaven tribesman dressed in a thobe and dusty suit jacket blocked the entrance to the shoe shop. "Excuse me," I said in Arabic, trying to push past him. I then saw a thin, razor-sharp silver dagger hidden behind his jambiya. He fixed his black, kohl-rimmed eyes on me and blocked my way. His towering presence was intimidating. "Happy Birthday to you—happy birthday to you," he sang in English. Where in the world would someone actually sing happy birthday to a total stranger?

"Happy birthday," I replied, and we both smiled. What I cherished about Sana'a was that nothing was predictable.

My last shopping trip in Sana'a before I went to Marib had been with Nathalie, an American friend, in a shoe store. For fun, we tried on fancy high heels. At the same store, the clerk remembered me and opened a box with a pair of black-velvet, high-heeled sandals bejeweled with rhinestones. "Princess shoes," Nathalie and I had called them. He placed a square of cardboard on the rough cement floor so I could stand on it and removed my shoes. I tried the high-heeled sandals on, thinking they would be of no use in Marib. Nathalie had bought a pair. "*Jamil*, beautiful," I said to the man and removed the shoes and returned them to the box.

Carrying the pink bag, I stopped at Khalid's shop, a small grocery store located near AIYS. Khalid stocked items for Western tastes, but I bought an ice cream bar, two eggs, and one yogurt. "How's Marib?" he asked.

"Fine," I replied.

"Better than Sana'a?" he questioned.

"No, very different," I answered.

33

LIVING TRADITIONS

There are many trails up the mountain,
but in time they all reach the top.
—ANYA SETON

People sat around the kitchen table talking, and I poured a cup of tea and joined them. One of the joys of staying at AIYS was meeting interesting researchers and scholars. After introductions, I listened to a woman's story:

Kawkaban, like other Yemeni villages, had schools for boys. Asma, a young girl, convinced her family and a few of the villagers to allow daughters to attend school after the boys finished lessons. Teachers agreed to stay and teach the girls. However, the families received harsh criticism from the more traditionally minded villagers.

Roles for girls in the village were clearly defined: they were to support the family by doing household chores, caring for younger children, and later marrying. Breaking long-held traditions was difficult, but a girl named Asma had the energy and resolve.

After Asma completed six years of elementary school, her family expected her to stay home. She had other ideas and persuaded her father to buy books so she could study at home and attend the year-end examinations. This way Asma completed intermediate classes while also attending to the duties required of girls.

The year she graduated from intermediate school, Asma's father insisted she marry. She obeyed, because to do otherwise would disgrace the family.

During the first years of marriage, Asma produced three children, two daughters and a son. A mother's value is in sons. When her son was born, her husband asked what gift she wanted. Women usually asked for

156

gold. However, Asma asked for his permission to continue her education. Although the request was unexpected, he agreed.

The closest secondary school was in Shibam. Asma walked down the steep, zigzagging mountain path in the morning and back up each afternoon. Without her husband's permission, she could not have gone. Without her mother and sister's help looking after her children, it would have been unworkable. Although exhausted, Asma finished the first two years of secondary school.

Successfully, she passed the examinations and became a teacher in the local girl's school. Her longtime dream to educate girls became a reality. However, her dream was not yet over.

Asma enrolled in Sana'a University. She could not be a regular full-time student because she lived in Kawkaban, worked, and was responsible for her family. Her professors lent books so she could study. They allowed her to take examinations at the end of semesters. Her husband agreed to travel with her to Sana'a to take examinations if she could earn the money. Asma weaves baskets in Kawkaban.

There are families in her village who will not allow daughters to attend the girl's school. To overcome this Asma will save money and build a mosque for the girls and women and this way teach them to read the Koran.

Listening to the story, I thought of students everywhere. How many had her ambition?

"Fathers think it is shameful for boys and girls to study together," the storyteller added. "They believe it is disgraceful for girls to have male teachers."

"Do you see many girls like Asma?" a bearded man asked.

"No," she replied. "Tribal traditions and extreme religious beliefs do not support education."

"Do you encounter other problems?" a young, sandy-haired woman asked.

"Revenge killings," she answered. "Tribal conflicts have always been part of Yemeni life, but now they prevent students from attending classes. Marib students could not take final examinations this year in Sana'a. Blood feuds force students to carry weapons, and if they are worried about being taken hostage or killed, study is unlikely."

"Let's go for fish," the bearded man, who I later found out was a photographer from Jordan, suggested to change the subject. "Anyone know a good restaurant?" We agreed on a neighborhood eatery. Someone at the table had been in Aden, where buying liquor smuggled from Djibouti was possible. Before dinner, we would drink gin and tonics. Marib seemed a million miles away. Then the phone rang. "Hello," I answered.

"Are you drinking wine?" Mohammed asked.

"Not yet," I replied. "But soon."

I had forgotten the early morning sounds of Sana'a. AIYS was located between two mosques, and the electric loudspeakers attached to minarets shook the foundation of the house starting at 3:30 a.m. Loudspeakers crackled to life with throat-clearing sounds followed by shouting that called believers to prayer. The daily wake-up warm-ups set the tone for more to come. Dawn clicks exploded from tiny-loudspeakers like scattered gunshots. Voices soared from minarets, the sounds so great that they virtually lifted buildings off the ground.

After spending more time in Sana'a, I would get used to the early morning call and sometimes could sleep thought it, but since I had just returned to the capital, I was practically thrown from my bed. I shut my eyes and whispered, "God is Great, Allahu Akbar. I am a spirit residing in a body." This happened five times a day and acted as reminders that we are in the presence of God.

After a breakfast of tea and bread, I met with Chris Edens and paid my room bill. "Do you think I'm suffering from Stockholm syndrome, identifying with my captors?" I asked. I explained my day-to-day life in Marib—locked in my room with no way of getting outside the gate without Mohammed. People believed I was a spy. Chris listened. The more I talked, the crazier Marib sounded—even to me. "I'm beginning to like Mohammed, and that worries me the most," I said.

"Do they want you to become a Muslim?" he asked.

"Yes, but I told Mohammed and Ahmed that if I became a Muslim, they couldn't come to my room," I replied. "They have not brought up the idea again."

"It sounds like you haven't lost total control," Chris said. "You're not following blindly."

"Not yet. But, I've stopped writing," I explained. "Writing was my life. I believed no matter what happened, I could afford pencil and paper. At Marib

Dam, I wrote a poem, but Mohammed and the driver quizzed me and wanted the pages. On a picnic, I read a book of Rumi's poetry and Mohammed saw the word 'wine.' He wanted to know what I was reading."

"Do you know the governor of Marib?" Chris asked.

"Yes, he came to see me, and we had tea at the hotel," I said. "He's annoyed with people at the American embassy because they telephone Dr. Mustafa instead of calling him to find out about me. I told the governor they should ask me how I am."

"That would be too direct," Chris said, laughing.

"Thanks for listening," I replied, feeling better after sharing my frustrations. "Oh, when I called from the telephone booth in Marib to reserve a room at AIYS, Mohammed wrote your telephone number on his hand."

Before walking to Suq al-Milah, the salt market, in old Sana'a, I changed money. The money exchanger on Gamal Street sat behind a partition of glass and next to him a boy, his apprentice, was chewing qat. Through a half-moon window, I slipped the man a recently dated hundred-dollar bill. He held it to the light. Fanning them as if he were shuffling a deck of cards, he piled a stack of thousand rial notes on the counter.

Main streets in the old city are oriented from east to west in order to capture the sunlight. Wandering through the narrow, twisted lanes, I noticed discarded plastic bags, bits of trash, empty water bottles, and a child's pink plastic sandal. Water escaped from a pipe, wetting the cobblestones. Stench from a wall where men and boys peed nearly knocked me over. A mob of children screamed, "Whatsoorname?" in high-pitched screeches. Little girls dressed in princess gowns shouted, "*Sura, sura, sura.*" They wanted photos taken. To children, foreigners are tourists with cameras.

Old Sana'ani families slowly moved away from the old city and built modern houses in Hadda, a newer section of Sana'a. They rented their traditional tower homes to villagers who take little pride in the houses or Sana'a as an UNESCO Heritage Site.

Shopkeepers in the suq lounged on cushions, chewing qat and not especially interested in customers—the drug's side effect. Hard-sell mentality is missing from the suq and shopping is relaxed. After a glass of tea opposite Bab al-Yemen, I walked along a back street and saw a group of children playing with matches. To avoid the growing blaze, I stepped around two boys, who picked up burning cardboard and hurled flaming paper in the air. Visions of the polyester baltu bursting into flame and melting made me pick up my pace.

Further along the alleyway, I heard footsteps echo from behind. A well-dressed man hurried past me, and I watched him approach a Western woman dressed in a long tunic. He pinched her butt. Her reaction was startling— she leapt into the air and ran toward him. Another leap and she landed on him, yanking his suit jacket up around his ears. The middle-aged man looked dazed. He never expected a woman to run after him—or catch him. His bulging eyes pleaded, and he whispered, "I'm sorry" in Arabic. She tugged his cashmere shawl and knotted it around his neck. He shuddered, appearing very small. She pulled the shawl one last time and let him go. He ran.

"Congratulations," I said to her.

"That's for all the Yemeni women who have to put up with this . . . crap," she said, unable to find a better word.

"Well, he won't do that again," I said.

"Don't bet on it," she answered.

On my way to Kamal's house, I walked by the teahouse near the institute where I lived my first summer in Yemen. The men—perhaps same men—sat on wobbly wooden benches, holding glasses of tea and conversations. During that first summer, a large black dog slept on pillows of trash sprawled across the walkway.

Stepping over the dog, I noticed gashes on his ears and blood on his matted coat. Too often boys poked him with sticks. Tired of tormenting the dog, they tossed stones at small cats hiding under cars. "Animals are gifts from Allah," I explained. They stared blankly at the foreigner talking gibberish.

In Arabic class, I told Kamal that I had seen a man on a motorcycle deliberately kick the black dog's private part as he passed.

"Was it the blind dog at the teahouse?" Kamal asked. Until then I had not known the dog was blind. Later, I found out the dog was blinded by boys holding hot coals to his puppy eyes. Not everyone believed animals deserved bad treatment. I met many kind Yemeni men and women who fed stray dogs and cats.

Banging on Kamal's blue metal door, I looked toward the upstairs window, and a dark, shadowy figure peered out. "*Ana*, I," I said, knowing women should not announce names in public. The door creaked open. I followed

Kamal's young son up two flights. On the third floor was a man I did not recognize. I said hello and shook his hand without thinking. He had probably washed for prayer, but I could not take the handshake back.

He escorted me to the mafraj, and I sat on low cushions covered with carpet runners. Kamal's voice preceded him up the stairs. Although Kamal is traditionally Yemeni, he is open to the West but does not embrace it completely. "You're more beautiful," he said from the arched doorway. He excused himself to pray.

Old Yemeni houses inside walls are adorned with Arabesque niches and small cupboards for storage made from *qudad*, a type of lime plaster resembling marble when polished. Ornate Koranic blessings written in raised qudad are part of the room's decorations. Seated alone, I looked through a stack of Kamal's books and magazines. It is most unusual to find an avid Yemeni reader.

Kamal again stood in the arched doorway, this time holding a tray and followed by the man that I had accidentally shaken hands with, his friend Hussein, a poet. Kamal's younger son cleared a low table and ran between the mafraj where we sat and the kitchen delivering food. He was perfectly happy to serve his father.

The son placed giant rounds of freshly baked bread on small tables. He sat plates of saffron rice, spaghetti with tomato sauce, fish, and mutton, along with a salad of sliced tomato, red onion, and cucumbers, on the woven dining mat on the floor. Last came the piping hot pan of bint as-sahin.

Kamal's wife could not join us. Hussein was not a relative. She and the children would eat leftovers in the upstairs kitchen. I remembered to take small portions, knowing they would go hungry if nothing was left.

After the meal, another son cleared the dishes. He returned, balancing three tea glasses and a pot of tea on a copper tray. A dish on the tray held bunches of tiny green grapes, which he placed in front of his father.

I excused myself and climbed the stone steps to thank Kamal's wife for preparing a wonderful meal. However, in most Yemeni households this would be impolite, because guests are to thank the man of the house for his hospitality. Kamal understood or accepted my bad-mannered Western ways.

Upstairs his wife mopped the gray concrete kitchen floor, her oversized brown dress hem soaked with water. Leaning over the mop, she hugged me.

I noticed her cotton headscarf damp with perspiration—a real-life Cinderella. "For you," I said, handing her a box of Galaxy chocolates.

When I returned to the mafraj, Kamal was busily removing pink plastic wrap from branches of qat. His son placed a black plastic sack of bottled waters and soft drinks at his feet. Hussein had disappeared.

"Last month I visited my village," Kamal said, passing me a soft drink. "Two of my brothers are getting married. Each of the brides gets half a million rials—it's crazy."

"Does a million rials include gifts for the brides?" I asked.

"No," he replied. "But both brothers are marrying at the same time—there'll only be one big party. That saves money."

Everyone agreed that bride prices were too high, but few challenged the long-held custom. I thought of Mohammed. "There was a newspaper article about group weddings, and the photograph showed one hundred grooms dressed in wedding costumes," I said.

"Group wedding are okay, but my brothers would not agree," Kamal replied.

In Yemen, religious sponsors held group weddings (men only) for as few as a hundred and as many as one thousand couples marrying at the same time. This assured that young people remained "virtuous" and "chaste" before starting families within the bounds of matrimony.

"If a couple divorces, can the bride keep the money?" I questioned.

"Usually, but it depends on the contract. In my brother's case, an additional fifty thousand rials must be paid if he wants a divorce, and it is no fault of his wife. But the money doesn't need to be paid before they marry—only if they divorce."

Our conversation ended because Kamal's wife entered the room dressed in a royal blue sequined ball gown with a plunging neckline. She was, indeed, Cinderella. "Wow!" I said. "You're gorgeous." Kamal translated my words. Her red lips smiled.

34

MARIB BY TAXI

Adventure must start with running away from home.
—WILLIAM BOLITHO

Friday mornings, before the noontime sermon, Sana'a sleeps. It is the only time during the week that the city is quiet. The AIYS residents were asleep, and I had the kitchen to myself. After lighting the stove, I set a pan of water to boil. I dumped bow-tie pasta into boiling water. Afterward, I sautéed chopped onions, garlic, tomatoes, and green peppers in sizzling olive oil. While stirring the sauce, I heard sounds on the stairs. "Hello," a man's voice called out.

Dane, a Dutch archeologist, worked in Sirwah, and the car had dropped him at AIYS. "Are you hungry?" I asked. "You're welcome to share."

"There are four of us," he answered, glancing over his shoulder. "They'll be here any minute—they're traveling in another car."

"I don't think there's enough," I said and dished up two plates. By the time we finished eating, the men had not arrived. "Where did you last see them?"

"In Marib. Maybe they were kidnapped," he said, laughing. Of course, it was possible.

When it was time to go, I found Mohammed with Shakeeb in the guard-house chewing qat. "Is that all you have?" he asked, eyeing my travel bag.

"Yes," I answered.

"Don't wear the veil until we reach the long-distance taxis," Mohammed said. Shakeeb passed Mohammed his Kalashnikov, and they kissed cheeks.

I followed Mohammed through the wooden gate. In the alleyway, he asked for taxi money. "Here," I said and gave him my wallet.

On Gamal Street, we waited for a taxi as drivers swerved this way and that, dodging pedestrians. "Why do they drive so wildly?" I asked.

"Vanity," Mohammed answered. "We learned the word in class."

"Yes, I know the word. What do you mean?"

"They need eyeglasses," he replied. "Yemeni men believed God made them as they are and there's no reason to put something on their eyes to see." Our taxi driver was no exception; he veered in and out of lanes of traffic and straddled the white lines.

I was the only woman traveling to Marib. I waited off to the side. Mohammed chatted with the long-distance taxi drivers. Shared taxis leave when full, and a driver hoped to convince Mohammed that we should ride with him. While I waited, a local taxi dropped four scruffy-looking armed men by the curb. A man spoke as he passed. Although I never understood what he said, Mohammed grabbed my black-gloved hand and hurried me to the taxi. I watched him count fifteen hundred rials for three seats.

Returning to Marib, I felt unexplainably happy. We were waved through the first checkpoint, and no papers exchanged hands. The first hour passed. Men smoked. Men chewed qat. Our driver and several passengers renewed qat supplies outside Sana'a. Men bought bottled water. Mohammed whispered to me in Arabic. I shook my head, because I thought he asked if I wanted water. Finally, I understood that he wanted out of the car. He leaned over and opened the door. Stepping out of the car, my sandals disappeared into a ditch of filthy water. Mohammed's eyes begged me not to complain. He jammed the Kalashnikov in my hand. I stayed by the car, clutching the rifle.

Mohammed returned with bottled water and a package of tissue paper and asked for my sandals. He wiped the sandals and tossed the pink paper in the ditch.

We traveled uphill on a road built by Chinese laborers. Looking out the car window over S-shaped curves, I saw a thousand shades of brown. Climbing steeply, the road zigzagged up the volcanic mountain whose sides were close enough to touch. Cars and trucks passed on hairpin turns. Drivers could not see. Blaring horns announced attempts at passing, but not everyone was successful.

Far below, a toasted desert awaited us, and I smiled. We barreled down the slanting switchbacks without guardrails, sliding on gravel patches. The taxi driver's bulge of qat grew with each bend in the road.

At numerous checkpoints between Sana'a and Marib, the taxi slowed and sometimes stopped when soldiers signaled for us to halt. Since Mohammed held the packet of photocopies, the military was unaware that an American traveled, and we avoided lengthy stops as soldiers checked and double-checked the papers. When non-Yemenis traveled, soldiers radioed to alert the military. If the car did not reach the next checkpoint, government officials were notified.

Darkness descended as we approached the outskirts of Marib, and the taxi stopped near a restaurant between two greasy tire repair shops on the main highway. Mohammed opened the car door and bent to pick up something on the sand. It was my gold earring. "Be careful," he scolded, as if I had dropped it on purpose.

"Thanks," I replied and held the earring in my black-gloved hand. Mohammed asked me to wait, and he walked to a pickup truck parked nearby and spoke with the driver. Mohammed gave the driver one hundred rials and returned my wallet.

"Thanks for going with me," I said to Mohammed at the guardhouse.

"Any service?" he replied. I shook my head.

Daood answered my first knock. "How are you?" I asked.

"Everything's good," Daood said, grinning. Zhara bristled like a bottle-brush and dashed around the room.

"Was she okay?" I asked. "Where are the sheets?"

"Accident," Daood answered. "The bathroom door was shut, so she couldn't get to her cat box."

"How was Sana'a?" he asked as we watched Zhara climb the curtains.

"I'm glad I went," I answered, "but happy to be back."

"Why?" Daood asked, looking confused. "No one likes Marib."

"I love the desert," I answered, opening a package of cookies.

Hearing crackling cellophane, Zhara's green eyes sparkled. I crumbled a cookie in her bowl.

"What's happened in Marib?" I asked, pouring tea.

"Nothing," he said. "Nothing ever happens here."

The next morning Mohammed said that something had happened in Marib. One soldier was stabbed and another soldier was shot. Checking for weapons, the soldiers had halted a car. The driver rolled down the window and stabbed the soldier in the stomach with a jambiya. Shots rang out from inside the car, hitting both soldiers and knocking them to the ground. The driver drove the car over the wounded bodies, grinding them into the pavement. "It must have happened after we passed last night," Mohammed said, visibly shaken.

"Did they catch the men?" I asked.

"Not yet," he replied. "But we know the village." Before the government bombed innocent villagers, the military found the killers dead in a car on the outskirts of Marib. No one took responsibility for the killer's deaths. The president had signed an order that carrying weapons in Marib was illegal. Guns are plentiful, and no one believed the numerous crackdowns made a difference. There are supposedly three weapons for every person in Yemen—twenty-three million times three. During the next twenty-four hours, thousands of weapons were confiscated at Marib's checkpoints, and this heightened tensions between military and local tribesmen. More soldiers guarded the Bilquis Hotel. Mohammed said we could not walk.

Automatic gunfire woke me before daylight the next morning. Mohammed shouted through the window screen, "Shut the window, keep down, and don't open the door!" I shut the window and pulled the blanket from the bed and sat on the floor. Zhara burrowed underneath. Eventually, I fell asleep. Much later, Mohammed knocked on the door with bread. "Is everything okay?" I asked.

"No problem," he answered. "But you can't leave the hotel. There are soldiers guarding Marib."

"How did so many soldiers get to Marib so fast?" I asked Mohammed.

"They were on their way to Saada for the war," he replied. At first, I thought Mohammed was joking about a war. One thousand Yemeni soldiers were reported to have died in Saada's war, but news from al-Jawf said it was upwards of three thousand. "Bodies piled in trucks and taken to hospitals, but few made it alive to Sana'a," Mohammed said. He had given blood twice.

Saada, an ancient town near the Saudi Arabian border, is the birthplace of Zaydism, a Shi'a sect that ruled Yemen for a thousand years. Yemen's last and final king, Imam Muhammad al-Badr, fled to Saada during the 1960s revolution and ruled from his cave stronghold in the mountains. He eventually lost control of Yemen. Government rule remains weak in the northern tribal regions.

A war is going on only a few miles away and people are dying, but there is no mention in the English-language newspapers. I cannot ask Mohammed questions, or he might think I am spying. We talk in circles.

35

BEDOUIN, RUSSIANS, AND *THE NEW YORKER*

Anything can be achieved in small, deliberate steps.
But there are times you need the courage to take a great leap.
You can't cross a chasm in two small jumps.
—DAVID LLOYD GEORGE

Mohammed, Salah, and Talib were why I was teaching in Marib. Locating three Bedouin in the desert—no permanent address and without telephones—in a tented camp somewhere between Marib and Shabwa seemed hopeless.

Then one day, Mohammed al-Baraki called when Mohammed and I were in the photocopy shop. "No, I'm not in Sana'a," I shouted Arabic into the phone, "I'm in Marib. Yes, yes, Marib. I am so glad Kamal gave you my telephone number."

Mohammed al-Baraki spoke Arabic too quickly, and I did not understand what he said, so I passed the phone to Mohammed. He scrunched up his face in disapproval at hearing a man's voice. I grabbed the phone back from him before he hung up.

"Where are you?" I asked. If I understood correctly, he was in Shabwa but would be in Marib the following week. We hung up.

"Who called?" Mohammed asked, his eyes narrowed to dark slits.

"Remember, I told you about Mohammed, Salah, and Talib. We crossed the desert last year," I said.

"Does Dr. Mustafa know?" he asked.

"Does Dr. Mustafa know what?" I answered impatiently.

"Does Dr. Mustafa know Bedouin telephone you?"

"They're my friends," I replied, astonished that we were having this ridiculous conversation. Men in the photocopy shop turned to stare at a veiled woman raising her voice in English. "Will you stop Mohammed from visiting me? Like you did my students?"

"I didn't stop your students," he said. "One wasn't your student."

Mohammed al-Baraki telephoned the following week and said he would be in Marib within the hour. "Come to the Bilquis Hotel," I answered in Arabic. I'll wait at the front gate."

Twice I changed clothes and settled on the baltu with chiffon overlay and lace at the sleeves and hem. Looking in the mirror, I applied lip gloss and tied my scarf. Slipping my feet into black sandals, I walked to the gate.

Facing Marib, I watched hazy outlines of buildings shimmer in the afternoon sunlight. Mountains obscured the desert beyond. Although I wanted to walk the desert with Mohammed and Talib after the camel trip, Abdullah Shaykh had stopped us. The last time I saw Mohammed was at the Land of Two Paradises Hotel, when I could not thank him or say good-bye.

A plume of smoke-like dust moved along the unpaved road and brought me back to the present. Driving a tan pickup truck, Mohammed stopped before the hotel gate. He got out of the truck, walked toward me, pressed his nose to mine, and kissed my cheeks— a traditional Bedouin greeting. I was both surprised and pleased. Men and women in Yemen did not greet each other affectionately in public.

"Please open the gate," I said to the guard. "He's my friend." The guard's eyes opened wide as if to say, "Obviously, he is your friend." "Where's Mohammed?" I asked, referring to my murafik. Mohammed sprung from nowhere before I finished saying his name. He led the way to my room, asked for the key, and unlocked the door.

Mohammed sat stiffly on the edge of the bed and Mohammed al-Baraki sat next to him. I sat on the floor at their feet. "How are Talib and Salah?" I asked.

"*Tamam*, good," he replied. While I made tea, Mohammed and Mohammed spoke Arabic. When Yemeni men meet, tribal connections are discussed— it is important to establish ancestral ties and determine who is who and from where. Kinship groups are the foundation of Yemeni society. A man's bloodline and his connections give identity. Tribes in Yemen trace their origins to Qahtan, son of Prophet Hud, the great-great-great-grandson of Shem, Noah's son and the ancestor of all South Arabians. The formal dance of language puts men either at ease or on guard. Unfortunately, in this case, Mohammed and Mohammed were in the second category.

After sharing a spiritual experience with Mohammed al-Baraki—sleeping under stars, drinking tea at dawn and meals at sunset, and crossing the desert, here I sat in a hotel room self-consciously trying to communicate using Mohammed as translator. Mohammed al-Baraki and I communicated better in the desert in silence.

For a whole year, I had looked forward to meeting Mohammed al-Baraki again and giving him the photographs, but now it felt strange. The situation was wrong. I wanted to speak with him alone to explain how the desert had changed my life and brought me to Marib and thank him a thousand times. I could not discuss our failed plans to walk the desert or mention meeting Abdullah Shaykh again in Marib or his death. "Here are the photographs," I said, pressing an album into his hand.

Smiles jumped to his face while thumbing through the photos. After he left, however, I found three photo albums on the desk. I ran to the gate, but by then he was gone.

While I stood in the driveway, the white hospital van drove through the arched gate, bringing the Russian doctor and four female nurses to swim. I followed the van. Although there were no formal introductions, I met the Russian women from time to time walking in Marib. Neither of us spoke the other's language, so we communicated in Arabic, which of course limited exchanges.

A waiter brought a tray of bottled Cokes and hung around listening. Taking a sip, I asked about their work at the hospital. Recently the most common patients had been women suffering gunshot wounds. Men delivered the women to the hospital and said "accidents." However, the nurses were doubtful.

"What do the women say?" I asked.

"Women do not disagree," they assured me, rolling their eyes. "Gunshot wounds for women are commonplace in Marib." Doctors at the understaffed medical facility helped those they could and others died.

While sipping my Coke, I recalled an incident, but I did not have the necessary Arabic vocabulary to tell the women: Weeks before, at a Marib restaurant, Mohammed and I were drinking tea after a meal. A man walked up to our table. "Who is she?" the man asked and poked his chin in my direction. Good at making up stories, Mohammed told him I was a Russian doctor. Instead of leaving, the man sat down, ordered tea for himself, and asked

Mohammed questions about his wife's operation. Mohammed said I was off-duty and would see him at the hospital first thing in the morning.

I wondered what tall tales Mohammed had told about me as I sat by the edge of the pool watching the women swim laps. My one-time swimming experience in Marib was a disaster—the hotel workers and soldiers gawked at me from the terrace when I removed my blouse and skirt, revealing a two-piece swimsuit. I had felt naked. I dressed immediately. I was glad the Russian women were comfortable wearing swimsuits, but I was not. The van driver sent a hotel worker to tell them it was time to leave. They got out of the pool, dried off, and dressed in casual clothes.

Before saying goodbye, they invited me to visit them and explained that they lived in an apartment on Marib's main street, but I had to come without the murafik. Without Mohammed, I could not get out the gate.

Alone, I hugged my knees to my chest and listened to the final call to prayer. The waiter hovered. "Can I ask you a question?" he said, holding an empty serving tray.

"Sure," I answered.

"I'm sick, what can you give me?"

"It depends on what's wrong." He had a headache. "I'll be back in a few minutes," I answered.

When I returned, the waiter and Mohammed were deep in discussion. "Here are the tablets," I said, placing two Tylenol in the waiter's hand. "Take one now and one before you sleep." Dispensing medicine meant a line would form outside my door.

"Shukran," he said. "American medicine is strong"—a widely held belief.

Mohammed had come looking for me when I did not answer his knock. "Did you think I'd run away?" I asked. "Jumped the fence?"

"Possibly," he answered. "Why were you with the Russians?"

"I saw the van," I replied. "The women came to swim. I miss talking to women."

"They'll give you a bad reputation," he said, squaring his shoulders.

"Why?"

"Everyone knows they . . . " He fished for the word. "Sleep with men," he replied.

"That's gossip," I said. "Or does someone sit outside their doors keeping count?"

Mohammed blushed. "They should get married," he answered.

"The doctor is married," I replied.

Mohammed shook his head no and sat on a poolside chair. "She used to," he paused and looked around, "swim with . . . a Yemeni," he said.

"You should ask the Yemeni," I replied.

"Muslims can have four wives," he added, as if that explained the situation. "Our Koran tells us."

"Muslims are supposed to have good reasons to take a second, third, or fourth wife," I replied. "Not boredom."

"Our way is right," he retorted, giving me an admonishing look that meant "you foolish woman."

"Polygamy, taking more than one wife, is difficult because Muslim husbands are required to treat all wives equally, which is virtually impossible," I said. "In olden times, the practice of multiple wives—as soldiers died in battle, leaving widows and children who needed male protection—served society. Islam did not invent polygamy. You can read about it in the Bible. Jews could have an unlimited number of wives. It has been practiced throughout the ages."

"But our Koran," Mohammed interrupted. "Americans have more than one wife!"

"Well, they cannot have two wives at the same time," I replied. "That's against the law."

"What if they travel?" he asked. "If a man is away a long time, he'll need another wife."

"If a woman travels, is she entitled to another husband?"

"No," Mohammed answered and stood for emphasis, his dark eyes angry, and he walked away.

Arguments with Mohammed were pointless because neither of us were likely to change the other's mind. We saw the world through cloudy cultural curtains. Our different views and "truths" were dictated long ago. Regrettably, cultural beliefs are difficult to discard. Perhaps it is easier to lift the veil on another culture.

Walking to class the next afternoon, there was no mention of the heated topic we discussed the previous evening. Although we would probably never see eye to eye about women's place in society because of our cultural curtains, the tension was gone.

In Yemen it was a given that men worked outside the home. Women generally stayed at home behind walls so that their movements were controlled. Of course, there were numerous exceptions of well-educated women in positions transforming society. In Marib, the three female health department workers, now students, were courageous because they attended English class with men.

No "male" or "female" signs appeared outside the health department bathrooms—work was men's domain. The assumption was that women would not be in the building. The female students never ventured down the hallway where the bathrooms were located.

At the class break, I had to use the bathroom. Looking through the frosted glass panels, I could see men inside. I waited while men—one after the other—washed their feet in the washbasin, getting ready for prayer. Finally, when it was my turn, the tile floor was flooded with water. I skidded to the toilet, lifted my baltu, and squatted. "Females have to put up with this," I thought. Then I remembered that countless schools do not have bathrooms for boys or girls. Boys use outside "facilities," which is impossible for girls. That is one reason families do not allow girls to attend school: there are frequently no bathrooms, but if bathrooms existed, they would be for boys. If my female students needed to use the toilet, they too would wait until they returned home. What did they do when they worked all day or had menstrual cycles?

The hem of my wet baltu created a muddy trail as I returned to class. "What do you want to be?" I asked the students and wrote the question on the white board. No one raised a hand. I asked another question: "What do you see yourself doing in five years?" No hands raised in the air. "Do any of you dream of becoming pharmacists?" I asked.

"That's impossible," Amal answered and then realized she had spoken aloud.

"Why?" I asked.

"Only men are pharmacists," Ahmed replied.

"Well, that might be true today in Marib," I said. "But women can change society by becoming pharmacists. Women work as pharmacists all over the world."

"You don't understand," Khalid said. "Yemen is different."

"If I have a medical question, I would prefer to speak with a female pharmacist," I explained. "Yemeni women might feel the same."

"No, they don't," he said.

"Can we hear from the women?" I asked. They remained silent.

On the conference table was a copy of the *New Yorker* dated August 2, 2004. Cheri had given it to me. "Look," I said and held the magazine to show advertisements of professional men and women in the workplace. The students seemed unconvinced.

"We can break stereotypes," I said, showing an advertisement. "In Sana'a there are women pharmacists."

When I placed the magazine on the table, Ahmed, sitting closest, picked it up. His eyes widened, and he slammed it on the table. Slowly I turned the magazine over. A full-page advertisement on the back cover for Altoids ("the curiously strong sours") was titled "Forbidden Fruit." The four-color spread showed nude Adam and Eve—holding Altoids chest high with a snake curled above their heads. The couple was adorned with green leaves in strategic places, and Eve's long, wavy black hair covered her breasts. "I'm so sorry," I whispered to Ahmed.

"That's okay," he replied. "But don't bring those magazines again."

The students were curious to know what was in the magazine. It seemed like a good time to end class. Ahmed would explain.

I bundled the *New Yorker* between notebooks and papers, hiding the "pornographic" advertisement as we retraced our steps to the hotel. The magazine incident would be at the top of the public security dossier, written in big red letters. I could not throw the magazine away or give it to anyone. I stashed it at the bottom of my locked trunk.

36

ENGLISH-ARABIC DICTIONARY

Every day of your life is a page of your history.
—ARAB PROVERB

"This is how Sana'ani women walk," Daood said, demonstrating by sashaying back and forth across the hotel's reception room. "You walk like a Marib woman," he said to me, "who carry things on their heads." "Carrying the burden of the world," I thought and sunk into the sofa.

Three dusty, armed Bedouin dressed in white thobes with bandoleers and long, curly hair entered the hotel lobby. Daood stopped mimicking women's walk and returned to the reception desk wearing a serious expression. The Bedouin wanted to swim, or maybe use the pool as a bath. After paying six hundred rials, Daood asked for weapons and received three assault rifles, two handguns, three jambiyas, and miscellaneous knives. He stored the weaponry.

The Bedouin marched to the pool, and sunshine streaming through thobes revealed stick-thin legs. I wondered if they swam in their underpants. "Do they swim in their underpants?" I asked. Daood nodded.

"Mohammed told us you have Bedouin friends," Daood said and flopped on an upholstered armchair with a smile.

"Anything else?" I asked.

"Nothing," he replied. "Oh, you like the desert."

"I love the desert," I answered.

"Why?"

"In the desert, I'm a grain of sand," I explained.

Daood stared. "Did you understand what I said?" I asked.

"No," he answered. "Do you want tea?"

"Yes," I replied. We sat outside on the concrete steps, silently drinking tea. Living outside my culture, I was often an observer, and chances of misinterpretation were great. Being observed, the same was true. I wondered why destiny brought me to Marib.

Thanks for tea," I said to Daood and stood. He remained seated. I walked along the curved garden pathway in the shade of trees to my room.

Turning the corner by the annex, I saw Zhara sprawled on the walkway. "What happened?" I screamed at the hotel workers cleaning rooms. The workers shrugged and pointed to the rooftop. "Did someone put her up there?" Zhara lay motionless. She was still alive, and I slid a piece of cardboard under her body and carried her to the room. When I turned her over, her hind legs flopped lifelessly.

One of the hotel workers ran to tell Mohammed. "Eggs," he said when I opened the door. "You feed her eggs. It helps a broken leg." I started to cry.

"She's young," he said, "don't worry." I was worried. I beat an egg with canned milk and put the saucer beside her. Zhara lapped the egg and milk and vomited yellow froth. Mohammed left.

Daood came immediately when I called, and we sat on the floor staring at Zhara. "Who is covering for you?" I asked.

"Saddam came on duty early," he answered.

I telephoned Dr. Hanafi in Sana'a. He diagnosed her best he could over the phone and suggested I keep her warm, and because she was young, he thought she would be okay. I wrapped a small towel around her and put her in the basket. Using the medicine dropper, I fed her milk. Zhara ate bites of tuna from my fingers, which was a good sign.

The next morning, she could not walk. Zhara pulled herself with front paws to the bathroom. I lifted her into the litter box, where she urinated.

After two weeks, she regained partial use of her hind legs, but Mohammed accidentally stepped on her. He of course felt terrible and apologized.

Holding Zhara on my lap, I reread pages of my "Desert Journal" and noticed the handwriting growing fainter, as if it were written in disappearing ink and would soon vanish from the page. I read, "We wander in desert after desert," and wondered why I had written the words and what they meant. My writing seemed like reminders of another life. My computer was broken. It did not matter—I had nothing to say.

Zhara's hind legs eventually healed, and she was back to her manic cat self. "I'll let you out later," I said as she frantically clawed the carpet by the door.

Mohammed knocked. He balanced three round loaves of bread in his right hand. Zhara took advantage and dashed between his legs.

A few minutes later, Daood knocked and held two hard-boiled eggs and slices of English teacake wrapped in white paper napkins. "Thanks," I said. "Come in."

"No," he replied. "I'm off-duty and need to sleep." The hotel staff worked long hours for meager wages and chewed qat when they could afford it or when wealthy Marib shaykhs brought them bundles of leaves. "I'd like to study English," Daood said, looking at his dusty brown leather shoes. He leaned against the doorjamb for support.

"Dr. Mustafa won't allow anyone in class that doesn't work at the health department," I explained. "Mohammed's the only exception. But I have a textbook, so that you can study."

"Thank you," he said, taking the book from my hand.

"Do you have a dictionary?" I asked. He shook his head. "What time will you wake up?"

"Before Maghrib," he replied. "I'll pray and have dinner."

"Will you be free at seven?" I asked. "We'll walk to the bookstore."

"Yes," he answered and looked up smiling. "I'm not on duty until ten o'clock."

That evening, before Daood was expected, I remembered buying my first Arabic-English dictionary in Sana'a. Yemeni Arabic is close to *fusha*, classical Arabic that I learned studying with Kamal. Since Yemen had been isolated until the 1960s, cut off from other Arab speakers, it maintained a language closest to the original.

During my first week of Arabic study, I used the Arabic-language section of the *Lonely Planet: Yemen* book as a guide. Writing the twenty-eight letters of the Arabic alphabet seemed simple. When Arabic alphabets become part of words, they change shape, depending on whether they are placed at the beginning, middle, or end of the word. Soon there were eighty-four Arabic letters, including a few variations, to memorize.

Vowels do not have to be written. For example, "book" could be written as "bk," which is easy if you know the language but difficult when you do not. To make matters worse, some Arabic letters are piggybacked one on top of each other, and I could not locate the letter "m" in the middle of words.

On Thursday at the end of the first week of instruction, Kamal assigned homework, and I needed a dictionary. Serious students at the institute turned to the pages of *A Dictionary of Modern Written Arabic* by Hans Wehr. What I did not understand was that to use the Hans Wehr dictionary, you must know Arabic—this I found out later. Arabic words are generally made up of three root letters, and you have to know or guess which three letters. I was not good at guessing.

After asking for directions to the bookstore and drawing a detailed map, I closed the institute's arched wooden door and confidently walked through the suq. Afternoons in Sana'a are the best times to walk because qat sessions have started and streets are empty. Only a few Sana'ani women were out, wearing flowing fabrics that resembled tablecloths on heads with long, paneled, patterned veils that were tie-dyed orange, black, and white over their faces.

Crossing a wide, arched stone bridge, my sandals slipped on the slick cobblestones. I skidded into oozing piles of garbage bags cooking in the sun. Looking up, I saw a tooth sign, which featured a hand-painted white tooth on a red metal square hanging by two wires from the corner of a building near a mosque, advertising a dental office.

In the vegetable and fruit suq, I stepped over squashed tomatoes and discarded fruit. Boys with wheelbarrows ran between the vegetable and fruit vendors shouting that they were available for hire.

I glanced at my map, and the gold suq was on my left. Shop windows overflowed with glittery jewelry. Gold is a sign of wealth for Yemeni women and is given as part of her bride price and later used as insurance if problems arise in the marriage. At this hour, the gold shops remained empty of customers, and shopkeepers lounged on tiled floors, stuffing qat leaves into mouths.

Crossing Abdul Mogni Street, I watched cars swerve and change direction randomly—no one stayed within the lanes. Joining a group of men, we crossed the street and climbed through a hole in the metal fence that had once been a center divider. Teetering on the concrete slab in the center of the street, we waited for traffic coming from the other direction to slow.

At the post office, I turned right and then left and walked past teahouses and two restaurants, both named Dubai. Eventually, I turned right and saw Dar al-Hikma ("House of Wisdom"), the bookstore, on my left.

Dictionaries sat on wooden shelves behind the checkout counter. "*Aw-fun,* excuse me," I said to the bookstore clerk, who wore a long white thobe and brown suit jacket. "*Min fadlak, shoofti,* may I please look?" He nodded and waved his hand for me to come behind the desk.

Inching my way between the desk and wall, I recognized the green book jacket. "That's it," I said, pointing to the third shelf. Standing on a wooden ladder, the clerk handed the dictionary to me. "Shukran," I said.

Opening the cover, I saw "twenty-two hundred rials" written in pencil. "Expensive," I thought at the time, but later I realized it was $13.50. "*Mafish falooz,* no money," I said to the smiling clerk, because I did not know how to say I do not have enough money. I set the book on the counter.

"Take the dictionary," he said in English and placed the book in my hands. "Pay me later."

"You don't know me," I replied.

"I know you'll pay," he said, exposing bits of green qat stuck to his teeth. That was the day I met Taha Hussein.

A knock at the door brought me back to the present. Daood and I walked to the hotel gate. "Where is Mohammed?" I asked the guard. He pointed the firing end of his AK-47 toward Marib.

Before Mohammed came into view, we heard clomping boots on the pavement. "Sorry," he said, shuffling past to the guardhouse. "I had to call my family."

Because Mohammed had gone to Marib with a group of soldiers, he was dressed in his uniform and changed into civilian clothes. Daood and I waited. Mohammed wore his uniform around soldiers but never with me. There was still so much I did not understand.

The bookstore was crowded, so Mohammed waited on the concrete steps, rifle ready. I found the *English-Arabic Readers Dictionary,* and the name was printed incorrectly on blue paper covers. The covers were stitched on upside down, but it was the only available dictionary. "*Arba,*" I said, holding up four fingers. After paying the twenty-four hundred rials, I gave Daood his dictionary. Outside, I gave Mohammed his. Of the two remaining copies, one I would keep, and the other I would give as a gift.

37

A RESTAURANT GUIDE TO MARIB

What is the use of running when we are not on the right road?
—GERMAN PROVERB

"Mohammed, why can't I walk to Marib with Daood?" I complained the next day. "If anyone asks, he'll say I am his aunt from Sana'a. I will wear my Sana'ani veil. Promise, I will not speak."

"If there's trouble, Daood can't protect you," Mohammed replied. "He's not a trained soldier."

"The shopkeepers in Marib would help," I insisted. "I am a woman."

"No one would help," he said sharply. I did not believe him.

Although it was Friday, Mohammed agreed to walk with me to Marib. He would not be hungry after chewing qat but said he would drink tea while I ate. The Salaam Restaurant, located near the suq, was open on Friday evenings. I had eaten at the restaurant several times: once with Abdulmalik my first summer; again with Abdulmalik, Mohammed, and Talib; and at a later time with Kamal and Ali.

The back section of the restaurant had long rows of tables covered with plastic cloth. White plastic chairs were arranged around the tables and extra chairs stacked at the edge of the room. Near the front of the restaurant where we sat were small tables for four. Mohammed sat in a chair so that he could see men approaching the restaurant through the window, and I sat opposite him with my back to the glass.

"What do you want?" he asked.

"I'd like a glass of white wine, please," I replied. Mohammed did not think my comments about wine were funny and ignored me.

A waiter came to the table, and Mohammed ordered foule and bread. Waiters did not need pencils or paper with few choices on the menu. Mohammed called him back and asked for an onion. The waiter brought two large red onions, cut into quarters, on a dented aluminum dish.

"Cheri's publishing a Sana'a tourist guide to restaurants," I said, noticing that the pillars holding up the buckling ceiling had recently been painted candy-apple green.

"What's that?" Mohammed asked.

"It's a book for tourists so they will know where to eat," I replied. "We could do one for Marib."

"Tourists don't decide where they'll eat in Marib," he answered. "They eat at the Bilquis Hotel—where it's safe."

"Safe and expensive," I added. The waiter set a metal plate of foule on the table next to the piping-hot circle of freshly made bread. Mohammed tore a piece of bread and scooped up a mouthful of beans. I flipped the veil over the back of my head.

"I'd like a Coke," I said to Mohammed. It was easy to get the waiter's attention—he was staring.

After the meal, I asked Mohammed to stop at the button and ribbon shop. "How did you know it was there?" Mohammed questioned, a suspicious glint appearing in his dark eyes. I could see his mind racing.

"By looking through the window," I said. "Why?" Inside the shop were boxes of buttons and spools of silk ribbons. Mohammed followed me through the door. I pointed to a cardboard box under the glass counter; it held a cluster of black buttons rimmed in gold. The small buttons were exactly right for my baltu. "*Bi kum*," I asked the price. Since I spoke directly to the clerk, Mohammed looked annoyed. The shopkeeper answered twenty rials and wrapped four buttons in a square of notebook paper. I put the shiny coins in his hand. "Can we to go to the tailor tomorrow?" I asked Mohammed.

"We can go now," he replied.

"But I need the baltu," I answered. "It's not the one I'm wearing."

The cool evening air was refreshing as we returned to the hotel, and Mohammed brought up the idea of publishing a tourist guide for Marib. "Would it make money?" he asked.

"It would be a joke," I said laughing. "But I'm willing to try eating in all the restaurants and write about them."

"The best restaurant is in the alleyway, under a wooden shelter," he explained. "Only on Fridays. They serve meat so you couldn't eat there."

"How many restaurants are in Marib?" I asked. He guessed twenty. This count included all sorts of places that served soft drinks and sandwiches. Maybe a Marib book on "fine dining" was a good idea, or at least a fun experiment. For two nights in a row, we walked to Marib for dinner.

On the second night, I carried my baltu and new buttons in a sack. We walked to a tailor located on an unpaved side street. His shop was a wooden frame covered with white cotton cloth. The tailor was from Taiz and a friend of Mohammed's, and I asked if he had given him the silver wedding ring. Mohammed pretended not to understand my question. The tailor made bound buttonholes, and he sewed buttons on my baltu. "Can he make me a cape?" I asked Mohammed.

"He's going back to Taiz," he replied. "Anyway, he only sews men's clothes."

For the next week, Mohammed was busy, so we were not able to walk or sample exotic "cuisine" in a Marib restaurant. My only outing was to and from class. During that week, a German tour group stayed at the hotel on their way to Sayun, and an assertive female artist demanded to sit outside the gate. She sat at the far edge of the fence, facing the uninterrupted desert with charcoals in hand, and I joined her, although the guard tried to stop me. I told him to come along. He did.

Freedom existed on this side of the fence. I watched the artist capture the desert in broad, dark strokes. "Will you be here tomorrow?" I asked, hoping she would say yes.

She shook her head and replied, "One day is enough."

The next afternoon, I sat in the exact spot by the fence, staring at a blank page in my notebook, trying to force a poem, hoping the desert would rekindle a spark. Nothing ignited.

"Why are you sitting outside the fence?" Mohammed asked.

"I'm going crazy," I answered. Mohammed, sensing my desperation, agreed to walk with me. The day was sunny but not hot, and we passed blue, open-front shops along the main street. A few men drank mid-morning tea in a restaurant and watched us as we passed. In Marib a woman on the street was uncommon entertainment. Approaching a small side street where on Thursdays the bakery—the only one in Marib—sold cakes, Mohammed stopped. I did not see or hear anything unusual, only two men getting into a Toyota truck. Backing up, the truck's tires squealed, sending clouds of dust into the air. Automatic gunfire from an approaching truck caused yellow flashes like bursting light before my eyes. The blue metal doors on shops slammed shut— the few people on the street vanished. Mohammed shoved me into a narrow space between two buildings. Standing in front, he snapped the loaded magazine into the Kalashnikov and leveled the rifle.

As quickly as it began, it was over. Bedouin fighting. A personal dispute. Nothing to do with us.

38

BLOWN BY DESERT WINDS

It is never too late—in fiction or in life—to revise.
—NANCY THAYER

Dressed neatly in a crisp white shirt, Daood sat behind the reception desk, his eyes red. "What's wrong?" I asked. He wiped tears on his shirtsleeve. Before he answered, a goat ran into the lobby. Her feet skidded on the slick tiles, unable to get traction, and she ran in place. We burst out laughing, which frightened the goat, and she peed.

"I'm off duty at two o'clock," he said. "I'll come to your room."

Befriending an American and her cat caused him untold trouble—people gossiped. I hoped I was not the source of whatever new problems affected him.

Daood arrived at my door with flat bread, cheese triangles, and an apple. "Your lunch," he said.

"Does anyone know you bring me food?" I asked. He shook his head no. Zhara was curled up on the bed, and he sat next to her. I offered tea. "Why the sadness?" I asked.

"I'm leaving Marib," he said, staring at his folded hands. "My father ordered me to Sana'a." His father had banished him to Marib as punishment and now wanted his return. Each month Daood had sent his father his meager earnings—he kept only a few rials for himself. The interpretation he knew of the Koran made him believe that to disobey his father was forbidden. Unraveling cultural customs from religion was complicated in Yemeni tribal society, since the two were intricately interwoven.

"You've been in Marib over two years—way too long," I said. "It's not a place for a young man."

"But I worry," he said tears brimming. "You and Zhara are alone."

"We'll be fine," I answered.

183

Daood kissed Zhara's head.

"You must be the only Yemeni who kisses cats," I said, smiling at the open affection he showed her.

"If Yemenis knew how special cats are, everyone would kiss them," he replied.

"Zhara is not your everyday—normal—cat," I added.

Before returning to Sana'a, Daood assigned Waheeb as his replacement. Waheeb worked at the hotel as an accountant and was his trusted friend—they were from the same village and shared a family name. Waheeb was busy with work and family—he and his wife just had a new baby girl. I did not want to bother him and relied on Mohammed.

"The next time cook goes to the suq," Mohammed said, "he'll take your carpets to the cleaners." Zhara had eaten plants and vomited green froth on the carpets. The cook drove the carpets and Mohammed to the cleaners.

A few days later, I asked Mohammed for the cleaning receipt. "It's in my name," he replied. "I'll pick them up."

"How much money do I owe?" I asked. Mohammed explained that dry cleaning in Marib was expensive, not like in Sana'a. He said the amount was sixteen hundred rials.

A week later, the carpets were not back. Waheeb walked to the cleaners and returned with the carpets and a paid receipt of eight hundred rials.

"What's wrong?" I asked Mohammed when I noticed that the right side of his face was swollen. "Come in."

"My teeth," he said, holding his face in both hands. He noticed the carpets on the floor. "Who picked them up?"

"Waheeb," I answered.

Mohammed had had teeth pulled at a military hospital in Sana'a, and his experience sounded like torture. The hotel receptionist suggested he go to a Syrian dentist in private practice. I went with Mohammed. The dental office was clean and equipment modern.

Dr. Baseer examined Mohammed. "How often do you brush your teeth?" he asked. Mohammed admitted to never brushing his teeth except at Ramadan, when he used a *miswak*, a stick for cleaning teeth and tongue. "Buy a toothbrush and toothpaste and start today," the dentist ordered.

At the market, I bought Mohammed his first toothbrush and toothpaste, and he carried them to the hotel in a bag, but I do not think he used them.

While crossing the road to the health department that afternoon on the way to class, walking haystacks called my name. "Are they the girls who cut grass at the hotel?" I asked Mohammed. Bundles of cut grass bobbed up and down as they ran to catch up. "What do they want?"

"They're too shy to speak to me," Mohammed answered. The giggling haystacks wanted photographs taken. The gardener told them I owned a camera. "Come this afternoon," I said. "I don't have my camera with me," and I opened my bag to show them that I carried only books and papers. The haystacks ran off in the opposite direction.

On the first floor of the health department, the doors were wide open. I glanced into rooms where men lounged on chairs and stretched on sofas. Not a soul looked to be working. Walking up the stairway, Mohammed stopped and talked with a military man while I continued up the stairs.

Armed Bedouin guarded Dr. Mustafa's office. One of the guards opened the door and let me pass. Students whom I had not seen since the first week of class sat in chairs and crowded together on a brown leather-like sofa. These students had refused to come to class without payment. International organizations working in Yemen had set precedents enticing Yemenis to attend workshops by giving money, and the men and women now expected to be paid. They wanted immediate payment, not something said to help them in the future. Most of the men were guaranteed positions at the health department and were paid regularly and did not have to do much in return. Low-level corruption trickled down from the top.

None of the men offered me a seat. I remained standing.

Ahmed, Dr. Mustafa's younger brother, held two phones—one to each ear.

My phone rang; it was Mohammed. "Where are you?" I asked. He explained that the guard at the door would not let him inside. Ahmed hung up one phone and shouted to the guard to let Mohammed in the office. For his age, Ahmed possessed a fearsome charisma that showed he was in charge.

"Dr. Mustafa will be here soon," Ahmed said and ushered Mohammed and me to an adjoining office. An enormous black desk took most of the floor space. Black plastic-leather upholstered sofas hugged two walls. I sat, jamming my legs against the glass-topped coffee table. Mohammed sat on the far side of the room, obscured from view. "Do you think Cheri bought his furniture?" I asked.

"Probably," he answered. We waited an hour. No magazines—few people in Yemen read. "We've waited long enough," I said to Mohammed. He did not reply.

"Let's go," I repeated and stood to see why he had not answered. Mohammed was sound asleep.

Dr. Mustafa yanked the door open, and his bodyguards followed. He clutched a mobile phone to his ear, wedged himself behind the big black desk, and sat in the swivel chair.

Leaning forward, he apologized: "Sorry, I'm late." His phone rang. Listening to a one-sided conversation, I heard that men had been killed in Sirwah, and retaliation would follow.

"When it calms down," Dr. Mustafa said holding the phone at arm length, "you will teach the nurses and midwives in Sirwah."

I nodded.

"Traveling to Sirwah is a problem—there is no car to take you," Dr. Mustafa explained when he finished the phone call.

"We'll hire a taxi—it's not far," I suggested. "Or I'll drive the taxi, and if you're worried, we could take two more soldiers."

"You can drive?" Dr. Mustafa asked, seemingly shocked by my revelation.

"Yes," I answered.

"Maybe Cheri will buy the health department a bullet-proof Toyota," he said, smiling as the picture of the Land Cruiser formed in his mind. "Her organization is worth multimillions."

"Why do you want to teach in Sirwah?" Mohammed asked as we walked to the hotel.

"Maybe the nurses and midwives in Sirwah would be more interested in learning English than the health workers in Marib," I said.

"I doubt it," he replied and plopped his black-and-white scarf on top of his head. I doubted it too, but at least I would have a change of scenery.

The ringing of the telephone woke me the next morning. "Mohammed al-Baraki," the male voice said when I answered.

"Ahlan," I said, feeling fortunate that he called when I was alone. "You forgot your photographs. When can you come to Marib?" He would be in Marib at four o'clock in the afternoon and bring a gift, or that is what I understood him to say. Mohammed made it clear that he would not come to the hotel. We would have to meet on the street at the main intersection in Marib.

This time, I would not tell Mohammed. In fact, I would write everything down—no slip-ups. Waheeb agreed to translate my words to Arabic.

"What are you doing?" Mohammed asked when he saw me talking with Waheeb in the hotel.

"We're exchanging words," I replied, turning to a blank page in my notebook and writing "cat." This satisfied Mohammed.

"It wasn't a lie," I said to Waheeb. "We're exchanging words—how do you write 'cat'?" Waheeb thought for a moment but did not pick up his pen. "CAT" I said again and wrote the word in capital letters. Three Arabic words appeared on the page: "*dim*," "*bis*," and "*qita*." "There are more," he said.

"Maybe Mohammed al-Baraki cannot read," I said to Waheeb.

"That's likely," he answered. All day, I thought of ways to sneak out the hotel gate without Mohammed or the guards knowing. Riding a camel across the desert seemed easy compared to walking less than a mile. "I'll come with you," Waheeb said. "You can wear my wife's baltu."

"If the guards stopped us, you'd be in trouble," I replied, declining his offer.

At 3:30 p.m., I had ran out of options and gave up trying to outsmart Mohammed and walked to the front gate. I could not think of any other way to get out without making trouble for others. "Mohammed al-Baraki will be in Marib at four o'clock. I'll meet him near the photocopy shop," I said. Mohammed did not seem surprised and slung his rifle over his shoulder. I followed.

"What are they doing?" I shouted when I saw men and boys hurl stones at the black-and-white mother dog and her six newborn pups. She laid in a ditch on the side of the road, protecting her babies. "*Kalb min Allah*, dogs are from God," I shouted. The men froze, not understanding why a crazy black-cloaked woman screamed at them. "Don't ever do that again," I bellowed in English, rushing toward them with my arms flailing. "God is watching you!" They ran.

Mohammed did not comment about my outburst. I could not tell if he was embarrassed. I was not looking for his approval.

We arrived at the intersection before four o'clock. Shortly afterward, Mohammed al-Baraki, driving a tan truck, made a U-turn and stopped. In the passenger's seat was Talib, more grown up than the teenager who traveled across the desert the previous year. Talib wore a gray-green cotton thobe and a red-and-white checked scarf tossed casually around his shoulders. His short, curly hair was uncovered. A silver band on his ring finger meant he was married. What had not changed were his laughing eyes. Talib opened the door and got out of the truck, and we touched noses while surprised men stood nearby and stopped to watch. Mohammed unselfconsciously did the same. Men stared from the photocopy shop, foreheads pressed against glass. "Your photos," I said and placed three photo albums in Mohammed's hands. Crinkly lines appeared in the corners of his eyes as he smiled, no words necessary.

From the men of the desert, I learned that love is without beginning or end—a timeless story. All the energy and time I spent planning what to say and do was unnecessary. Waving to Mohammed and Talib as the truck sped across the desert kicking up dust was not good-bye—there are no good-byes.

39

Princess Shoes in a Fish Restaurant

The human heart at whatever age, opens only to
the heart that opens in return.
—Maria Edgeworth

Mohammed stood outside my door, looking sheepish. "Where have *you* been?" I asked, irritated that he had gone off without telling me.

"I didn't think it would take so long," he replied, staring at his unlaced boots. "We had to protect the tourists."

"Why didn't you leave a note and explain that you'd be away?" I asked. "You didn't answer your phone."

He started to say something and stopped.

"Ahmed drove me to class," I shouted and slammed the door. This was not the first time Mohammed had disappeared. My emotional outburst showed that I cared more for Mohammed than I admitted to myself.

The next morning, Mohammed knocked. "I'm not home," I shouted. He left.

After I was sure he had gone, I sat outside on a patch of dried yellow grass while Zhara hid behind the hedge and stalked small desert birds. The flowers I had recently planted were gone; the goats had eaten every one. The naughty goats stood on tiptoes—like ballerinas—and ate the plants growing in clay pots on the window ledge. Zhara was frightened of the goats and ran when they came into the garden. I heard a noise and thought it might be the goats, but it was Mohammed.

"Are you talking to me?" he said, standing behind the hedge.

"Yes," I answered. "Go away."

"Will you go to Sana'a on Wednesday?" he asked.

"I'm planning to," I replied.

"What time?

"Ask Ahmed."

189

Wednesday morning, the car was crammed with people hitching a ride to Sana'a. I sat in the passenger's seat next to Ahmed. Mohammed and two armed guards huddled in back with three men and a teenage boy. On the first bend in the road, the teenager traveling in a car for the first time vomited. Mohammed kindly helped the boy and cleaned the car.

Ahmed stopped at the al-Jawf turnoff, and Mohammed left his Kalashnikov with a mechanic, an ex-military friend who worked at a car repair shop. He motioned for me to roll down the window, so I did. "Your scarf," he said, pointing to my bag. He hung the extra black scarf I carried in my bag on the window to block the sun.

Ahmed dropped Mohammed and me at AIYS. "Here's money for your room and food," I said. "See you Friday."

"Can we have dinner tomorrow night?" he asked. "Sana'a has good fish restaurants."

"Okay," I said, knowing my anger was pointless and childish. "What time?"

"Six o'clock," he replied, smiling.

Thursday evening, Mohammed waited outside the gate at six o'clock, and we walked along Gamal Street to the fish restaurant. "Can I look at shoes?" I asked. The store was crowded with weekend shoppers—pieces of cardboard littered the floor so customers would not dirty their socks while trying on shoes. "May I try on the sandals?" I asked the clerk and pointed to a pair of black velvet high-heeled sandals decorated with rhinestones inside the glass case. He found a pair, size 38.

There were no chairs. I balanced on one foot and then the other. "*Momtaz*," Mohammed said. "Wonderful."

"They are princess shoes," I explained. "In my whole life I have never bought such a beautiful pair of impractical shoes."

The clerk asked if I wanted them wrapped. "I'll wear them," I replied. He wrapped my practical, flat-heeled, black leather sandals in brown paper, and I left the shop wearing bejeweled, velvet high heels.

Although the high heels were beautiful, it was difficult to walk on the cracked sidewalks and potholed streets. The fish restaurant on Kuwait Street did not warrant princess shoes. I stepped over puddles of spilled tea and clumps of tissue that dotted the concrete floor. Stained Formica tabletops were covered with fish bones and wadded-up newspapers. Before I sat on the bench, Mohammed wiped it with tissue and dropped the soiled wad on the floor with the others. He selected the fish.

While waiting for the fish to cook, Mohammed said he wanted to explain why he had disappeared. Two summers before, he had met a young European woman. She traveled with her family throughout Yemen after completing an Arabic course in Sana'a. Mohammed was one of the military guards assigned to the family, and he and the girl became friends. "She spoke beautiful Arabic," he said with a faraway look in his eyes. On the last evening in Sana'a, she and her family invited Mohammed—none of the other soldiers—to join them for dinner at the Sheraton Hotel.

Mohammed believed that his fate had changed and she would invite him to travel with the family to Italy. He borrowed money to buy new clothes and his first pair of leather shoes. He went to the Sheraton Hotel at the appointed time, but the military guards on duty would not let him through the gate. They would not take a message to the family.

"What did you do?" I asked.

"I waited by the gate all night," he replied. "Maybe she would find me."

"Did she?"

"No."

"This explains you disappearing?" I asked.

"Maybe she'll come back," he said wistfully. "I go if Italian tourists travel."

Whenever Mohammed bought chocolate candy bars, I noticed he chose the brand Linda. Although I wanted to ask her name, I did not. "Thanks for explaining," I said and changed shoes before we walked back to AIYS. I told him, "A famous poet, Rumi said, 'Break my heart or break it again so I can learn to love even more the next time.'"

"Is that the book you read with the word 'wine'?" he asked. I smiled.

Staying an extra day in Sana'a was a luxury, and I decided to get a manicure at the Taj Sheba Hotel. My appointment was for Friday morning at nine o'clock. "*Marhaba*, hello," a worker at a fruit juice stand called when I passed.

"*Marhabtian*, double hello," I replied and ran into a string bag of oranges hanging from the juice stand roof. We both laughed.

Boys saw me bump my head and looked up. They were holding hands and dressed in white thobes with miniature jambiyas tucked into embroidered belts. "Old man," one boy said in Arabic.

"Not old man," I corrected. "Old woman."

"Young woman," they said as their faces turned red. "Yes, young woman."

Greeted by the hotel attendant, I walked through the revolving door and glanced at the cakes and pastries in a refrigerated glass case, but I kept going and turned left past the reception desk and down a corridor to the beauty salon. Irene, the beautician from India, worked miracles on nails. When the manicure was finished, I did not want to smear the clear polish and waited on the plaid sofa for my nails to dry and Irene to bring the bill.

A woman covered in black entered the salon. We exchanged greetings in Arabic. She sat in the red-leather swivel chair with her back to me and removed her black face veil and scarf. Long, copper-colored, hennaed hair cascaded to nearly the floor when she loosened the clip. Turning to face me, I saw red-rimmed eyes that looked like she had been crying. "Can I get an appointment?" she asked in English.

"I don't work here," I said, fluttering my hands to show her I had had a manicure. "Irene will be back."

"My hair needs a touch-up," she said, taking a brush from the counter and running it though her hair. "Where're you from?"

"Hawaii," I answered.

"That's paradise," she said. "Are you a tourist?"

"We're all tourists," I replied.

She smiled, thought for a moment, and quoted an Arab proverb: "Be in the world, but not of the world."

"Did you study abroad?" I asked, surprised by her command of English.

"My husband and I attended graduate school in New York," she said. "We lived in America twelve years—that's where our children were born. We're U.S. citizens. How do you like Sana'a?"

"It's good," I answered, "but I live in Marib."

"My God!" she exclaimed, leaning forward in the chair. "I'd never go there in a million years. Marib is awful, and people are crazy."

"Marib is different," I acknowledged, knowing I could not change her conviction that only gun-toting, backward people lived in Marib. Stereotypes have truth, but not the whole truth.

Our conversation lulled, and she faced the mirror. Gazing into the looking glass, she pulled a tissue from a box of Fine on the counter and dabbed her eyes. "My daughter's getting married next week," she spoke to the mirror. "Her birthday was this week—she's eighteen."

"Congratulations," I said, thinking I should respond.

"The wedding will be in Saudi Arabia. My daughter's marrying a very wealthy Saudi. For three weeks, I've literally lived at the Saudi Embassy, getting signatures on documents—we needed visas," she said. "They send me home for yet another document or photograph—it's exhausting."

Since she was speaking to the mirror and not to me, I remained silent, not wanting to break the spell.

"Finally, I shouted at them, 'I cannot do this any longer—we need our passports.' Then the passports are finished." She brushed her hair, showing me strands of gray. "These gray are from the Saudis," she said, and then she whispered, "I'm losing my first born." Her voice was strained. "Because of stupid Yemeni tradition, my daughter must marry."

Irene returned with my bill.

"My hair needs a touch-up," the woman said to Irene. She composed herself, squared her shoulders and sat tall in the chair.

The drama I had witnessed was confusing and left me feeling sad. The slice of chocolate cake I had promised myself after the manicure was no longer appealing. Walking across Tahrir Square, I thought of Yemeni-Americans caught between two very different cultures.

On Fridays, stores in Sana'a opened in the late afternoon. I had two hours to shop before returning to Marib. Shumaila Hari, the largest supermarket in Sana'a, sold groceries and produce on its first floor and clothing, shoes, and assorted items on its second floor. They stocked a wide selection of cheeses, and that was the reason it was on my to-do list.

Sana'a taxis are old, banged-up white cars with yellow license plates. I shook my head no when the driver of a shiny, black Mercedes with a blue license plate stopped and offered a ride. Soon a battered white station wagon with a dangling yellow license plate honked. I waved him to the curb. He leaned over and rolled down the window. I asked how much to Shumaila Hari—250 rials. I opened the rear door and sat in the backseat, brushing qat leaves aside. Empty water bottles littered the floor.

"Where are you from?" the driver asked.

"America," I answered. He seemed jarred by the fact I had volunteered my nationality.

"I don't like American politics," he said, looking in the rearview mirror. "But Americans are nice. Are you a Muslim? You cover your hair."

"Not yet," I replied.

"I was born here, that's why I am a Muslim. It's not a choice for me," he added.

"Are you married?" If I answered yes, he would ask where my husband was and why he let me out alone, unprotected. If I answered no, I was suspect or fair game. Either way, doomed. "No," I replied.

"I want to go to America," he said, speaking to the rearview mirror. "Getting a visa at the American embassy is really difficult. If I had an American wife, it would be easy. My friend from Taiz married an American—they live in Detroit." I nodded.

"I'm not married yet," he explained. "I'm almost thirty. Marriage is expensive—one of my friends paid half a million rials to marry a girl from Ibb. For American women, you don't pay anything—they are cheap," he laughed. "Don't take that wrong."

He quit looking in the rearview mirror and turned to face me. "Anyway, I would like to marry an American."

"Stop," I yelled as the traffic halted. At the very last second, he slammed on the breaks. Stopped at the red light, he focused his full attention on the conversation of marriage. "Go," I said when the light turned green.

"I want to marry an American so I can travel to the U. S. and make money."

"It's not that simple," I replied.

"If I'm married, I'll get a green card and work—make money," he said. I kept quiet.

He faced me again, "She doesn't have to be young—maybe fifty years old. Or even older is okay. It doesn't matter about age," he said.

I did not reply, which did not seem to matter, because he continued. "My American friend, Andy, lived in Sana'a and said he was a Christian, but he was a Jew. Do you know him? Why would he say he was Christian?

Jewish tourists and researchers traveled to Yemen and probably did not advertise religious beliefs due to the general sense of dislike and intolerance toward Israel. However, ancestors of the Yemeni Jews, legends explained, settled in Yemen three thousand years ago as merchants sent by King Solomon, following the footsteps of the Queen of Sheba on her return trip home.

In the 1940s, over 100,000 Jews lived in Yemen, but near the end of the 1950s, only a few hundred remained scattered in Amran and Saada. Yemeni Jews had traveled to Israel, transported on flights that were for months, even after completion, kept secret. Later identified as "Magic Carpet" flights, they left Aden, Yemen, and brought Yemeni Jews "home" to the new state of Israel by British and American transport planes. Today it is rare but not impossible to see Yemeni Jews—men with long, curly earlocks, an outward sign of their Jewish faith. However, the women appeared identical to Yemeni females.

In al-Ga'a, the old Jewish Quarter of Sana'a, houses were one story with deep dugout basements because Jewish homes could not tower above Muslim neighbors. If Jews passed Muslims riding donkeys, they had to dismount so as not to appear taller. Jews were not allowed to carry weapons. During his reign, Imam Yahya (1904–1948), signed a Letter of Protection for all non-Muslims in Yemen, saying, "We cannot hinder what their [Jewish] religion allows." The imam gave Jews the right to solve problems among themselves. Wine making and drinking wine was strictly forbidden for Muslims, but it was allowed in Jewish homes.

Yemen's finest silver jewelry—fashioned by Jewish silversmiths—still brings the highest prices in the suq and is sought by collectors around the world. Marjorie Ransom, a friend and longtime collector of silver jewelry, invited me along on several silver-seeking expeditions. Once in Amran we attended a Jewish wedding, but we were there on the wrong day to see the bride dressed in her silver. The all-female bridal party was similar to Yemeni gatherings held in small villages under tents, indistinguishable from other villages throughout Yemen. The only difference there was a synagogue where boys studied the holy book.

Two blocks from Shumaila Hari, the driver turned to face me. "One more thing—she needs to be healthy," he said.

"Yes, health is important," I sighed, glad to have something to add to the conversation.

He stopped the car in front of the market, "My name is Mohammed," he said and extended his hand. I shook his hand and wished him well, "You'll find an American wife, inshallah, I said, getting out of the taxi and paying the fare.

"Do you really think I will?" he asked hopefully.

"Anything is possible, God willing."

40

CLASSICS AND CAMOUFLAGED CARS

A book is a garden carried in a pocket.
—ARAB PROVERB

Back in the Marib classroom on Saturday, I cautioned my six students, "There is danger in not reading," speaking in a low voice. I noticed that when I spoke softly, they listened. "If you don't read, you'll limit yourselves to knowing only ideas of like-minded people. To be educated, you have to read and expose yourselves to a variety of opinions. Education allows you to live in a much larger world. Lack of education narrows horizons and choices."

They looked skeptical. "What if it's against Islam?" Ahmed asked.

"I'm not encouraging you to read anything against your religion," I assured them. "Reading is a way to open minds along with developing new vocabulary and sentence patterns. If you don't read, you won't write well."

I lost the students. Okay, I started over, "How many of you read an hour a day in English? Do any of you read an hour a week?" No hands shot in the air. "Do you ever read?"

The students did not make eye contact. "Why?" I asked.

"It's not our habit," Khalid answered, speaking for the group. "We don't read in Arabic either."

"That's not true," a male student replied. "I read Arabic newspapers." He did. I remembered seeing him squatting on the cement steps of the health department, reading a newspaper. What had caught my attention was the fact that his lips were moving. While reading English or Arabic, they all moved their lips.

"Maybe chewing qat takes our time," Khalid added.

"You only read because I assign homework?" I questioned. "Not for fun?"

"Reading isn't fun," they said.

196

How could I make reading fun? Perhaps reading in Arabic was difficult because of its formal style. Reading from the student's point of view was a chore or waste of time. I was not giving up. Exposing students to good literature in English would change their minds. The bookstore in Marib did not carry literature in English.

I telephoned Taha Hussein at the Dar al-Hikma bookshop in Sana'a. His bookstore stocked abridged English readers for ESL students—literary classics would be right for their level. I ordered ten titles and expected students to share and discuss the books among themselves and read for fun, not for homework. But they did not read.

"Mohammed," I asked as we walked to the hotel, "did you finish *Sherlock Holmes*?" He looked straight ahead without reply.

"Did you even open the book?"

"You have to say it's for homework," he answered. "Or we won't read."

"But I want the students to experience reading as fun," I explained.

"No one thinks reading is fun," he said. "They already told you."

I was not listening. I did not want to hear that reading was worthless.

"Can't you walk faster?" Mohammed whined.

"Why rush?" I replied, irritated because I would never make a difference in the students' lives. I wasted their time and mine. Who was I kidding? I came to Marib to help improve lives, thinking I knew best.

"Hurry," he ordered.

"I'll hurry," I said. "Watch me." I turned and walked in the opposite direction.

Mohammed followed me to the intersection near Hant Supermarket. A car painted camouflage colors stopped with two military men inside. They spoke to Mohammed and offered him a ride.

"I want to walk," I told Mohammed, feeling uneasy. But Mohammed opened the door and slid across the backseat. I slid in next to him.

The man quizzed Mohammed about where he was from and how long he had been in Marib. Then the man asked questions about me. Mohammed gripped the Kalashnikov, and I knew something was wrong.

"Where are you going?" Mohammed said as the car turned right on the dirt track toward the desert. "We're going to the Bilquis Hotel."

The driver muttered to himself but did not change direction. Mohammed released the safety on the Kalashnikov with a loud click. The driver must have heard the sound because he veered back onto the paved road. He drove to the hotel but stopped halfway up the driveway before reaching the gate. We got out and walked.

"Who are they?" I asked, concerned because Mohammed did not turn and walk to the gate. He watched until the camouflaged car disappeared in clouds of dust. I noticed there was no license plate.

"I need your phone to call Dr. Mustafa," he said. I opened my purse and handed him the mobile phone. "No, I'll use the phone in your room."

Mohammed's usual calm voice sounded agitated when he spoke with Dr. Mustafa, explaining what had happened. "I'll stay until Dr. Mustafa calls," Mohammed said and leaned against the bookcase.

"Want cookies and tea?" I asked.

"No," he answered. I opened the package of cookies, and Zhara jumped on the bookcase. I crumbled a cookie in her bowl. Mohammed did not pay attention to where he placed his hand. Zhara danced up and down on tiptoes and hissed. "No one will bother you with her around," he said and quickly moved his hand away from the dancing cat.

"I didn't want to ride in the car," I said. "Something wasn't right—I trust my intuition."

"Dr. Mustafa's finding out who they are," Mohammed replied. "What's intuition?"

"My inner voice," I said, pointing mid-chest. "Here."

"I'll be back," he said. "Don't open the door." When Mohammed returned, he was dressed in a military uniform. This time he sat stiffly in the chair with his Kalashnikov on his lap.

"Who were the men?" I asked.

"No one knows them," he replied. "Dr. Mustafa's guards are looking for the car, and if they drive through one of the checkpoints leaving Marib, the military will remember them."

Mohammed heard the next day that the car was stolen and belonged to someone in Sana'a. "Dr. Mustafa doesn't want you to walk," Mohammed said. For two weeks, Rafallah shuttled us to and from class. I never found out who the men in the camouflage car were or what they wanted.

41

ISOLATED LIVES

To travel hopefully is better than to arrive.
—ROBERT LOUIS STEVENSON

"You're in Yemen?" I said, shocked to hear Nathalie's voice on the telephone. Our last time together was in Sana'a shopping for princess shoes a lifetime ago. "Guess what? I finally bought the shoes."

"I gave the shoes away," she replied, her voice tinged with sadness. "I never wore them."

Nathalie was in Sana'a at AIYS after spending three weeks on the island of Soqotra finishing field research for her dissertation. "Can you come to Marib?" I asked, holding my breath and hoping she would say yes. More than anything, I missed being with Westerners who understood Yemen—men and women, but especially women friends who knew the people and country and did not totally romanticize or criticize experiences as some tended to do.

In only two days, Nathalie would return to America; she could not visit Marib. Our telephone conversation would be our connection. In Yemen, we led isolated lives—Nathalie on Soqotra and me in Marib. The places were similar due to remoteness, mountainous terrain, basic ways of life, a lack of foreigners, an abundance of camels, and unpaved roads. Soqotra was an island and Marib an island onto itself.

Six million years ago, Soqotra's landmass separated from the African continent and now resides as an island in the Arabian Sea. It's a botanist's dream—a paradise of plants. Over eight hundred plant species are cataloged, and of those, two hundred are endemic. Soqotra's emblem, the dragon blood tree (*Dracaena cinnabari*), with its limbs reaching for the sky, resembles an opened, windswept umbrella. The image is stamped on Yemen's twenty-rial coin. Written accounts of Soqotra are rare, but the Sabaeans (the same people who ruled Marib) controlled the island for a time. Alexander the Great in 330

BCE settled a colony on Soqotra. In 52 CE, Thomas the apostle founded a Christian community before sailing to India. In the thirteenth century, Marco Polo visited Soqotra and commented on the number of Christians.

As an anthropologist, Nathalie lived on Soqotra for a year and was sensitive to the lives of the villagers. She questioned how she might be disrupting their lives or contributing to a sense of lack of self-worth among the people. While doing research, Nathalie remained in a remote community in which she was suspect as an outsider. Harsh conditions in the village made her life difficult and at times downright unpleasant.

With the telephone to my ear, I listened to Nathalie's story:

> Although I did not want to sell my car last year when I left Soqotra, the shaykh's son hounded me. He promised that if I sold the car to him, I could use it when I returned. He wrote that in the contract that we both signed. Other people on the island were willing to pay more money for the car, but it seemed wise to keep a good relationship with the shaykh's family.
>
> When I arrived this summer, I called the shaykh's son to tell him I was back and asked to use the car. "I'll stay in Hadibu a few days, but I'll need the car to travel," I explained. He yelled at me, saying he never promised I could use his car.
>
> Ali, a friend, said I could borrow his car, but that is not the point—the shaykh's son promised. The reason I was back on Soqotra was to finish translating poems, and the only translator in the capital said he would help me, but he had business on the other side of the island. However, if I drove him, he would do the translations.
>
> Our first day away from Hadibu, we stopped in a village that hugged a mountainside and drove on a rough dirt path to a small cinder-block house. The translator called the owner's name in a loud voice but did not approach the house. A woman covered in black answered the door, but before we could enter the house, she went to get her father so he could sit with us, since her husband was traveling. Women have to watch reputations.
>
> While we spoke with her father, the woman stayed in the other room. I could smell incense wafting through the curtain room-divider. The men

and I ate rice mixed with goat's milk, and after serving us tea, the father returned to his house. The woman did not enter the room where we worked translating poems. At nightfall, she passed sleeping mats under the curtain without a word.

The translator and I were to sleep on separate mats in a screened-in porch attached to the main house. Before going to sleep, I heard the translator brushing his teeth—no one uses toothbrushes in Soqotra.

Inside the main house, I heard a mattress sliding on the floor, and just as I was falling asleep, I saw the translator get up from his mat and push the curtain aside and enter the woman's room. He returned some time before morning, and I wondered if I had dreamed it or if it really happened.

The next morning, I asked him, and he said, "Yes. Her husband was away." We traveled around the island, and the same thing happened night after night. He explained that he carries his toothbrush and uses it when he sleeps with a "friend."

One afternoon, we drove to a village, and one of the villagers was very ill. His sons arranged to take him to a doctor in Hadibu. The translator, being a good friend, paid for the car. That night he slept with the sick man's wife. "How can you do that?" I asked him. "You helped her sick husband and then . . . ?"

"I give with one hand and take with the other," he replied.

My last days on the island, I was again saying good-bye. The women in the village where I had lived for a year acted unfriendly. We sat in a circle in a small room blackened by smoke, but no one touched noses with me. I gave them the gifts I had brought from America. My neighbor had been eyeing my gold earrings. I took them off and handed them to her. She had earlier asked for the princess shoes, which she was wearing.

"We have nothing to give you," they said. "We're unfortunates." Then a villager asked her daughter to bring me a present: the woven dining mat. The girl brought the food-stained mat—not a new one—as a farewell gift. One woman stiffly shook my hand. I had no idea what had happened.

Later I found the reason for the changes in the village. A teacher from Aden had sent a message to the villagers:

1. Do not speak with non-Muslims.
2. Do not offer food to Jews who visit the island.
3. Do not allow men and women to sit together.
4. Do not speak any language other than Arabic.

He delivered these commands as if they were direct quotes from the Koran.

Before leaving the village, I visited the leader's house to say good-bye. He invited me inside, and we sat together. He never offered tea. "You won't need your mobile phone, since you're leaving Yemen," he said, extending his hand, expecting I would give it to him.

"I'll use it in Sana'a," I explained. I gave him gifts for his wives and children.

"The best gift for you," he said, "is to become a Muslim."

42

Women over Sixty

*Our lives begin to end the day we become silent
about things that matter.*
—Martin Luther King Jr.

"We'll have a meeting in Marib on Wednesday if we get security clearance to travel," Cheri said on the telephone. "What can I bring from Sana'a?"

"Cat food, please," I replied. "I heard Whiskas reached Sana'a."

"Your computer is fixed," she added. "It only needed cleaning—there's no charge." Having a computer did not make much difference. I was not writing.

Cheri arrived on Wednesday with gifts of homemade pumpkin soup, lettuce from her garden, two packages of cheese, fresh baked chocolate chip cookies, and Zhara's first can of Whiskas cat food.

I opened the cat food, waving the lid. "You'll love this," I said and placed the dish of food on the bookcase. Zhara jumped up, sniffed the food, and raked her paw in the air, covering it with imaginary sand.

"Why?" I asked. "This is real cat food!" Zhara hopped off and eyed Cheri's chocolate chip cookies.

"Later," I said and put the plastic, zippered bag on the top shelf of the bookcase.

Cheri had meetings in Marib, and afterward we planned to have lunch in the hotel dining room. I did not dress in black because I knew Cheri would object, believing that, as a Western woman with feminist ideas, I should be setting standards of freedom of choice for Yemeni women. I wore a turquoise print skirt and white mid-length-sleeved blouse. I was looking forward to getting together for a social lunch. Cheri waited for me in the hotel reception area. "I thought by now you'd have married a Marib shaykh," she said as we walked to the dining room.

"I've met a few," I said laughing. "The last one, with wispy orange hen-naed hair, was nearly toothless—he tried to entice me by trading his old, dent-ed Toyota truck in exchange for marriage. Although I was tempted, I said no."

"Marib must have lots of interesting men," she said.

"Look around," I answered. "How many do you see?" She glanced around the empty hotel dining room.

"How could I possibly meet men?" I asked. "I'm locked up. The only men I see are hotel workers and soldiers. Oh, and Bedouin who use the pool as a bathtub."

"What about Shaykh Salah from Baraqish?" she asked, raising an eyebrow.

"We had tea at the hotel," I answered. "He wanted money to build a clinic and elementary school in Baraqish. I gave him your telephone number."

"So you meet men!" she said, as if catching me in a lie.

"Well, yes, I guess so, and when I find the right shaykh. . . . The Shi'a sect of Islam has a temporary marriage contract. It's called *mut'ah*, an enjoyment marriage, contracted for a specific period of time—an hour, three days, a week, a month, whatever. The couple is legally married. The couple agrees to the start and stop date and what is required of each. Neither can inherit from the other unless that is part of the contract. Marrying a Christian or Jew is permitted—people of the Book."

"Would you marry someone for a short time?" she asked, perhaps sur-prised by the idea of a short-term marriage.

"Maybe," I replied. "At least it would give me something to write about. Thanks for the wonderful gifts of food, that was thoughtful."

"Did you like the cookies?" she asked. "I brought the chocolate chips from America."

"I didn't have one yet," I answered, knowing the cookies sat on the top shelf of the bookshelf. I pictured Zhara munching cookies while we ate our salads.

After lunch, I returned to the room to get my baltu and scarf, but first, I put the unopened package of chocolate chip cookies in the refrigerator.

"Are you still wearing that black thing?" Cheri asked. I nodded. Moham-med Hani drove us to Marib because Cheri wanted sweets to take to her staff in Sana'a. Two truckloads of blue uniformed soldiers followed our car. Mohammed sat in the back of Cheri's car and directed Mohammed Hani to the open-air, lean-to candy shop opposite the qat suq. It was the first time for me to see the store.

Mohammed Hani parked on a dusty, unpaved road next to a vacant lot covered with weeds waving in the wind. Men who were crossing the vacant, sandy ground and those in the suq gawked as we got out of the car followed by armed soldiers.

"Fudge," Cheri said and pointed to a thick chunk of swirled dark brown and white candy behind a partition of glass. The shopkeeper with velvet brown eyes sliced samples for us to try—the fudge was sugary. Cheri bought a big sack of candy. The clerk wrapped my small purchase in waxed paper. "You could make a fortune here," Cheri said. "Marib lacks everything. Why don't you open a bakery—bake cakes and cookies?"

"There is a bakery that sells cake on Thursday. Cheese is what I miss," I said.

"Someone makes cheese," she replied. "Look at all the goats!" Of course, she was right about the goats, but I had not found cheese for sale in Marib. Mohammed overheard our conversation and thought that cheese-making might make money. Taiz was famous for its smoked goat cheese rounds. By the time we returned to the hotel, he apparently lost interest because he did not mention the cheese business again.

"Your earring," Mohammed said and picked my gold hoop out of the dust as I waved good-bye to Cheri. "You're going to lost it."

"Yes, some things disappear, and there's no getting them back," I replied.

This reminded me that the general had borrowed my camera to photograph his men. "Can I get my camera tomorrow?" I asked.

"We'll go to his house," Mohammed replied.

The general's two-story, gray, cement-block house surrounded by a tall, cement block wall was located on the outskirts of Marib toward the President's Palace. Standing in sand outside the double metal blue gates, Mohammed told me to knock. "Only women will be home. They won't answer if they hear a man's voice," he said.

"What do you want me to say?" I asked. "Should I say I want my camera?"

"Just say hello," he replied.

I banged on the metal gate with my hand, shouting "Marhaba." I turned to say something to Mohammed and saw three men and a boy watching us. They leaned against a wooden fence. I tried again. "Marhaba," I shouted and pounded harder. A wizened old woman opened the gate about an inch. Her dark, leathery skin draped in folds, and two beady eyes like pebbles stared from behind curtains of flesh. She looked scary.

"Is the general home?" I asked in Arabic.

"No, she replied, shaking her head. Loose skin jiggled. She closed the gate.

"Wait," I said in English, and she came back. "Mohammed, you explain." As he approached speaking Arabic, she slammed the gate and listened from inside—she was not about to talk with a man she did not know. Her reputation was at stake. Finally, it was settled. Mohammed would return in the evening when the general was home. We left.

"Don't you think that's carrying the man-woman thing a bit too far?" I asked, laughing. "She's got to be over one hundred years old!"

"You're right, women over sixty don't have to cover," he said. "They're no longer considered . . . you know . . . like women. You understand?"

"If you mean the women are past childbearing age and considered useless in this society, I understand," I replied, no longer smiling. "But I don't agree. Women in their sixties are just coming into their own. We need to reinvent ourselves at each stage of life and make plans as long as we are still breathing."

"Why are you angry?" Mohammed asked, nervously adjusting his scarf.

"I'm angry for all the women over sixty who are treated unfairly," I shouted. "And for women who believe that life stops if you aren't popping out babies."

43

SUPERSTITIONS

Everything can be told. It's just a matter of starting,
one word follows another.
—JAVIER MARÍAS

Before class, Amal asked if she and the women could see me on Thursday. "Yes, of course, but I thought someone told you not to visit me," I answered.

"He called Nura," Amal explained, keeping her voice low, "but Asma will not join us—we're three, and they won't know."

"Do you know who called her?" I questioned. Mohammed and Ahmed entered the classroom, and Amal rushed to her seat. I wrote sentences on the board, and when I turned around, I said, "Please pass in your homework." Ahmed was busy copying Khalid's homework. "Ahmed," I reminded, "homework's done at home.

"Please begin all English sentences with capital letters," I said, pointing to the sentences on the board. "Each sentence ends with a period, a question mark, or an exclamation point." I erased the sample sentences.

"Turn to page sixty-two." Getting books out and finding the correct page took five minutes. "Is everyone ready?" I asked.

"Sorry, I have to go," Ahmed interrupted, holding a phone to his ear. He shrugged his shoulders, grabbed his Kalashnikov, and spoke rapid-fire Arabic as he crossed the floor. Two male students whom I had not seen for weeks waited at the door.

"Come in," I said. They sat on the men's side of the room and wanted to know if they had missed anything important. "We're on page sixty-two."

"Jamila, can you come to the board and write a sentence from your homework?" She did not answer. "Is it okay if Amal writes your sentence?" I asked. Amal shook her head. "May I write your sentence?" I wanted the women to

207

shine in class to build self-confidence, but standing out as "stars" was not a part of the culture.

When we practiced new vocabulary aloud, I had to put my ear to veils. The women did not want the men to hear. It was exhausting, teaching two classes and running between the men and women.

"Mazen, wants to come to class," Khalid said when he finished writing sentences using the new words. "Is it okay?"

"Of course," I replied. Mazen was one of the better students in English but seldom came to class. His father, a powerful shaykh, undermined his son's success by scheduling errands during class time. Maybe insecure fathers were threatened or jealous of their sons' opportunities for education when they themselves had not learned to read or write.

On Thursday morning, Mohammed brought bread, and I told him the female students would visit in the afternoon. "I'll let three women in the gate," he said, "not four."

At four o'clock, there was a knock at my door, and three women dressed in black with veiled faces stood outside. I was delighted to see them. After tea and cookies, Nura, who spoke English well, told a story about her great-grandmother who had lived in Sana'a when it was a small collection of tall tower-houses with walled gardens, and the gates of the city locked at sundown:

Khulud, her great-grandmother, married at thirteen years old, and her first baby was born a year later, but it did not survive. Five of her pregnancies ended in death. She blamed fate for the terrible curse—the evil eye. Her husband blamed her and was prepared to take a second wife.

Then a miracle happened. Khulud became pregnant again, but this time, the midwife placed a baby boy in her arms. Her female relatives scattered rue to protect her and the child. They burned frankincense to drive the evil spirits away from the house. When she asked to be alone with her baby, the women were shocked by the strange request but respected her wishes and left.

After giving birth, a mother should not leave the house for forty days—and of course, she should never leave alone. However, she remembered stories told in hushed tones about secret rituals when women gathered. Khulud dressed in a long cloak and fastened a scarf around her hair.

A veil covered her face. Her newborn she wrapped in an old tattered blanket. Her husband was away on business and would not return until evening.

Carrying the baby, she walked down the flights of stone stairs, opened the heavy wooden door, and stepped into bright sunlight. The marketplace near her house was crowded. "Allahu Akbar" sounded from the minaret.

Men entered the arched doors of the whitewashed mosque. My great-grandmother waited on a side street, and when men exited the mosque, she held out her hand. The first man passed without giving her money. An old man, who looked as if he could least afford to give away money, gave her five rials. Others put coins in her hand. She hurried to another nearby mosque.

After the seventh mosque, she counted the coins in her leather purse. Next, she visited seven marketplaces. She extended her hand in silence. Yemeni women never ask for money.

By afternoon, her purse was full of coins and the gold suq crowded. She entered a gold shop and pointed to a small gold baby bracelet and tiny gold baby ring. The clerk wrapped the jewelry in a velvet bag. She paid for the purchases with the money she collected at the seven mosques and seven suqs.

At home, she placed the golden bracelet on her son's wrist and the ring on his finger. Although exhausted, she was grateful to have performed the first part of the ritual. Seven days needed to pass.

Her husband returned home that evening and was overjoyed with his healthy son. "Why aren't the women of our family present?" he asked, shocked that she was alone. His wife explained that to protect her child, she had asked them to leave. He doubted her reasoning, so he sent for family and friends to come at once. Soon the house filled with women. Big brass incense burners blazing with frankincense perfumed the room. Musicians sang songs and played drums. Trays of raisins and almonds sat on low tables. Sweetened tea flowed into glasses. Although the women commented on the baby's gold jewelry, the mother gave no words of explanation.

On the seventh day, she removed the gold jewelry and walked upstairs to the roof with the gold bracelet and ring in her hand. From the rooftop, she flung the bracelet and ring into the air and watched as they bounced on the ground far below. Whoever found the gold jewelry would say a blessing, and the blessing would be bestowed upon her son. The ritual was completed.

"That's a wonderful story," I said. "Did the baby live?"

"Yes. If the baby hadn't lived, I couldn't tell the story," Nura replied, laughing. "The baby was my grandfather."

"Have you written the story?" I asked, wondering if it could be published in Yemen.

"No," she replied.

Old practices remain deeply embedded within Yemeni culture, but men and women did not usually admit to being superstitious. Nevertheless, people sprinkled ashes on floors, tossed salt over shoulders, broke eggs in the corners of rooms, bought potions to purify houses and rid them of jinni and jinn. Sweet basil sprigs were tucked into clothes and behind ears for good luck. Cats in Yemen have seven, not nine, lives.

44

WITHOUT WORDS

There is only one journey: going inside yourself.
—RAINER MARIA RILKE

"I can't write," I said, shutting my eyes and feeling like a failure. "No words."

Mohammed brought the daily ration of bread, noticed my tears, and came inside. "Writing beautiful words about Yemen—foreigners will read the books and come to Yemen and think you lied. Yemenis will never read them," he said.

"Yemen is unique—a place like nowhere else. I'm not making that up," I said. "Sana'a is the safest place I have ever lived. I have walked across the city at midnight with never a concern for personal safety. I could count a stack of money on any street corner of Sana'a, and no one would bother me. Yemen, at least Sana'a, is not a place to fear. Someone needs to write about the good, and not just picture books about the natural scenery and ancient sights.

"No one cares about Yemen," he replied. "The aid people say they want to help Yemenis, but they help themselves by driving new cars. They don't ask what Yemenis want—they tell us what we need."

"I care," I added.

Mohammed dismissed my outburst with a wave of his hand. "You should be married," he said, "then you wouldn't be sad about not writing." He stood to leave and asked if he could borrow my phone.

Mohammed returned after lunchtime, holding a scrap of chicken wrapped in a flap of flat bread for Zhara and my phone. "Can I come in?" he asked. He seldom missed an afternoon nap, so there was cause for apprehension—something was up.

"Sure," I said, opening the door wide. Mohammed sat on the chair. I cut the chicken into pieces with scissors. Zhara jumped on the bookcase and ate from her dish.

211

"Here's your phone," he said, returning it. "I called my family."

"Is everything okay?" I asked.

"Yeah," he replied, sounding American. But only sounding so—his reasoning switched to Yemeni. "I told my dad and 'wife' I'm going to marry you," he said matter-of-factly. "Both agreed. My dad said you could teach English and make money for our family while my other 'wife' takes care of the house in the village. We'll have two homes—one in the village and one in Taiz."

"I am supposed to live in Taiz and teach?" I questioned. "Is that right?"

"I'll stay with you half the time and half with my other 'wife' in the village," he said dreamily. "Having two wives, I'll be fair. On weekends, you can come to the village, and we will sit together—a wife on my right and a wife on my left. You'll both pass me the best qat." He went on and on about chewing qat with wives on each side.

I stared at a carpet stain that seemed to grow. "Mohammed, you've painted an unrealistic picture. I'm not marrying you or anyone—I don't want to be married."

"Everyone wants to be married," he said, wide-eyed, not believing my words.

"I thought your 'wife's' bride price hadn't been paid and the marriage was off," I said.

"No, when we get married, I'll pay for her," he said assuredly. "She's happy to have you live with us."

"She doesn't know me," I replied.

"But I tell her about you," he said.

"I'm much older," I answered, knowing his argument about Khadijah, the first wife of Prophet Muhammad, and his only wife for twenty-five years. "Life is not as simple as it was in the Prophet's time."

"Then I'll marry you for six years—that way you'll still be young. We can go to America, and I'll make money. We can end the marriage contract after six years."

"What about your Yemeni wife?" I asked. "What about being fair?"

"She'll stay in Yemen and take care of my father and the children. She knows that I'll come back rich."

"Mohammed, I don't want to marry you," I insisted.

He seemed unfazed. "Okay," he said, gathering his thoughts. "How old is your stepdaughter?"

His proposal was so outlandish that I was stunned and just stared at the carpet stain. "I have to get away from Marib," I thought. "Think about this," he said and stood to leave.

A few minutes later, a knock on the door. I assumed it was Mohammed, coming back for another try. Opening the door, I came face to face with a tall, handsome, well-groomed Bedouin wearing a spotless white thobe and a neatly pressed suit jacket with a light brown cashmere shawl draped over his shoulders. Even his brown leather sandals were polished without a speck of dust. "Yes?" I said, seeing the pistol tucked in his belt.

He did not speak English. I was surprised the guards had not stopped him from coming to my room. If I understood correctly, he wanted me to see a collection of women's handicrafts. He had organized a cooperative in Harib and was asking for my help. He wrote his name and phone number on a piece of paper. "*Ta'al*, come," I said, reaching for my room key and shutting the door. We walked to the front gate so that Mohammed could translate. "What's your name?" I asked, and he responded.

"Mohammed, this is Nasser," I said, introducing them. They regarded each other, but did not shake hands. I had wanted to visit Harib ever since a friend told me a story about two young cousins—women from Harib—impersonating soldiers. I wanted to write a story, and I needed to see Harib.

"Dr. Mustafa will give his permission," I assured Mohammed. He shook his head. "Why can't we go with Nasser now? It feels right!"

"No," he replied, turning his back on me and putting an arm around Nasser's shoulder, leading him away. Watching Nasser get in his truck, I felt life diminish. Now I was really, truly, completely hopeless, because without writing, I had nothing. I crumpled the paper with Nasser's phone number and stuffed it in my sweater pocket.

When I opened the door, the telephone was ringing, and I prayed it would be Nasser telling me to climb the wall so he could meet me on the other side. But it was Marjorie Ransom, my American friend calling from Sana'a. She was going to pass through Marib on her way to Sayun. "Should I take the bus?" she asked.

"The bus is comfortable for men because it stops for tea and bathroom breaks. But women, when I traveled, stayed on the bus. We didn't get off.

If you go to the Marib long-distance taxi stand, you can buy two seats for five hundred rials each and sit by the door. You will not be pressed against a man—put your bag between you and your seatmate. How long can you stay?"

"Just overnight," she answered.

"Hurry. Please hurry," I said.

45

SPELLS CAST

Life shrinks or expands according to one's courage.
—ANAÏS NIN

Marjorie knocked at my door just before noon the following day. "I won't pay any more money," she said, "to the military man standing outside my door." Mohammed stood between Marjorie and the disgruntled soldier.

"Come in," I said to Marjorie, who for the first time wore a long, black baltu, her curly auburn hair partially hidden beneath a black lace scarf. I stared at her outfit.

"I know I said I would never be caught wearing this black thing," Marjorie said and laughed, bunching up fabric with both hands.

"It makes more sense traveling," I replied. "Mohammed, please tell the soldier that Marjorie won't pay any more money," I explained and shut the door. Soldiers hope for extra money guarding tourists between al-Jawf and Marib, but it is unusual for a foreigner to travel in a shared taxi. The Yemeni government demands that foreigners use armed escorts when they travel between al-Jawf and Marib. The government is supposed to pick up the tab, but it does not. Everyone knows soldiers need money for meals and qat. The guard had unfortunately encountered Marjorie, a remarkable woman who spoke Arabic and knew the ins and outs of Yemen and just how much to pay.

"I'm so happy to see you," I said. "I don't know where to start."

"Let's start with lunch," Marjorie replied. We sat on the floor in my room and made sandwiches of sliced tomatoes and cheese triangles pressed inside flat bread. Marjorie listened to my complaints. "I don't have friends—not one. I have stopped writing." Then I told her about Nasser's visit and not being able to travel to Harib.

"Will you last?" she questioned.

215

"I suppose," I answered. "Let's go out to dinner tonight. I'll show you Marib."

"Give me Nasser's telephone number," she said and wrote it in her notebook. "I'm interested in handicrafts—maybe I could photograph women in Harib wearing silver jewelry." Marjorie's interest in silver jewelry has taken her all over the Middle East searching for unique pieces, which she exhibits in museums around the world.

"Don't go to Harib without me," I begged.

After lunch, Mohammed knocked. He stepped inside the door while I tied my scarf. "Wait outside," Marjorie told him.

Mohammed walked Marjorie and me to the health institute. "You can't go anywhere without him?" she whispered, leaning closer as we walked away from the hotel. "I couldn't stand it."

"Me too," I said. At least with Marjorie, I laughed. Alone, it was not funny. I wanted to tell Marjorie about Mohammed's marriage offer, but I could not find words to describe the indescribable.

In the mornings, nursing students worked in Marib's hospitals, but in the afternoons they attended classes. "Today is English class," I explained to Marjorie as we walked. Female students squeezed through the door in twos and threes, bumping and pushing. Although it was an all-women class, more than half of the students kept the black face veils in place. In Marib, some girls never take off veils—even at home. Maybe no one sees their faces after they turn ten or eleven years old.

Only three out of the twenty-two students had completed the homework assignment. The photocopied medical book we had to use was too advanced for the basic level students. I wrote medical vocabulary on the white board that rolled across the floor when I pressed hard. "Mona," I said, calling names from the list of students.

"She's in Sana'a," a veiled voice answered.

"Ghadeer," I called, looking around the room. Although she was in class, she could not answer because she was giggling hysterically. "Can anyone make a sentence using the word 'malaria'?" I asked and wrote it on the board. "What causes malaria? How does a person contract malaria?"

A black-gloved hand shot in the air. "A contract is an agreement," a black-veiled voice answered.

"Yes, you're right," I said. "However, in English some words are spelled the same and pronounced differently—such as the word contract. It can mean to contract a muscle to make smaller.

When it's cold, muscles contract. A person contracts a disease—'to catch.' And contract is a written agreement, as you said. Please make a sentence using the word 'malaria.'" No one wanted to try.

After class, Mohammed waited outside the door to escort us to the hotel. "Would she like to see the dam?" Mohammed asked, avoiding speaking directly to Marjorie.

"Good idea," I said. "Who will take us?"

"Ahmed will drive Dr. Mustafa's car," he answered.

On the way to the dam, Marjorie asked to stop at the Dubai Hotel and check the room rates. Three men chewing qat lounged in the hotel lobby and did not look up when we entered. Mohammed asked them to show us a room, and begrudgingly, the youngest man put down his bag of qat and picked up the key from a cubbyhole, and we followed him upstairs. The basic room had a fluorescent light, a double bed with a well-used sheet, a chair, a cupboard, and a prayer rug.

"Why isn't she staying at the Bilquis?" Mohammed whispered.

"Marjorie wants to be close to the bus station so she can walk. She's traveling to Sayun in the morning," I answered.

"But she can't walk alone in Marib," he said, alarmed by the idea.

"She'll be fine," I answered. "Or you can go with her."

The price of the room was an outrageous three thousand rials, but Marjorie would stay only one night, and the hotel was behind the bus station. Down the hallway, we passed an open door next to Marjorie's room, a qat chew in full swing. Shaykh Salah had rented the room to host a party; an arsenal of personal weapons leaned against the walls. Hotels in Marib had few guests, and renting rooms to well-to-do shaykhs was a way to make money. Men waved bundles of qat as enticement for us to join the gathering. Mohammed could not resist and dashed in for a leafy branch. "You can stay," I said to him. "We'll go with Ahmed." Although Mohammed wanted to stay, his duty was to guard Marjorie and me. Unhappily, he hoisted his Kalashnikov, and we rejoined Ahmed, who drove to the new Marib Dam.

A white military bus loaded with policemen had arrived just before us, and the men clamored down the concrete steps of the dam dressed only in underpants. They were eager to swim. They seemed oblivious to the dead fish that floated on the surface of the brown, frothy water. "It doesn't look clean," Marjorie said, watching thick brown foam lap the concrete sides.

"The water is infested," I replied. "Anyone with an open cut or scratch is sure to be infected with bilharzias."

"Why does the military let them swim?" she asked.

"Good question," I answered. Workers at the health department knew the water was infected. They reported many cases of bilharzias.

Dusty shades of lavender and pink stretched across the sky as we watched swimmers climb the concrete steps. I wondered why the health department did not post warning signs. Lack of information limits choices.

"We should go," Mohammed said, shouldering his rifle. He walked on ahead while two soldiers appeared out of nowhere and followed behind. "Always being watched must get old," Marjorie said. "He keeps an eye on you even when he's in front."

"He's got eyes in the back of his head," I replied.

Ahmed drove to the bus station and blasted the horn. "Does he expect someone to come outside and sell tickets?" Marjorie asked laughing.

"Yes," I answered. "That's how it is done in Marib." No one appeared, which meant the bus station was not open for business.

"Can we walk from here?" I asked Mohammed.

"Why walk?" he asked, wondering why anyone would walk when a car was available.

"Let's walk to the restaurant," I insisted and asked him to open the car door. Unwillingly, he agreed.

"There are no girls or women anywhere," Marjorie commented. "Not a single one." We followed Mohammed along a dusty footpath through the suq and past the padlocked Internet café and turned right on an unpaved road that led to the Salaam Restaurant. "Let's eat outside," Marjorie suggested, seeing tables and chairs on the cement landing in front of the restaurant. Mohammed was not happy for us to be out in the open on the "terrace" but relented when workers from the Bilquis Hotel pushed tables together and joined us. The men sat nearest the street.

After stuffing ourselves with foule and flat bread, we finished with glasses of sweetened tea. Yosuf, one of the hotel workers who spoke English, told a story about his lunch with a famous Marib shaykh:

The shaykh lived in a palace, and we sat together in a spacious room in a large circle on the carpeted floor. Boys carried heaping trays of rice and placed them on colorful woven mats. Soon stacks of flat bread and platters of salads covered the mat. When the shaykh said begin, we tore bread and scooped up rice. Salads we ate with our fingers. I overheard a boy ask the shaykh if he should bring in the chickens. "No, no," the shaykh replied, shaking his head. Later the boy asked again if he should bring in the chickens and the shaykh answered, "Not yet."

The rice and salads were nearly finished, and the boy asked a third time if he should bring in the chickens. This time the shaykh said, "Yes, it's time for the chickens," and the boy opened the door, and ten chickens marched into the room and began eating the rice and salad that had spilled on the floor.

"What's the shaykh's name?" we asked, laughing. "It's not true."

"This is unusual for Marib," I whispered to Marjorie.

"What?" Marjorie asked. "Laughing and having fun?"

"Most unusual," I replied.

Marjorie remembered she needed to buy a bus ticket. Everyone at the table had the bus leaving for Sayun at different hours. "Can't Marjorie go by taxi?" I asked.

"There are no shared taxis between Marib and Sayun," they answered.

"Maybe she can hire her own taxi," Yosuf said and went to speak with the drivers parked a few blocks from the restaurant. A driver agreed to take Marjorie to Sayun first thing in the morning for eight thousand rials. Mohammed was relieved that the driver would pick her up at the hotel so he did not have to guard her when she walked to the bus station.

On the way to the Dubai Hotel, we stopped at the suq to buy apples and bananas for Marjorie's journey. Mohammed carried the carton of bottled water on his shoulder and told the hotel worker to take it to Marjorie's room.

I hugged Marjorie goodbye as we stood near the backdoor of the hotel. "Thanks for coming to Marib," I said. The fluorescent lights colored us eerie shades of blue-gray.

"I'm sorry to leave you with him," she replied, glancing at Mohammed.

"He's okay," I said.

The next day Marjorie telephoned from Sayun. "The Dubai Hotel charged three thousand rials for the room, but no soap, no towel, no toilet tissue, and only one dirty sheet on the bed," she fumed. "When I asked why service was so bad, they told me none of the items were standard—the management refused."

"How was the taxi ride?" I asked.

"Oh, that was great," she answered. "The driver was a stitch. He told marvelous stories and already introduced me to a silver dealer in Sayun, who invited me to the wedding tomorrow. I'll meet women wearing silver." When Marjorie and I hung up, I realized how often things come together in Yemen, as if magic spells had been cast. We meet the right person at the right moment, and doors are thrown open. This happens in other places as well but seems more noticeable in Yemen.

46

PRE-ISLAMIC GLASS BEADS

To love oneself is the beginning of a life-long romance.
—OSCAR WILDE

"Your AIDS test is not in the file," Dr. Mustafa said to me loudly enough for the Japanese tourists, who happened to be in the hotel's reception area, to hear.

"That's because I don't need an AIDS test," I answered.

"All foreigners need AIDS tests," he said. "I've checked."

"Not if we're over sixty years old," I replied. Older Japanese members of the group relaxed and bowed heads in my direction. I returned the bows.

My last AIDS test was at Modern Clinic in Sana'a. I had first telephoned Kamal: "How do I say 'sterile needle' in Arabic?" Inside the not-so modern clinic, people exchanged money for papers through a half-moon window. When it was my turn, I paid one thousand rials. "Go to room number eight," the clerk said in English. Over the door was a hand-lettered sign reading, GET AIDS HERE. I wish I had had my camera.

In Yemen, foreigners under sixty years old applying for visa extensions or work permits must have AIDS tests. A female nurse dressed in a white nurse's uniform and black face veil wore yellow rubber gloves and tossed my passport into an overflowing basket. "Can you write your name in Arabic?" she asked, handing me a label. I did.

Men and women eventually separated into two lines and were sent to different parts of the room. Our women's section was half-hidden from prying eyes behind a white sheet. A white uniformed nurse wearing a black headscarf and a black face veil pointed to a wooden chair. I sat. Her yellow rubber-gloved hand placed a plastic package in my lap; the seal on the needle was not broken. I had already forgotten the Arabic words for "sterile needle." Reusing needles was standard practice by health-care workers in Yemen.

221

I rolled up my sleeve. A nurse tightened the rubber tube around my upper arm. She knotted the tube and tore a wad of white cotton from a spool. The cotton fell to the floor. She bent over to retrieve it but noticed I was watching. She took another piece of cotton, moistened it with alcohol, and swabbed my inner arm. After cleaning my arm, she probed my vein with her yellow-gloved finger. She took off her yellow gloves, exposing red, chipped fingernails, and removed the syringe from its package. Then, she probed my vein with the tip of her ungloved finger and plunged in the needle. I thought of the sign above the door.

I watched Dr. Mustafa walk to the reception desk and use the hotel telephone to call the health department in Sana'a to see if I needed an AIDS test. While waiting for him to return, Mohammed entered the lobby.

"When was your last AIDS test?" I asked Mohammed.

"I never had one," he answered.

"Didn't you get tested when you joined the army?" I asked. He shook his head.

"Maybe if I give blood," he replied. Yemen's blood donations are screened 50 percent of the time. AIDS is an ongoing health concern in Yemen. Lack of education compounds its spread, and most of the cases are transmitted through heterosexual relationships and blood transfusions. Less than half of the health-care workers receive basic information concerning AIDS.

Greed as well as ignorance contributed to poor health care in Yemen. When the recent polio epidemic broke out, vaccines were distributed without cost by international agencies, but the vaccines did not reach the intended children living in desert regions. Yemeni authorities stored the vaccines until the dates expired and threw them away, keeping the money earmarked for the doctors and nurses administering medicines. International agencies later learned what had happened and sent new vaccines and their own health-care workers to villages to give inoculations. When I asked a health-care worker what he thought of authorities preventing medicines from reaching the children, he answered, "People needed to make money."

"At the expense of children's lives?" I asked, astonished. He shrugged his shoulders but did not reply.

Dr. Mustafa found out on the telephone that I did not need an AIDS test and left.

"Dr. Mustafa thinks you'll stay in Marib," Mohammed said as we walked to class. "He spoke with Cheri, and she said you can renew your contract."

"Well, I won't," I replied.

"Where's your earring?" Mohammed asked, noticing my scarf had slipped back on my head, exposing my ear. I was not wearing a face veil to keep it in place. I retied the scarf and fastened it with a pearl-tipped straight pin. The earring was finally gone—disappeared. It had wanted to leave for a long time.

"I'll buy a new pair of earrings in Sana'a," I said.

"What can I get you for Eid?" Mohammed asked.

"Nothing," I answered.

"An Eid gift," he repeated. "Everyone gets new clothes."

In class during the afternoon, I congratulated the six students for their amazing progress. Khalid had not been able to stay within the lines on the first day but was now creating orderly sentences. The women wrote flowery paragraphs—not quite English, but close. Ahmed and Mohammed spoke with each other in English during class—at least they practiced.

After class, Mohammed suggested we have dinner at the restaurant where heat from the brick oven warmed the room. The weather was becoming increasingly cold. We scooped beans with freshly baked flat bread, the food delicious and filling. I shook crumbs from my baltu and walked to the sink. After washing hands, Mohammed paid the bill. For the first time, he did not ask for my wallet. "Thanks," I said outside the restaurant and pulled the thin, wool scarf around my shoulders.

"Let's stop at the fabric shop," he suggested. It was filled with shiny, brightly colored fabrics decorated with sequins and "jewels"—over the top for most Western tastes. "Do you like any of these?" Mohammed asked. For a ball gown, I knew where to shop. Maybe I had lived in Yemen too long, but a bolt of black velvet with red roses caught my eye. It reminded me of Mexican velvet paintings. I fingered its plush softness. "Do you like it?" Mohammed asked.

"Plain black velvet might be better," I said, walking to the other side of the store. A Moroccan-styled hooded cloak was what I wanted. In winter, I could wear it over my baltu to keep warm. "How much is the velvet material a meter?" I asked.

Mohammed repeated my question to the shopkeeper and he answered, "Seven hundred rials a meter." With dramatic flourish, the shopkeeper unrolled the bolt of cloth.

"I'll come back," I said.

"Is that what you want?" Mohammed asked. "You really like black?"

"Well, the bright red rose print is gorgeous, but I can't imagine walking to Marib wearing it," I said.

"No," he replied, shocked that I would even suggest wearing the fabric in public. "That's for the bedroom."

The next evening we walked to Dr. Mustafa's house located on a dirt road near the center of Marib a mile from the hotel. I needed his signature on the forms so I could travel to Sana'a for Christmas. A crescent moon was the only light. Walking after sundown, I shivered and thought more about the Moroccan hooded cloak. Cold wind whipped my veil aside. Mohammed tied his scarf so that his face stayed hidden. "I didn't know Marib would get this cold," I said, patting my gloved hands together.

Mohammed did not reply, having been alerted to a car parked on the road. "Stay," Mohammed ordered. Although I did not want to stand alone in the shadows, I stopped. He pointed the rifle at the side of the car. The headlights flashed twice. Two tall Bedouin dressed in light-colored goatskin robes got out of the car. Mohammed kept his distance and waved me forward, telling me to walk on ahead.

"Who are they?" I asked when he caught up with me. By his silence, I knew he was troubled. We soon approached Dr. Mustafa's two-story, cement-block house. I was surprised it looked "normal"; a rope swing was even attached to a tree. Guards recognized Mohammed, and they let us pass. We walked up a long dirt driveway.

"What are you doing?" he asked.

"There's a rock in my sandal," I said, standing on one foot and trying to shake it loose.

Mohammed knocked at the brightly painted blue front door. Dr. Mustafa was not home, but a boy invited us inside. Mohammed pointed up the stairs.

I made my way up the wooden stairway cluttered with women's shoes. Some of the soles faced skyward—I thought of Amal. On the second floor, I saw women seated on low couches inside a room to my right. I knocked. A pretty woman with an ample bosom dressed in too-tight purple satin sat near the door and opened it with her bare foot. I took off my shoes and entered the room.

Women in party dresses were seated on low couches lining both sides of the room. They leaned against pillows and stared, but no one spoke. In front of the couches were small, mahogany, short-legged tables. I did not know where to sit, or even if I should. "Marhaba," I said.

A woman with skin the color of coffee and bright green eyes sat near a panel of windows and patted the couch. I took it as a sign to sit. She offered her long-fingered hand, which I kissed. When she turned her head so I could kiss her other cheek, I saw a scar from her eye to her mouth that had been carelessly mended, like the seam of a rag doll.

Seated opposite and cradling a toddler, a woman introduced herself as Ahmed's wife. Her shiny, dark hair pulled back in a loose bun emphasized her long neck. She wore an elegant, champagne-colored, scooped-neck, long-sleeved dress. She was the only woman wearing heavy make-up. Her scarlet lips were not smiling.

"How do you like Marib?" an older woman with henna-dyed hair asked.

"Tamam, good," I replied and realized her dress was made from the black velvet with red roses that I had admired in the shop.

"Are you a Muslim?" she asked.

"Inshallah, God willing," I answered. Glasses of tea along with baskets of popcorn stacked on a tin-plated copper tray arrived. A young girl set the tea and a popcorn basket on a table near my feet.

"Ahmed wants to go to America," his wife said, sending her young son away and smoothing wrinkles from her skirt. "Will you help him?"

"I can't help anyone go to America," I replied.

"Won't you take Ahmed and Mohammed when you leave?" she asked, leaning forward.

"No," I answered, surprised by her question. She smiled for the first time. Her intelligent eyes sparkled when she realized I was not taking her man to America.

Dr. Mustafa's wife entered the room and introduced herself—her frizzy, hennaed hair showed under a midnight blue semi-hat that looked like a crown. Her sleeveless, blue velvet dress was decorated with antique, hand-painted beads sewn on the bodice. Antique beads are not supposed to leave Yemen—but of course, some travel. I had seen beads for sale in shops in Sana'a. She wore heavy silver bracelets studded with turquoise nuggets on her upper arms. I thought of Marjorie.

She seated herself next to Ahmed's wife, and she looked at me a while before asking her first and only question: "Do you swim in the hotel pool?"

"No," I answered, thinking what an odd question that was. Although I had not realized that the women in the room were listening for my answer, I heard a collective sigh.

"You're a good woman," she said. Conversation exhausted, we sat in silence, and I ate popcorn and drank tea. Mohammed sent a boy to the door to let me know it was time to leave.

Walking down the wooden staircase, I watched men crowded around Dr. Mustafa as he passed green two-hundred-rial notes to men. Hiring bodyguards must get expensive. I wondered who wanted to harm him. Mohammed, standing at the foot of the stairs, waved the signed document—Christmas in Sana'a.

PART VII

THE END OF THE JOURNEY

47

CHRISTMAS

*We must pass through solitude and difficulty, isolation and silence,
to find that enchanted place where we can dance our clumsy dance
and sing our sorrowful song.*
—PABLO NERUDA

"Visit your family in Taiz while I stay in Sana'a," I said to Mohammed.

"If I go to Taiz," he answered, "I'll need gifts."

"Your Christmas bonus," I said and gave him an envelope. "I would like to buy you a warm Christmas jacket in Sana'a."

Walking to the taxi stand the next morning, I braced myself against the cold wind. Marib looked especially drab and colorless. A steel-gray mist obliterated the mountains. Underneath my polyester baltu, I wore double sweaters and a woolen skirt. The thin, black, cotton gloves did not keep my hands warm. I was thankful the veil covered my face. My black, leather sandals had stretched to accommodate two pairs of socks, but my feet felt frozen.

Under Mohammed's futa, I noticed a pair of baby-blue sweat pants. He clutched the lapels of his thin, blue sport jacket with his free hand. In his other hand, he held a plastic bag containing gifts for his family. The black-and-white scarf was draped over his head like a tent. I saw that he was quivering from the cold. Neither of us spoke. Sunlight skated slowly over the mountains on icy feet.

A dark-blue Land Cruiser stopped, and the driver rolled down his window. Puffs of frozen air escaped from Mohammed's mouth when he spoke. I thought the driver stopped to ask directions, but Mohammed opened the car's rear door and got in the backseat. I followed.

"Is he taking us to Sana'a?" I whispered to Mohammed when we passed the checkpoint leading out of Marib.

"Naam, yes," he replied in Arabic.

The next time the driver stopped or spoke was when we reached the military checkpoint before entering Sana'a. He told Mohammed to leave his rifle. Mohammed traded his rifle for a piece of paper. When he returned to the car, he sat on my glasses. "They're bent," I said, holding them by a twisted arm.

"Will he take us to AIYS?" I whispered when the driver stopped near the gas station on Hadda Street.

"No," he answered. "He thinks you're Yemeni but you've lived abroad. That's why your Arabic is mixed up."

Mohammed opened the car door and we got out. He suggested we cross the street and go to Shumaila Hari. We checked our bags at the store's entrance, and I followed him upstairs. "Why are we here?" I asked, removing my black face veil.

"My jacket," he replied. Mohammed tried on several Chinese-made, down-filled jackets and chose a russet-colored jacket with taupe lining. "Do you like this one?"

"Yes, it's nice," I replied, watching him admire himself in the floor-length mirror. A young female clerk asked if I was Mohammed's grandmother. "Do you see a family resemblance?" I asked.

"No, I wondered why an old woman would buy a young man a jacket?" she replied.

"Then that is the question you should have asked," I said.

Mohammed smiled broadly, marveling in the mirror. The salesclerk cut the dangling tags. I paid.

"Thanks for the jacket," Mohammed said, still admiring himself. "I'm beautiful."

"You're welcome," I said. "But in English you can't call yourself beautiful."

"Why can't I?" he asked. I did not know, but thought it had to do with our culture teaching us that loving ourselves was narcissistic.

Sana'a was warmer than Marib, so the black cashmere shawl I had stored inside a rose-pink metal trunk at AIYS would keep me warm. I asked Shakeeb to bring the trunk to my room.

When I turned the key in the lock and lifted its lid, memories floated out. My shawl was on top. I thumbed through the *Lonely Planet: Yemen* book and read the words *mumkin sura*—may I take a photo—scribbled on the last page. Names of places I had visited were checked off. Business cards toppled out. Folded between pages was "Bullies and the Elephant," a story I collected at Yirfus Mosque near Taiz, about Shaykh Ahmad bin Alwan, a Yemeni Sufi. I read:

> "Give us money or food," the bullies shouted. "Or our elephant will uproot trees and destroy your homes."
>
> Of course, the villagers were afraid. They gave the bullies whatever they wanted. Soon the villagers ran out of things to give. "Let the elephant ruin our village," they said. "We have nothing left."
>
> The bullies knew the villagers told the truth. "We have blackmailed the people of the village," the oldest bully said. "All except one."
>
> "Who did we miss?" the others asked.
>
> "Shaykh Ahmad bin Alwan," he replied.
>
> "But he's a Sufi," they said.
>
> "What difference does that make?" the older bully replied.
>
> "Maybe he'll pray," they answered, "and ask God for help."
>
> "Well, so what?" he said. "Ahmad bin Alwan is old and weak—no match for us or our elephant."
>
> When they arrived at Shaykh Ahmad bin Alwan's house, he was working in his garden. "Welcome," he said.
>
> "We want money and food," they shouted.
>
> "How dare you ask for money and food," Shaykh Alwan scolded. "You're strong and capable of work."
>
> "Keep your advice," the bullies shouted. "Give us what we have asked for or our elephant will uproot your trees and destroy your house."
>
> The bullies realized he would not obey, so they hit the elephant with a stick. "Tear down the house!" they yelled.
>
> The elephant charged the house. Ahmad bin Alwan raised his arms above his head. The elephant sunk into the ground, and all that remained were the two ivory tusks.
>
> Afterward, the bullies knelt on the ground. "Please forgive us," they said. Of course, Ahmad bin Alwan forgave them, and the boys left the village believing in miracles.

Neatly folded underneath the *Lonely Planet* was Abdulmalik's blue scarf, the one I had worn while riding the camel. A zippered plastic bag held stones, and each contained a story. I found blue slate from Haraz at a religious site while researching the book on Queen Arwa. Two black volcanic stones from Bir Ali were from the storage site on the southern tip of the incense road in ancient Qana. A petrified, white, conical-shaped stone was the image of a sea creature said to have fallen from the sky during the sixth century when Abrahah journeyed through Amran on his way north to destroy the Ka'bah in Mecca. The green petrified fossil fern I bought from a boy selling trinkets in Na'it. An amber-colored stone the color of honey was from Wadi Doan in the Hadramawt. My most prized possession was the Neolithic spearhead Talib discovered in the sands between Marib and Shabwa.

I skimmed the lined pages of the gray al-Jadeed notebook that contained my first writings in Arabic. I remembered how hard I studied. Underneath the notebook was the *Hans Wehr Arabic-English Dictionary*, the one I never used. Pressed between pages of the dictionary was a red rose from an unknown Yemeni woman who placed it in the fold of my notebook while I wrote a poem on the steps of Dar al-Hajar in Wadi Dhahr near Sana'a. Her soft, dark, velvet eyes smiled from behind a black veil—no words were necessary. Inside a plastic sleeve was the CD, a gift from a taxi driver when I mentioned I liked his taste in music. The trunk was full of random acts of kindness I had experienced in Yemen. Repacking the memories, I locked them in the trunk, realizing that memories are what matter.

"May I speak with you?" I asked Chris Edens and ducked my head to peer through the miniature door into his office. He stopped what he was working on and invited me inside.

"Do you know of a house for rent?" I asked.

"What are you looking for?" he replied.

"Something small near AIYS," I answered. "It needs to be furnished. Oh, and I have a cat."

"Michael's returning to America for a few months; she might sublet. She has complained about her place being noisy. In Tahrir Square there are boys playing ball at all hours. Here's her telephone number," he said, writing it on a note pad.

After introducing myself to Michael on the phone, I asked if she might consider subletting her apartment. She was open to the idea. We set a time to meet. Although we had not met before, I knew it was her walking toward me in Tahrir. She wore a hooded robe made from the colorful fabric Sana'ani women draped over their heads.

Michael and I walked to Beit al-Moayad, a five-story house located behind Parliament. It had once been a family home but was now divided into three separate apartments. From the outside, the gray-brown, cut-stone and mud-brick house with *mashrabiyah* (intricately carved wooden latticework covered windows) was beautiful.

We entered a narrow alleyway. She unlocked a black metal gate, and we stepped into a paved courtyard. To the left, behind a wrought-iron fence, was an overgrown garden with a huge tiled fountain. An arched, wooden door several inches thick and studded with hand-wrought iron nails led to the stairwell. The heavy door creaked and sighed on its hinges . . . when opened.

Walking up three flights of stone steps, we came to another arched, wooden door studded with similar iron-nails, and Michael inserted a huge, antique metal key to turn the complicated lock.

The one-bedroom, one-bathroom apartment was charming. An architect by profession, Michael had remodeled the small kitchen—her personal touches said "home." While she brewed tea, I looked around and felt comfortable and hoped she would let me stay. Michael carried the teapot and cups on an antique copper tray. I followed her through the wide stone hallway with glass-fronted bookcases along one full wall.

"This I'm taking," she said and stopped at the bedroom door and pointed to an antique wooden chest next to a queen-sized bed.

"It's beautiful," I said. "Where is it from?"

"The Hadramawt," she replied. "Old treasures are disappearing."

The mafraj—her living room—was furnished with low couches that lined the three white walls and were upholstered in bright, lapis-blue fabric. A large, heavy, wooden table with sawhorse legs and metal braces was set against the windows to the right of the door—it was a workspace that held her laptop computer, a landline telephone, a gooseneck office lamp, miscellaneous books, and magazines.

In front of the couch was a carved, antique, wooden Yemeni table with drawers and a "secret" hiding place. Michael placed the tea tray on the small table and poured tea. "The rent is $210 a month," she said. "Utilities are extra—water and electricity cost about $15 a month. The house telephone I don't use, but take the number," and she wrote it on a slip of paper.

"I'm interested," I said. "But I have a cat."

"That's not a problem," she replied. "When do you need the apartment?"

"I'll leave Marib the middle of January," I said.

"What are you doing in Marib?" she asked. Her face suddenly looked concerned.

"Teaching," I answered. "I went to make a difference and to say thanks to the Bedouin but somehow I lost myself."

"It's none of my business, but from the way you look, I'd say stay at AIYS until I leave the first of January. Move in then," she added.

"I can't quit," I said.

"If you change your mind, let me know."

"It's a lovely apartment," I replied, feeling sad to say good-bye and glancing through the large window at rooftops that stretched all the way to old Sana'a. "Thank you so much."

Walking to AIYS, I wondered what Michael had seen in me. It is hard to know how we appear to others.

The phone was ringing when I walked up the AIYS stairs. "Hello, Mohammed," I said upon hearing his cheery voice. "How's Taiz?"

"Merry Christmas," he shouted. "You say Mary, mother of Isa, for Christmas?"

"What?" I asked. "No, no, we say '"merry.' It means happy. Not 'Mary,' Jesus's mother's name."

On Christmas Eve night, I fastened my baltu and wrapped the black cashmere shawl around my shoulders. There was a Christmas party being hosted by French couple Marylene and Remy; they enjoyed opening their home and bringing people together. The house was a five-minute walk through the alleyway. Marylene and I had met because of our interest in Queen Arwa, an Islamic queen who ruled Yemen for fifty years during the last years of the eleventh century and the first years of the twelfth century.

An informal dinner for fifteen was served on large woven mats placed on the floor of the mafraj. A tall, wrought-iron form in the shape of a big bell with hooped-stays was made to hold skirts to infuse them with incense, but on this occasion it was decorated with lighted candles to serve as the Christmas tree. Most of the guests spoke French. I listened. We avoided the lighted candles as we reached from low cushions to refill plates. After dinner, French pastries and coffee were served. Marylene asked about living in Marib. "It's more difficult than I imagined," I answered.

"Remy and I said you were crazy to go," she added. "We worry. You do not look like yourself—a thin ghost of you sits here. When do you return to Marib?"

"Tomorrow," I replied, feeling the weight of the words.

Lights from the dim street lamps glowed in the alleyway and created slanted shadows, but I was still able to see my feet on the narrow road. I passed tea-drinking soldiers guarding the political prison. "Good morning," one man said as I passed. He was right—it was past midnight.

On Christmas morning, Mohammed waited in the guardhouse, slumped on low cushions with his head against the wall and his eyes closed. He has traveled overnight from Taiz in a shared taxi. "Merry Christmas," I said. "Let's have breakfast."

"Okay," he replied. We crossed Tahrir Square, and Mohammed stopped at the Dubai restaurant, thinking we would have foule. I kept walking. "Where are you going?"

"It's Christmas," I said. "Follow me." The Taj Sheba's lobby was gaily decorated with twinkling Christmas lights as we walked through the revolving door. Surprisingly, the lobby was crowded, not with foreigners but with Yemeni men dressed in Western suits. "What's Dr. Mustafa doing here?" I asked Mohammed.

Dr. Mustafa was startled to see us, too. "Can you join us for Christmas breakfast?" I asked.

"Thanks," he said looking at his watch. "Our meeting begins in a few minutes." On the way to the coffee shop, I read the announcement for the Health Director's Conference listed on a signboard. An Indian waiter seated us at a table beside the window overlooking the garden. Another waiter brought coffee, tea, and menus. "Have whatever you want," I said. Mohammed studied the menu. "I'm having an omelet, toast, and orange juice."

The waiter came for our order. "Do they have foule?" Mohammed asked. I checked the menu, and yes, they served foule.

"Why don't you have waffles or pancakes and eggs too?" I insisted. "What kind of juice do you like?" Mohammed ate his pancakes and eggs with a spoon and scooped foule with bread.

"Is there time to fix my glasses?" I asked, placing my napkin on the table.

"Okay," he replied and stood to leave. "That won't take long."

A shopkeeper took one look at my glasses and excused himself. He returned with a container full of cloudy liquid and dipped the glasses into it. He manipulated the frame until the lenses popped out.

"What's he doing?" I asked Mohammed. "Tell him to stop." Mohammed remained quiet. The glasses looked to be broken beyond repair, but within seconds he reinserted the lenses, wiped them on his red and white checked scarf, and handed them to me.

"How much do I owe?" I asked.

"Nothing," he said. "If you need another pair of glasses, come back."

"He didn't even know it was Christmas," I said to Mohammed.

Rain was falling when we left Sana'a. The storm got worse as we drove into the desert. Soon rain mixed with sand obliterated the road, and a raging windstorm tossed the car—like a toy—back and forth. Sand pelted the windshield and pitted the glass. The driver had to use his scarf to wipe the windshield every few minutes because the wiper on his side was broken. Rains came in torrents and washed out sections of the road. We kept driving into ditches, which caused the car to bounce and shake. The men wanted to stop and wait out the storm. The driver thought stopping would be more dangerous. The men chanted, and faith carried us forward.

Stars twinkled in the clear evening sky just before we reached Marib. "How was Christmas in Sana'a?" Mohammed asked, walking to the hotel.

"Good," I replied. "How was Taiz?"

"Fine," he answered.

Before I had time to tell Mohammed I had rented Michael's apartment, a blue-and-white Toyota police truck mounted with a heavy-caliber machine gun stopped on the road a few feet ahead of us. Mohammed grabbed my arm, and we hurried to the right through the nearly deserted suq. At the teahouse, Mohammed called for Rafallah. He came for us using the back roads through the desert, avoiding the main street, as we listened to gunfire. Rafallah did not know who was fighting and thought nothing of it, accepting the occurrence as part of everyday life in Marib.

Zhara ate Christmas dinner, a bowl of Whiskas dried cat biscuits, as I un-packed my bag. "We'll leave Marib soon," I told her. My telephone rang. It was Daood wishing us a happy Christmas and asking if it was raining. I pulled the drapes aside. "No, It's not raining here," I said.

"Did you tell Dr. Mustafa you're leaving Marib?" Daood asked.

"I've told him," I replied. "But I don't think he is listening."

"What about Mohammed?"

"Of course Mohammed knows I'm leaving."

"Mohammed told Khalid and Ahmed you're taking him to America."

"Well, I'm not," I said. After we hung up, I wondered how many people Mohammed had told that he was going to America.

48

WINE AND CHEESE

How is it that in a moment of inspiration you extract
water from the heart of a stone?
—NIZAR QABBANI

"When will you leave Marib?" Waheeb asked, standing in the lobby holding a stack of accounting books.

"The middle of January," I answered. While we were talking, a telephone call came from Marylene in Sana'a. "Yes, I'm back," I said. "Thanks for a lovely Christmas party." She then asked if I could host a friend of hers from the World Bank named Oliver. "Sure, he is welcome."

Oliver called later that day and asked what he could bring. "I was just in Sana'a and don't need anything," I explained. "Ask for me at reception when you arrive; someone will show you to my room."

Saying that I was looking forward to Oliver's visit was an understatement. I told Mohammed that Oliver was coming. "Who's Oliver?" he asked.

"A friend of a friend," I replied. "I don't know him."

"Why are you so happy to see someone you never met?" he asked. I could not explain.

Oliver, a French-American who did not speak a word of Arabic, arrived the next day in a shared taxi. It is against Yemeni law for foreigners to be unaccompanied in Marib. He could not explain in Arabic where he wanted to go. At the police station, he found someone who spoke English, and the police truck delivered him to the hotel. After checking in, Oliver came to my room and put his backpack on the floor. "Probably smells the cheese," he said, staring at the wild cat unzipping his bag. "She's clever."

Four legs clawed the air as I picked Zhara up. "Sorry," I said, shutting the bathroom door with her inside. "She's excitable."

Oliver brought gifts of cheeses, a large bar of Belgium chocolate, a half bottle of white wine, a book, and an infectious laugh. Our lives were worlds apart, but seated on the floor of my tiny room in the middle of the desert, we shared stories and laughter. "A book you might like," he said, handing me a selection of stories, including excerpts of *Alice in Wonderland* by Lewis Carroll. I read:

> 'Would you tell me, please, which way I ought to go from here?'
> 'That depends a good deal on where you want to get to,' said the Cat.
> 'I don't much care where—' said Alice.
> 'Then it doesn't matter which way you go,' said the Cat
> '—so long as I get somewhere,' Alice added as an explanation.
> 'Oh, you're sure to do that,' said the Cat, 'if you only walk long enough.'

"Thanks," I said, closing the pages of the book. "I have been asking Alice's question. It seems to be a reccurring theme."

Mohammed knocked at the door. He and Oliver had met at the hotel entrance when the police dropped him off. He glanced around for Zhara. "She's inside the bathroom," I said.

"Let her out," Oliver said. "I like cats." Mohammed lifted his eyebrows and opened the door. Zhara raced around the room on hind legs, front paws clapping. "She's a wind-up toy." Zhara jumped on the bookcase and watched us with half-closed eyes like the Cheshire Cat.

Oliver unpacked his French guidebook to Yemen with highlighted must-see places in Day-Glo orange. "We can do those this afternoon—we've already asked a friend to drive us," I said.

"What else do you suggest?" he asked.

"Maybe Rafallah can take us to Sirwah. We can have a picnic tomorrow," I said to Mohammed.

"Talking about lunch," Oliver said, "break out the wine and cheese." Mohammed looked startled hearing "wine" but did not leave. I sliced apples and pears and put them on a plate. The cutting board held two kinds of cheese. I cut the flat bread into triangles with scissors and poured three glasses of water and two glasses of wine. We toasted. Mohammed anticipated that we would fall flat on our faces after finishing the bottle. We disappointed him.

After lunch, Rafallah drove us to old Marib Dam. Oliver and Mohammed climbed gigantic blocks of hand-hewn stone. They wandered about the area and looked at remains of the ancient sluice gates that had once turned fields green. I heard shouting when one of them found an inscription on stone in an ancient south Arabian language.

The afternoon sun warmed the rocks where I sat.

"It makes you feel insignificant," Oliver said, joining me on the rocks.

"That it does," I agreed.

Mohammed looked uneasy. I trusted his intuition. "We should go," he said.

"Have you written about the desert?" Oliver asked as we walked to Rafallah's truck.

"I haven't written in Marib," I answered, feeling ashamed of the wasted time. Then I remembered a story I had collected on the camel journey. "I'll read it to you, if you'd like."

"My privilege," Oliver said and climbed in the back of the truck with Mohammed. I sat beside Rafallah and he drove to the hotel.

Oliver and I ate dinner in the hotel dining room. "Why didn't Mohammed join us?" he asked.

"People gossip because they are jealous," I answered. "It would make life more difficult for him."

After dinner, Oliver remembered that I promised to read the story. "Can I walk you to your room?" he asked.

"Sure," I said and explained how the story came to me:

One night while we crossed the desert, we camped at an oasis with date palms and a huge *birka*, an underground spring and storage place for water. We spread our blankets on the sand, and transparent white spiders joined us. I drank tea standing up. I did not want to sit on a blanket with spiders. While Mohammed al-Baraki told us how water holes in the desert were created by falling stars, a man appeared out of nowhere.

He sat on Mohammed's blanket and asked questions. Mohammed told him I was a writer. Of course, Mohammed saw me writing in my notebook, but I never told him I wrote books. The man asked me in English if I collected tales. I told him I did. He said a German woman—an author—thirty years before had sat with him night after night, and he told her stories.

"Didn't it surprise you that a man dropped out of nowhere to tell you a story?" Oliver asked.

"Yes, but that often happens. What really shocked me was he spoke English," I said unlocking my door and wedging my foot in the opening so Zhara would not dash out.

"Would you like tea?"

"No, thanks," he replied.

"Why don't you sit here," I said and moved the chair away from Zhara, who was sitting on the bookcase.

I read the title of my story, "A Journey."

Wind whipped dark storm clouds that gathered on the horizon.

Raindrops pounded deep holes in the sand.

Pools of water collected in the holes on the desert floor.

The pools flowed together creating a fast moving stream.

The stream became larger and wider but stopped when it reached the sand dunes.

"It's impossible to cross the desert," the stream cried watching its water soak into the sand.

"I cross the desert and so can you," said the wind.

"That's easy for you to say," the stream replied. "You can fly."

"Come with me," invited the wind. "But I'm afraid," said the stream.

"One thing for sure if you stay where you are you'll vanish," answered the wind.

The stream was quickly disappearing into the sand.

"Okay," said the stream. It took the risk and traveled with the wind. Changing into vapor, it traveled across the desert.

In the sky, the vapor became clouds.

Dark clouds moved silently and swiftly across the sky. Raindrops fell.

Pools of water collected on the sand.

The pools joined together creating a fast moving stream.

The people who lived on the other side of the desert called the stream a new name—but that was the only change.

"That's a lovely story," Oliver said. "I've heard or read something similar."

"When the man told me, I wondered if the German woman hadn't given him the story. It's so unlike anything I have collected in Yemen."

Oliver made a fast move and leaned back in his chair, which alarmed Zhara. She jumped off the bookcase, lowered her head, and flattened her ears. Her eyes looked hard. "She means business," Oliver said.

"She's scared," I replied.

"I'm scared," he said, moving to the door. "I wouldn't want to meet her in a dark alley."

"Yemenis say they would rather fight a leopard than a wildcat," I said.

"Are there leopards in Yemen?" he asked.

"Only a few," I replied. "Killed for pelts or hunted by farmers as pests. Arabian Yemeni leopards bring high prices when sold to wild animal parks and private collectors."

"Desert wildcats are disappearing too, but for different reasons. Wildcats searching for food come to the hotel, and the females sometimes mate with domesticated cats—which gives us Zhara."

Zhara was impossible when upset, and if I tried to touch her, she attacked me. Oliver opened the door and slowly let himself out. "Sleep well," I said.

By the time I showered and brushed my teeth, Zhara was asleep on the bed. Whatever crossed wires in her head that set her off were now uncrossed.

The next morning, I packed the picnic lunch, and everything was ready at nine o'clock. Mohammed knocked and told me that we couldn't take the food with us.

"Why can't we have a picnic?" I asked. Mohammed gave a vague answer and shuffled away—scraping his sandals on the walkway—and went to get Oliver. Maybe he thought Oliver and I would open a bottle of wine and toast the Sirwah spirits.

Rafallah waited in his parked truck next to the annex. As I unpacked the picnic lunch, the three came to my room. "Would you like an orange?" I asked, emptying fruit into a bowl.

Rafallah examined my knife. Obviously, he thought the blade was dull because he removed his jambiya from its sheath and sharpened the knife on the J-shaped dagger. Then he sliced through the thick, orange skin separating it into four even sections. Without spilling a drop of juice, he opened the sections and ate the orange.

Mohammed and Oliver climbed in the back of the truck. I sat in the cab next to Rafallah. "Stop at the guardhouse," Mohammed yelled, pounding on the roof. He jumped out of the truck, went inside the guardhouse, and returned with a borrowed scarf to wrap around Oliver's head and face. When I looked through the window, I saw two Yemeni brothers.

Rafallah stopped the truck outside Sirwah Temple. "Wow," Oliver gasped, standing back staring at the temple ruins. "How old is it?" He flipped though his guidebook, searching for Sirwah. "Oh, my God, it flourished in the eighth century BCE."

Sirwah, of all the wondrous sights in Yemen, had a similar effect on me. It is dazzling. "Wait until you see inside," I said, and we followed Mohammed through the gate. The ibex lined up shoulder-to-shoulder—chiseled from light-colored stone—were identical in appearance and had once decorated the top of the temple. Artists thousands of years ago created these animals, and by laying our hands on the carved stone, we reached back in time.

"I'm blown away," Oliver exclaimed, turning this way and that, taking in the awesome site. "Maybe we live in a technological age, but these guys knew art."

Mohammed wanted to show Oliver the underground passages, which we had crawled through on our last visit. "I'll wait here," I said, standing in the shade next to stone inscriptions.

"No," Mohammed replied, waving his Kalashnikov.

Rafallah was waiting for us in the truck when we finished. I wondered if he identified with his ancient heritage or just took it for granted as he drove the ribbon-like road back to Marib. The smooth, dark, volcanic mountains and valleys without plants and trees looked desolate, but the area was once a fertile garden that thrived with the help of abundant rainfall. Over thousands of years, weather patterns changed, desiccating the land. Given time, it will change again. I remembered the words of al-Hamdani, a tenth-century Yemeni scholar: "If the kings of Sirwah and Marib can disappear, who can hope for lasting security in the world."

Oliver planned to return to Sana'a by bus, but the Marib-to-Sana'a bus did not leave Marib until four o'clock in the morning. Foreigners cannot travel by bus at night. The bus company would not sell Oliver a ticket. However, they might make an exception if he paid double the price.

Oliver and I ate lunch in the hotel dining room, and afterward he hurried to his room to shower and collect his belongings. He would return to Sana'a by shared taxi.

The hotel reception was empty, and I sat on the imitation-leather sofa to wait. Recent kidnappings meant fewer tourists in Yemen. Oliver was the only Western guest at the hotel. "Is your friend checking out?" a male receptionist I had not seen before asked.

"Yes," I replied.

He offered some unsolicited advice. "Men shouldn't go to your room. People talk."

"People with nothing better to do," I thought but did not say.

Oliver paid his room bill. Raising my veil, I glanced at the receptionist, but I could not think of anything to say. I confirmed his belief that Western women were immoral. Oliver and I walked to the guardhouse.

Mohammed, Rafallah, and five soldiers squatted in the driveway, eating with their hands from a round, metal communal pan filled with yellow-tinted rice and chunks of gray meat. They asked us to join them. Politely we refused. We walked away so that Mohammed could finish his lunch without feeling rushed, but we managed only a few steps up the driveway before Mohammed called, "Finished," waving greasy hands.

We watched men wash by dipping a can into a metal drum of water and pouring the water over their hands. Taking sips from the can, they swished water in their mouths and with their fingers cleaned teeth and lips and then spat the water on the ground. "These guys have hard lives," Oliver said. "I want to leave Mohammed money. Probably they're just thankful to have water."

A tanker truck delivered water every few days and filled the metal drum. Whoever was on duty got soaked because there was no hose. The soldier opened the valve on the back of the truck, and water gushed. Oliver was right: they led difficult lives, and they were thankful.

49

DIPLOMAS

No problem can be solved from the same consciousness that created it.
—ALBERT EINSTEIN

"Oliver's smart," Mohammed said as we watched the taxi speed down the highway on its way to Sana'a. "He made me think."

"Oliver's educated," I said. "He reads."

"Do you think Yemeni people are kept ignorant on purpose?" Mohammed asked. "If we had education, maybe it would be different—but now, the shaykhs control everything. We obey their rules or they jail us. Shaykhs keep big militias—armed soldiers who take our land and livestock. They do whatever they want."

"Can't people complain to the government?" I asked.

"They control the government—there are no laws in Yemen." He spoke cautiously.

I wanted to ask questions but decided it was not wise. "Can we stop at the gold suq? I'd like to look at earrings." I said. Two jewelry shops side by side operated as moneychangers and a taxi delivery service across Yemen. I tapped the glass counter with my finger and asked to see a pair of plain gold hoops. The storekeeper took the earrings from the case and set them on the counter. "Do you like these?" I asked Mohammed and held the gold hoops to my black-chiffon covered ears.

"The one you lost was nicer," he replied. "Let's go." The next store had similar plain gold hoops and a pair of twisted gold wires. The clerk weighed the twisted wire earrings on a scale—I watched the number stop at 5.4 grams.

"Can you ask him to hold them?" I said to Mohammed, but he was already outside on the street.

"You didn't ask the price," Mohammed said.

"Gold is gold," I replied. "There's a set price."

"There are no set prices in Yemen," he scoffed. "He'll charge what he can."

"Mohammed, maybe he's honest," I said. "You see the world through dark-colored lenses."

"What does that mean?"

"I'll tell you a story," I said. "This is how I remember it."

Once upon a time, a family moved from a village in the valley to a village in the mountains. At the crossroads, they stopped to speak with an old man. "What kind of people live in the mountaintop village?'" they asked. "We're moving there."

"What kind of people lived in the village you came from?" the old man replied.

"Mean and stingy folks—they would steal the thobe off your back."

"Well, that's the same kind of folks who live up there," he said, pointing to the mountain.

The next day another family passed the crossroads, leaving their village in the valley for one higher in the mountains. "What kind of people live in the village on the top of the mountain?" they asked the old man at the crossroads.

"What kind of people lived in the village you came from?"

"They are the nicest people you would ever want to meet," the family said. "We're sad because we have to leave."

"Well, the mountaintop village has the same kind of people—kind and friendly," he said smiling.

"The story doesn't make sense," Mohammed said and kicked a stone in the road.

I wanted to believe that people were honest, but it was becoming more difficult, and that is why I told Mohammed the story—it was a reminder for me. He knew his culture and was probably right. I had not lost myself all at once—it was going slowly.

The next morning, Dr. Mustafa called from the lobby telephone. "Come now," he said. I twisted my hair in a bun and tied my scarf. A baltu hung by the door, and I put it on and walked to the hotel. When I arrived, Dr. Mustafa was by the reception desk talking on the hotel phone. "Sit over there," he said between conversations.

He soon joined me. "Mohammed told me you're leaving," he said, and his eyebrows formed a straight, dark line above his eyes.

"Yes, the middle of January," I replied. "Cheri sent a letter explaining my contract ends."

"I don't remember," he replied.

"Mohammed Hani brought the letter," I added.

"Why won't you stay?" he asked.

"I can't," I said. Saying "sorry" came to mind, but I was not sorry.

"Maybe you'll change your mind," he said forcing a half laugh that was not a laugh. He stood to leave, and the bodyguards followed like worker ants, single file out the door.

On the way to class, I told Mohammed that Dr. Mustafa came to the hotel. "I saw him," he said. "What did you say?"

"I said I'm leaving."

At the gate of the governor's compound, a soldier stopped Mohammed. "Go ahead," he said. "It's safe." Of course it is safe, I thought, seeing a dozen armed soldiers guarding the gate and walls.

The female students sat quietly talking. Khalid looked up guiltily while trying to quickly finish his homework. "It is fine," I said. "Class hasn't started. Finish your homework." Ahmed and Mohammed arrived, giggling and nudging each other. "What's going on?" I asked. They were laughing so hard that neither replied.

"Take out your sentences," I said, ignoring the laughter.

"Have Ahmed read his sentence," Mohammed said and held his hand over his mouth and tossed his head back.

"Okay, Ahmed please read your sentence."

"It's snoring and cold in Boston," he read. It was difficult to keep a straight face—I dared not look at Mohammed.

Amal called me with a wave of a hand. "What's a microwave?" she whispered. "I can't find it in the picture."

"Does anyone know what a microwave is?" No hands went up. "On page 101 they're having a 'yard sale' and the microwave is on the table. Can you find it in the picture?"

"What's a yard sale?" Khalid asked.

"When you sell things you no longer want. It's called it a 'yard sale' because items are sold in people's yards, and sometimes in garages. Then it's called a 'garage sale.' We have not answered Amal's question. Sitting on the table is a microwave. Does everyone see it? Food is cooked or warmed in microwave ovens—it is a very, very fast cooking oven. I saw them for sale in Sana'a."

"You mean the television?" Mohammed said as he and Ahmed burst out laughing.

"Yes, in the picture it does looks like a television," I replied. "But the word 'television' is not one of the choices."

I wrote "tuna sandwich," "vegetable soup," and "iced tea" on the board along with words from our textbook. "Please write complete sentences using one of the following words in each sentence: 'usually,' 'frequently,' 'seldom,' or 'rarely'." Explaining "iced tea" and why anyone would drink cold tea took ten minutes. I walked around the classroom and peered over hunched shoulders as students created long, complicated sentences, stringing words together, even if the sentences ended up as nonsense. Mohammed covered his writing with his hand. Ahmed had drawn a television set and underneath printed the word "microwave."

While I wrote the homework assignment on the board, Khalid asked if we would have a graduation party. "Yes, but let's discuss the party next class," I said, feeling tired.

"When do we get diplomas?" Ahmed said, raising his hand. Diplomas—pieces of paper—seemed more important than learning to the students. "Today, I spoke with Dr. Mustafa. Diplomas will be signed by the governor of Marib and Dr. Mustafa. You'll get them," I replied, irritated by the repeated question.

"You don't understand," Khalid said. "Yemeni employers want diplomas—the more the merrier. They don't care about education—only diplomas."

"No," Ahmed interrupted. "First, they care about connections—family name, friends in government, money, and then they'll look at diplomas."

"What if you're qualified for a position—really smart?" I asked.

"Then you won't get the job," Khalid said, shaking his head at my naiveté. "If you show you're clever, the boss will think you'll take his job. He'll never hire you."

"I'll never understand," I said as Ahmed drove Mohammed and me to the hotel. "There must be people who want to make Yemen better."

"There are," Ahmed said, "but people can't change things. They can't even feed families." Mohammed did not want to be a part of the conversation and jumped out at the guardhouse. Ahmed drove on the dirt track to the annex.

"Dr. Mustafa doesn't want you to leave," Ahmed said as I opened the car door.

"It's past time for me to go," I said, standing in the cold. "The hotel is my prison. I am under house arrest. I cannot teach students who want to learn English. I came to Marib believing I would make a difference, enjoy a social life, meet interesting people, and spend time in the desert. But I'm locked in my room."

"Don't cry," he said.

"I'm not," I said, brushing away tears.

The bathroom window was open, and Zhara pressed her nose against the screen as I passed. "Hi, kitty-kitty," I said. By the time I turned the key in the lock, Zhara was at the door and ran between my legs.

Yogurt and flat bread sounded unappetizing as I searched the refrigerator. Pushing aside a can of tuna, I found Oliver's chocolate bar.

The hot plate acted up, shooting blue sparks when I plugged it in. While waiting for the water to boil, I ate the chocolate bar. Afterward, I opened the door and called for Zhara. "Here kitty-kitty-kitty." She did not come. I wanted her in before Hamza, the nighttime guard, came on duty. He sat in a white plastic chair by the annex and faced my bathroom window until sunup. Whenever we met, he asked the same questions: Where is your husband? How much money do you make?

I opened the door, and Zhara ran inside. Mohammed was behind her. "Will you take Zhara with you?" Mohammed asked.

Yes," I answered.

"I'll bring her to my village," he said. "She is not normal."

"I know," I answered.

"Here," he said, handing me a purple plastic bag.

Inside the bag were four-and-a-half meters of black velvet for the Moroccan cloak. "Mohammed, thank you!" I said, overwhelmed by his generosity.

"You're welcome," he replied, grinning. "We'll go to the tailor tomorrow."

"New Year's and Eid come together this year," I said.

"The Russians had a New Year's party at the hotel last year. They were so drunk they had to stay at the hotel all night."

"How do you know that?" I asked.

"We watched them."

"You stood outside the dining room?"

"No, we hid in the bushes."

Hamza was on duty when Mohammed left at ten o'clock. I wondered what words he added to the police reports.

50

CELEBRATIONS

The last of the human freedoms is to choose one's attitude
in any given set of circumstances.
—VICTOR FRANKL

"Zhara is fine, crazy as ever," I said to Daood on the telephone. "I'm watching her dig through the trash. Now she is running with a candy wrapper in her mouth. She jumped from the bookcase to the bed and is doing her circle dance on tiptoes!"

I told Daood that Mohammed offered to take Zhara. He became furious. "He'll drop Zhara in the desert," he shouted. "He wants you to think he likes her, but he doesn't. I'll take her."

"Zhara stays with me," I replied, noticing the bites and scratches on my hands and arms, wondering if she would ever outgrow her wildness. "Daood, someone's at the door, I'll call later."

A hotel worker delivered a package mailed from *Saudi Aramco World*, a magazine published by Saudi Arabia's national oil company. I had ordered journals to use in class as teaching aides. I wanted students to read, and reading about Islamic culture might inspire them.

That afternoon, I excitedly passed the journals out in class. Students found them too difficult. When I paraphrased an article, I was surprised to learn that they did not know the names of Arab scientists. "Do you study science?" I asked. "The Islamic world once stretched from Spain to Samarkand and by the twelfth century was far ahead of Europe in mathematics, astronomy, medicine, physics, and chemistry."

"Where's Samarkand?" Ahmed asked.

"In present-day Uzbekistan," I answered. "It is your heritage, and you should be proud. Zabid right here in Yemen, attracted great minds from all over the world. Scholars discussed law, mathematics, poetry, and history.

Where is your questioning spirit? Prophet Muhammad said, 'Search for learning even as far away as China.'"

After class, I followed Mohammed to the tailor. He walked fast, ignoring my comments about the students, lack of curiosity. Mohammed entered a tailor's shop on a side street a few steps ahead of me. I took out the picture of a Moroccan cloak and placed it on the worktable. At first, I thought the tailor did not understand. "Women don't wear this," he said to Mohammed and flicked the paper with his hand in disgust. It landed on the ground. The tailor never acknowledged me. For him, I did not exist.

"Well, I won't wear the Moroccan cape for New Year's," I said. We walked to the Salaam Restaurant, and Mohammed ordered foule and bread. I wanted to know why the tailor refused to sew the cape. Mohammed did not talk.

"Our relationship isn't healthy," I said. "You want money, and I want out of the gate. We're in a codependent relationship." I gave Mohammed my wallet, and he paid the bill. Leaving the restaurant, I thanked the cashier, speaking to him for the first time. He smiled and handed me toothpicks.

"Are you angry?" Mohammed asked.

"No," I replied. "I'm tired. Well, maybe a little angry. Why didn't you explain to the tailor what I wanted?"

"He wouldn't sew it," Mohammed said, his eyes flashing. The conversation was finished.

The desert wind blew cold, and the warmth from drinking tea quickly wore off. I clapped my gloved hands, hoping to create heat. Diamond-like stars twinkled in the black sky. "Aden," Mohammed announced, "has New Year's parties. There are clubs near the water with music, and people dance. You can buy alcohol."

"Let's go," I said, smiling at the idea of dancing and drink—it seemed a lifetime away. "Can we take the bus?"

"Yes,' he said. "But you'll need Dr. Mustafa's permission."

"There's always a catch," I said, realizing that freewill had gone from my life.

Aden for Mohammed held a fascination. He and his wife had either lived or spent holidays there—the story was unclear. Aden was also the favorite vacation spot for Eid, and thousands descended upon the southern coast. I did not want to celebrate New Year's in Aden or Sana'a. Staying in Marib and

partying at the Bilquis while soldiers watched from the bushes felt wrong. My
New Year's celebration included Mohammed. I could not leave Marib without him.

"I would like to walk the desert," I said. "Ahmed promised a camping trip."

"It's too cold," he answered.

"Have you been to Sayun?" I asked.

"No, only to Shabwa," he said. "Three months I worked as a guard for a
French archaeological team."

"Please tell Dr. Mustafa we need papers to travel to Sayun," I said, regain-
ing a sense of freedom.

"We'll take the bus," he added, smiling. "You won't wear a veil—Sayun
is safe."

"If it's safe, I won't need a murafik," I replied.

"But I'll protect you," he added. "Between Marib and Sayun, it's not safe.
Women can't travel alone—how would you buy food or water?"

"Women travel the world alone," I reminded him.

"Yemen's different."

"That's for sure."

The next day, I asked Waheeb if he would mind feeding Zhara while I
traveled. He answered by telling a story about Prophet Muhammad: "A kitten
had fallen asleep in the fold of Prophet Muhammad's billowing sleeve, and
instead of disturbing the sleeping kitten, he cut off the sleeve." So Waheeb's
answer was yes. Muslims feel that imitating the prophet's life is living the
ideal way.

Cans of tuna and mackerel were stacked on the bookcase next to Zhara's
bowls. Post-It notes were pasted around the room: "Don't let her out," "If
Zhara gets out, pull ribbons to entice her inside."

"Mohammed, I don't want to travel by bus. We can take a taxi, like Marjorie," I suggested. Mohammed's heart was set on traveling by bus—there
would be comfortable seats and perhaps Indian movies. After a dozen reasons
why we could not go by taxi, he said he would check.

That evening, Mohammed and I walked to the long-distance taxi stand.
He wanted to speak with the taxi drivers alone. "If they suspect you're not
Yemeni, they'll say no or charge higher rates," he advised. While talking to the
taxi drivers, he glanced in my direction, either to keep an eye on me or explain
something to the drivers. They also turned to look.

Mohammed returned to where I waited. "A driver will take us for ten thousand rials," he whispered. "The others want more."

"Did you tell them Marjorie paid eight thousand rials?" I asked and realized how foolish my words sounded. "Okay, tell him to come to the hotel at 5:30 a.m." Mohammed returned to the group of tea-drinking drivers and confirmed our plans.

The next morning it was dark when I walked to the front gate. Mohammed was asleep with the blanket pulled over his head. None of the soldiers stirred. I dialed Mohammed's mobile phone. It rang. The ringing did not wake him. However, the noise woke a man sleeping on a nearby cot. He shook Mohammed so hard I thought the bed might collapse. Mohammed leapt out of bed, fastened the futa around his waist, and slipped his feet into sandals. He was ready.

We waited at the gate. No taxi arrived. Mohammed dialed the phone number, but the phone was switched off. He hoisted his rifle and unlocked the gate. I followed him to Marib.

The taxi drivers uncurled themselves from backseats, having slept in the cars all night, and spoke with Mohammed. Our trip looked doubtful. The regularly scheduled route was Marib–Sana'a–Marib.

"Let's have breakfast," Mohammed said. "If someone is interested, they'll find us." After foule and bread were slapped on a metal-topped table, I ate with the veil in place and listened to deafening screams of men ordering food. Mohammed ate, washed, and when he returned from the basin, said, "He'll take us for nine thousand rials."

"Shouldn't we look at his car before we decide?" I asked.

"They're all the same," Mohammed replied, and I followed him to an open window, which served as a store in the suq to buy bottled water. The dingy white station wagon had its share of dings and dents but otherwise looked fine. I sat in back. Mohammed and his Kalashnikov sat in the passenger's seat.

Just before the first checkpoint leaving Marib, a car pulled alongside and honked. The driver yelled out the window for us to stop. Mohammed told our driver to pull over. It was the no-show taxi driver who had agreed to take us to Sayun. "Do you want to go with him?" Mohammed asked through the open window. "He's insisting."

"*La*, no," I answered and rolled up the window.

We traveled a straight, black, stretch of road across hard-packed, uninteresting desert—no golden sand dunes in sight. The vast, flinty, featureless desert was the color of dirty dishwater. Breaking the monotony were fire-breathing dragons—tall smokestacks spewed columns of fiery plumes, the result of burning oil. Oil companies had existed on the edge of Marib since the mid-1980s, but it was the first time I saw them.

At military checkpoints on the road every few miles, Mohammed handed official documents signed by the governor of Marib and Dr. Mustafa. When soldiers asked questions, Mohammed explained I worked for the Health Department in Marib. They waved us through.

Our taxi driver had not eaten breakfast and stopped at a one-story, whitewashed restaurant at the side of the road thirty minutes outside Marib. The restaurant would not have looked out of place in Malibu if only it had striped umbrellas.

We had a second breakfast of scrambled eggs with tomatoes and green peppers, foule, and freshly baked flat bread. I removed my veil. "This is the cleanest restaurant I've ever eaten at in Yemen," I exclaimed. Tea was served in clean glasses with no chipped rims. "I'll have to remember this place for the *Marib Guide to Fine Dining*."

We drove for about a half hour, and Mohammed asked the taxi driver to stop. "Why are we stopping?" I asked, seeing that we were in the middle of nowhere.

"Get out," Mohammed said and opened my door. Wind whipped my scarf and baltu as I stood in soft sand on the side of the road. The taxi driver got out, opened the rear door, and sat in the backseat. "You're going to drive," Mohammed said.

"I am? Why?" I asked. I sat behind the wheel and moved the seat forward so I could reach the pedals. I checked the gearshift, stepped on the clutch, and shifted into first. The car lunged forward.

"I told the driver if you drove, you'd feel happy," Mohammed explained. "Maybe you'll feel free. He knows Marib is not easy for a woman."

"Thanks," I said. "Are you checking to see if I can drive?" Mohammed laughed. When I looked in the rearview mirror, the taxi driver had fallen asleep. He slept until I ground the gears at the next checkpoint. Soldiers were surprised to see a veiled woman driving a taxi, but they waved us through when I handed them official papers.

After five hours, we arrived on the outskirts of Sayun and were met by palm groves and low-rise mud-brick architecture—a welcomed oasis. Without hotel reservations, we stopped in the middle of Sayun and looked at several basic hotels, but no rooms were available.

"There's a new hotel on the way to Shibam," a hotel clerk said, and the taxi driver took us there. Mohammed's single with shared bath was sunny and clean with a window overlooking a palm grove. He had two sheets and a thick blanket. My spacious room with two single beds and similar blankets had an attached bathroom.

Although it was the last day of the year, the weather was sunny and warm. I wore one sweater under my baltu. "You've bought a new shirt," I said, noticing yellow plaid under Mohammed's jacket. "Does it feel strange to walk on the street without your rifle?"

"Feels good," he answered. "Sayun's safe—not like Marib." We walked on a dirt path next to a wide, paved road. Rows of date palms lined the sides of the streets, and wind rustled the fronds. Cars moved slowly. We found a suq with shops selling Chinese merchandise. Mohammed wanted a futa made in Indonesia. For centuries, Yemenis have had close ties with Southeast Asia, including India, Indonesia, Singapore, and Malaysia, traveling there for business and pleasure and acquiring great fortunes and Asian influences, which they brought back to Yemen.

We passed restaurants, but none looked special enough for New Year's Eve. "Let's eat at the hotel," I suggested. A waiter dressed in a clean white shirt and black trousers asked where we wanted to sit. "It's up to you," I said to Mohammed. He pointed to a square table near the wall that was set for four. The waiter removed two of the place settings and brought bottled water and two menus.

Mohammed ordered grilled fish, and I asked for the same. We shared a mixed *mezza*: plates of hummus, olives, stuffed grape leaves, tabouli, and flat bread.

"That was delicious," I said, wiping my mouth with the cloth napkin.

The waiter brought tea in small, gold-rimmed glasses. "Want desert?" I asked.

"Yes," he said, smiling. The waiter brought a star-shaped cream-custard on a plate with two spoons. We toasted each other's good health and wealth for the coming year with water.

"Sleep as late as you want," I said. "See you next year."

Mohammed realized that next year was tomorrow and laughed. "Sweet dreams," he replied. Walking to my room, I knew Mohammed and I had allowed ourselves to be vulnerable, and that is one definition of friendship. I hoped to remember that our souls only see friends if we look with our spiritual eyes. We are all in this together.

51

TARIM

I don't want to come to the end of my life
and find that I have just lived the length of it.
I want to have lived the width of it as well.
—DIANE ACKERMAN

At nine o'clock the next morning, a knock at my door. "Yes," I said.

"It's Mohammed," he answered.

"Meet me in the restaurant," I replied. "I'll be there in fifteen minutes."

"I'm going to reception to check my Kalashnikov."

"How did you sleep?" I asked as we walked to the dining room.

"I love my room," he said, beaming. "The shower has hot water."

Our breakfasts were included with the price of our rooms. We sat at a table bathed in sunlight. A basket of bread, a dish of strawberry jam, a platter of cheese triangles, and olives were placed before us. Tomato-and-onion omelets came next. Mohammed ordered coffee, and I had tea. We ate the bread in the basket, and the waiter brought more. Dusting crumbs from my baltu, I asked Mohammed what he wanted to do besides seeing Shibam, which would take half a day.

"We'll find something," he replied. A German tour group was finishing breakfast, and we wished each other Happy New Year.

Outside the hotel, a Yemeni driver stopped on the highway and offered us a ride. He had lived in Detroit and proudly showed us his Michigan driver's license. He would not take money and said he was glad to help Americans because they had helped him. Meeting Yemenis that had lived in America or had relatives who lived in America was common.

Walking through Shibam's gates, we were greeted by the thousand-year-old, whitewashed, mud-brick mosque, its minaret poking a hole in the sky. Shibam is a compact collection of stone-foundation and mud-brick skyscrapers rising from the desert floor. They looked to be leaning against each other for support, like old friends. Roofs are all the same height and seemed to touch—hopping from one rooftop to the next seemed possible. Narrow alleyways untouched by sun except during midday were filled with raggedy children, goats, chickens, trash—and, for me, antique stores.

"I'll look quickly," I said to Mohammed, seeing antique wooden chests stacked in front of the doorway of an old house. One small wooden chest was especially handsome, with inlaid brass designs. "Isn't it gorgeous?" I said to Mohammed, probably too loudly because the storekeeper appeared.

"Open it," the storekeeper said. I opened the lid—inside was a removable wooden tray with small compartments and below a storage area and secret hiding place.

"What was it used for?" I asked.

"To hold ink and writing instruments," he replied.

"A writing box," I shouted to Mohammed. "Look." Turning the chest over, I saw that the wood was in wonderful condition. Even its heavy brass handles matched.

The storekeeper returned inside to help someone who asked a question in Italian. "How much do you think I should pay?" I asked Mohammed. "Maybe it's a magic writing box. I'll be able to write again."

The antique shop was on the first floor of an old house made from rough stone. It had few windows, so it was dark inside. Customers browsed in shadows. "Excuse me," I said to the man. "How much is the small (I stressed the word "small") writing box?"

Before he answered, Dr. Selma al-Radi from AIYS grabbed my arm. "Too expensive," she said, smiling. "What are you doing in Sayun? I thought you were in Marib."

"Just a short holiday," I replied. "This is Mohammed." I introduced him to Selma and her four female colleagues who were working to restore the Al-Kaf Palace in Tarim.

"It's New Year's Day. Join us for lunch; we're staying at the Al-Hawta Palace. Do you have swimsuits?" Selma asked.

I turned to Mohammed. He looked pleased, and I said, "Yes, we would love to join you." Neither of us had swimsuits, but sitting in the sun by a pool would be relaxing. "Come with us," Selma insisted. "We have two vehicles."

Selma, a renowned Iraqi archeologist and art restorer, has been the driving force behind restoration on the Al-Amiriya Mosque in Rada, Yemen since the 1990s. She has trained Yemeni artisans to reclaim age-old procedures to restore ornamentation on the mosque and madrassa to authentic magnificence. Through her dedication and hard work, she is preserving what might have been rubble and ruin. "We are in great company," I whispered to Mohammed.

Selma stopped her car at the entrance to the Al-Hawta Palace Hotel, once a Sultan's palace, located halfway between Sayun and Shibam. Two white-uniformed men held the double wooden gates ajar for the car to pass into luxury.

The compound, surrounded by a tall mud-brick wall, was built with defense in mind. The elegant palace itself is constructed of thick, mud-brick, whitewashed walls. Antiques are placed artfully throughout as reminders of a past when wealthy sultans used the impressive rooms to entertain. Manicured gardens and green lawns tended to make us forget that we were in the middle of the desert. At the edge of the garden was a jewel-like swimming pool where guests relaxed. Mohammed and I walked along a shady, palm-lined stone walkway to the pool. We sat in padded chairs near the water, shaded by blue-and-white striped umbrellas, while the women went to their rooms and changed into swimsuits.

"Well, I don't need my baltu," I said and removed it. Relaxing on a chaise-lounge, I pulled up my long skirt, exposing white legs. "Why don't you take off your jacket?" I said to Mohammed, who turned his head to answer, but the shocked look on his face said it all. Two women walked toward us wearing skimpy, brightly colored bikinis. Mohammed dropped his gaze but from time to time stole glances as they swam. Selma wore a more conservative, dark, one-piece bathing suit, but for Mohammed, who was used to women covered in black, these mermaids were nearly naked.

Three men—an architect, engineer, and an art historian—who worked on the restoration project in Tarim joined us. "Do you want lunch inside or outside?" Selma asked. Everyone voted for lunch on the terrace café by the pool.

Mohammed sat between the art historian and a bikini-clad woman who had put on a pink cover-up. "What are you having?" she asked Mohammed. He stared at his menu. "Did you decide?" she asked again. He shook his head.

"The hamburgers are good," she said, before adding, "The cheeseburgers are awesome!"

He ordered a cheeseburger and an iced tea. "Have you eaten a burger before?" she asked.

"No," he replied. "It's my first time. And my first iced tea, but I learned about them in English class." Mohammed fumbled with his hamburger, since he was not sure if he should pick it up with his fingers or use the knife and fork. But the woman cut it in half, and he managed just fine.

"What did you think of your first cheeseburger?" she asked when he finished.

"I don't think I'll have another one," he replied.

The afternoon went too fast, and New Year's Day ended. "Would you like to see our project in Tarim?" Selma asked.

"We planned to go to Tarim tomorrow," I said, fastening my baltu. "Seeing the Al-Kaf Palace would make the trip even better." Selma gave directions from the Tarim shared-taxi stand. Inshallah, we would see them around ten o'clock.

"Did you have fun?" I asked Mohammed while we waited on the main road for a taxi. Sunset colored the desert shades of toasted brown and burnt ocher. A soft chanting indicated the time for prayer.

"Yes," he said, smiling, lost in his own dream as shadows from the palm trees lengthened. "This is the happiest time of my life."

52

MUD MANSIONS

The journey is the reward.
—CHINESE PROVERB

After breakfast, we planned to check out of the hotel, and I carried my small bag to Mohammed's room. I waited in the hallway. The door was open, but he was not inside. His bed was already made, the blanket neatly folded, and sandals placed under the table. On a wooden stand beside the bed, the Koran lay open. His yellow checked shirt hung on a hanger. Seeing his neatness surprised me. This side of his personality I had not known.

Mohammed came out of the hallway bathroom dressed in an undershirt and trousers. He had already showered and shaved. "I'll miss my room," he confided.

We stored our belongings at the reception desk and walked to the taxi stand. The taxis for Tarim left when full. We waited twenty minutes. I sat beside the window, and Mohammed sat in the middle seat next to a man. "Maybe you should cover your hair," Mohammed whispered. "Tarim is strict." I tied my black scarf around my hair and tucked in loose strands as the taxi traveled a narrow road through a sheltered valley. Both sides of the road were bordered with date palms gardens.

The taxi stopped at a grassy square. We walked around, admiring the small town. Tarim was once a great cultural and educational center for Sunni Islamic teachings, with 365 mosques and celebrated libraries. Over the centuries, religious groups that viewed Islam from different perspectives destroyed libraries and manuscripts. Today the Al-Ahqaf Library houses volumes of religious manuscripts and remains an important place of scholarship.

Religious bookstores lined the street opposite the library. At a small restaurant, we had tea. Men were obviously curious why Mohammed and I were together, but no one asked. While drinking tea, we studied Selma's map.

Afterward, we crossed the road, following the map, and headed toward old mud-brick mansions. "I can't believe there are so many mud palaces," I said. "The money it took to build the mansions, but no one lives in them now."

"They're falling down," Mohammed said, pointing to a house missing its roof.

We rounded a corner and saw Selma's car parked in front of the most beautiful mud-brick palace. Busy workers emptied buckets of sand and carried water for cement. "Hi," I said to a woman that we had met the day before. Today she wore baggy pants and a man's long-sleeved shirt with a turban wrapped around her head. "Is Selma here?" She pointed to a staircase that led to a second-story landing—an Art Nouveau, glassed-in porch with ornately carved decorations. We climbed the steps and Selma gave us a tour. The house had more than one hundred rooms, including several huge ballrooms. Ceilings and walls had collapsed, but that did not detract from the house's splendor.

How many palaces still stand in Tarim?" I asked.

"Jean hasn't completed the survey," Salma answered. "But if the old mansions are not restored, they'll all soon be piles of dust. We're trying to save this one, but there is little financial support for such projects."

"More people would be involved if they knew about the mud palaces—these are masterpieces," I said. "Why are they abandoned?"

"Families fled during the war, and people can't afford to maintain them," she answered. We thanked Selma for showing us the work of art and for her part in trying to save the mud palaces of Tarim.

"The mud palaces will disappear—return to the earth," I said as we walked to the taxi stand.

"Yes," Mohammed replied.

"In America there is a magazine, *Architectural Digest.* Maybe they would be interested," I said. It seemed such a shame the mud art structures would disappear.

A small restaurant near the taxi stand was open, and we stopped for lunch.

"I didn't find out the price of the antique writing box in Shibam," I said, eating a plate of yellow rice with a spoon. Mohammed ate rice with his hand. "Can we go to Shibam?"

"There's not enough time," he answered.

"I'll call Selma," I said and dialed her number. "Owning the wooden chest might help me write." I asked Selma to buy it.

"How will you get it?" Mohammed asked.

"Selma will have it delivered to AIYS."

Back in Sayun, we walked to the long-distance taxi stand, but there were no taxis going to Marib. "We have to get back," Mohammed said, sounding anxious. "Wait here."

By the time he returned, ten taxis were lined up, all traveling to Al-Mukalla. "We can't get a taxi to Marib for any price."

"What'll we do?" I asked.

We walked to the bus station and found rows of small shops that sold bus tickets. Mohammed asked at the first shop, but the man saw me and said he would not sell a ticket to a foreigner traveling at night. Mohammed went directly to the bus station, but they sent him back to the ticket sellers. Beggars hung around outside the bus station and asked for money as we passed.

"No taxis—no buses," I said to Mohammed. "We'll stay in Sayun?"

"Do you have your lithma and gloves?" he asked.

"No, they're in my bag at the hotel," I replied. We walked to the hotel, and I put on my black veil and gloves. We returned to the bus station. Mohammed asked me to wait outside, but I felt uncomfortable standing alone. Soon I was not alone but surrounded by beggars asking where I was from. They knew who was behind the veil—a foreign face. They had seen me earlier. Trying my best to ignore them, I did not answer.

"What took you so long?" I asked. "Did you get tickets?"

He pointed to his pocket, and I saw ticket stubs. "My friend bought them," he replied. "I had to pay extra."

The money seemed unimportant, so I did not ask the price. "When do we leave?"

"Our bus leaves at ten o'clock, inshallah," he answered. "We need to be here a half hour early."

We walked to the Sultan's Palace. Now a museum, it resembled a white, layered wedding cake with its edges decorated with blue icing. Steps led to the museum's metal gate, but it was now padlocked. The guard said the museum would open at nine o'clock the next morning. "We might still be here," I whispered to Mohammed.

"Let's have tea," Mohammed suggested, and we crossed a wide street, heading for an open-air juice and tea restaurant.

"We have four hours before we leave," I said, noticing an antique shop. Ignoring my idea to shop for antiques, Mohammed continued to the open-air restaurant. Seated at the far end of the communal concrete table were a group of soldiers. They knew a Yemeni woman would not drink tea at a restaurant with a man and asked Mohammed who I was. He explained I was an American and taught English for the Health Department in Marib.

"Can I look at the antique shop?" I asked. "Now that my identity is settled." Mohammed nodded.

Prices for the antique wooden bowls and hand-painted porcelain dishes were reasonable. The collection of silver jewelry was nice; I thought Marjorie must know the shop. The small wooden boxes were not as beautiful as the ones in Shibam. "If you're looking for antique chests," a Yemeni said, "there're stores in the old suq."

"Where's that?" I asked. The man walked outside with me and pointed to a street behind the tea and juice bar.

Mohammed seemed in good spirits talking with the soldiers. "I'm going to the old suq," I said, interrupting him. "I'll be back in a few minutes." Mohammed stood and said good-bye to the soldiers. "I'm sorry," I apologized for disturbing his lively conversation as we walked the winding paths of the suq. Nothing especially nice was for sale—the stores mainly sold Chinese merchandise. A shop sold shawls from India. Another sold pearls and "silver" jewelry blackened with motor oil to look old. "There's nothing here," I said, but I spoke too soon. Stacked in front of an old, rundown, whitewashed store were wooden chests. We went inside. One whole wall had antique wooden chests stacked from floor to ceiling. Begrudgingly, Mohammed asked the owner if he could take them down. The owner telephoned his son.

Mohammed glanced at his watch, but I knew we had time. One by one the son lowered the heavy chests, spilling clouds of dust over the room. Although I was wearing a veil, the shopkeeper surely knew I was not Yemeni by my excitement over old chests.

"Which do you like?" I asked Mohammed. He remained silent. Two of the nicest chests were also the largest. One was a missing its brass hinge, which would be hard to replace. The other—the biggest—was decorated with brass nails in circle designs on the lid and front panel. Its sides were edged with brass. When I lifted the lid, I saw wooden drawers on each side and the not-so-secret hiding place—a false bottom. "How much?" I asked Mohammed.

Mohammed stared at me. "You're not buying it?"

"Maybe," I said. "Please ask the price?"

"No," he replied. "It's too big."

"I like it because it's big," I said. "I'll use it for storage." It reminded me of the antique wooden chest in Michael's apartment. "Please ask how much." Mohammed remained silent.

Finally, I spoke to the storekeeper.

The price was four hundred dollars. Michael had paid three hundred dollars for hers. "Offer two hundred dollars," I whispered to Mohammed.

"How will you get it to Marib?" he answered, annoyed.

"On the bus," I replied. We settled on $250. The owner's son, with Mohammed's help, wedged the wooden chest in the trunk of a white car—it was so big that two-thirds hung out, so the man drove slowly.

At the bus station, two workers helped Mohammed carry the chest to the bus. I paid one thousand rials for oversized luggage. "See, it's easy," I whispered to Mohammed.

Exactly at ten o'clock, the bus pulled out of the Sayun station, and we were on our way to Marib. Since I was traveling as a Yemeni woman, I could not speak. Mohammed passed me a stick of gum. After chewing the gum, I took it out. The gum stuck to my veil, making a mess. Mohammed could see what had happened but, of course, could not help. I tried not to laugh, but I could not contain my giggles. Mohammed and I glanced at each other, and we burst out laughing. No one seated around us seemed to notice.

Halfway between Sayun and Marib, the bus stopped, and we got out. Men stood in line for tea. For the first time, I noticed that two women were on the bus. They got off, and together we walked to a bathroom, which was really a primitive stall with a hole in the ground.

Mohammed waited with the two male protectors near the bathroom. I followed him to the back of the restaurant. He opened a blue metal door, and we entered a small room that looked like a horse stall. On the earthen floor was a rectangular woven mat. Mohammed squatted. I sat on the dining mat.

Mohammed answered a knock at the door and took a tray from a man's hands. The foule and bread were delicious; we had not eaten since breakfast. "I had a wonderful time—it was like a honeymoon," Mohammed said, finishing his tea. I replaced my veil and we returned to the bus. A honeymoon? Had I missed something?

The bus arrived in Marib at about three o'clock in the morning, and after a short stop at a restaurant, the bus would continue to Sana'a. We stood on the side of the highway in the dark, shivering. Mohammed could not leave me to look for transportation, and it was too early to call Rafallah. We could not walk with the heavy chest. Finally, a driver in a battered old pickup truck stopped. Mohammed hauled the heavy wooden chest into the truck's bed. We climbed in back and sat on top of the chest. The driver drove to the hotel and dropped us off. Mohammed pounded on the wooden gate that barred entry to the hotel at such an early hour and woke the guard, who then helped carry the chest to my door. New Year 2005.

53

THE LAST SUPPER

*To be yourself in a world that is constantly trying to make you
something else is the greatest accomplishment.*
—RALPH WALDO EMERSON

The long-awaited graduation party would be in the hotel dining room. "What
do you want for the lunch?" Hisham asked.

"Fish, meat, pasta, salads, and fruit and cream caramel for desert," I read
from my list. "Bottled water, tea, and coffee." He estimated the price per person to be between ten and twelve dollars.

For gifts, I ordered six hardback copies of *Longman's Contemporary English Dictionary* from Taha Hussein at Dar al-Hikma in Sana'a. "Aren't you
giving money?" Mohammed asked. A slow shake of my head told him no.

"Can we walk to Marib?" I asked Mohammed. "I need wrapping paper
and cards." From his smile, I knew he envisioned cards stuffed with cash. "But
I wanted to walk," I said to Mohammed when he knocked to tell me the car
was waiting along with Ahmed.

After buying wrapping paper and cards from a kiosk on the main street,
we drove to an open-air teashop. Mohammed wiped dust off the wooden
table and benches with pink tissue paper before we sat. Ahmed shouted our
order. The waiter placed three scalding glasses of sweet, milky tea on the tabletop. Wrapping a tissue around a glass, Ahmed handed mine to me. Holding
the hot tea warmed my hands.

When I looked up, Mazen, the student who had dropped out of class,
stood beside the table. "Join us," Ahmed said and screamed for another tea.
Mazen hesitated but sat down.

"When's the graduation party?" Mazen asked, looking at me.

"Thursday," I said. "But it's only for the six students."

"I helped you," he said, raising his voice. "Do you remember?"

"Yes, of course I remember," I answered, sensing his anger. "Thanks for your help."

"I don't care about the party, but I want my diploma," he said and leaned across the table menacingly.

"Everyone wants a diploma, but only the students who completed the course get them."

"You could give me one," Mazen said, raising his voice. Hearing his aggressive tone, Mohammed clenched his tea glass. Ahmed remained silent.

"No," I answered. Mazen slapped the table with the flat of his hand. The table wobbled, and tea spilled.

Mohammed half stood, and his thighs nudged the table forward, "She already explained why you can't have a diploma," Mohammed said calmly. "Yelling at a woman in public is not right."

"I'll get my diploma," Mazen shouted and stormed off.

"Does he really believe he'll get a diploma?" I asked.

"Yes," Mohammed answered. I looked at Ahmed, who nodded. "Teachers are afraid of students with powerful families. They might lose their jobs. Bribing teachers is common, because they change grades for money. Mazen's father could cause trouble."

"What kind of trouble?" I asked. They did not answer.

During the week, students I had not seen since the first week of class called to ask about my health and ended conversations by demanding diplomas. Students knocked on my door, waving money.

On Tuesday evening, Mohammed and I were to have our "last supper." I was sealing the envelope with Mohammed's gift of two months' salary when he knocked. "General Shamlan called," he explained, dressed in uniform. "I can't go to dinner."

At seven thirty, Mohammed knocked again, this time dressed in a yellow plaid, long-sleeved shirt and brown slacks fastened with a black belt. I was boiling eggs. "We can go to dinner," he said, patting his arms to keep warm. I unplugged the electric hotplate.

"Why aren't you wearing your jacket?" I asked.

"My friend took it to the laundry," he replied. "I'll pick it up in Marib."

Mohammed seemed distracted as we walked. He stopped outside the photocopy shop. "Wait," he said. He left me standing in the dark on the side of the road. After a thousand lectures about the dangers of Marib, I stood alone. Neon lights from the shop's window cast ghostly shadows on the street as Mohammed spoke with a man inside the shop. I watched silhouettes create a kind of puppet show.

I took one step and another and another until I reached the intersection and crossed the street. It was exhilarating. I felt tingly. I turned right at the first side street and recognized the apartment building where Dr. Mustafa had suggested I rent a flat. Across the street, men were drinking tea in an open-air teashop. They did not seem to notice me. Feeling invisible, I took a seat at an empty table. A waiter with a soiled white apron asked if I wanted tea. I nodded. He set a pink plastic cup with a matching saucer on the table; the cup held cardamom-flavored milk tea.

An alluring Egyptian video was playing on a television that sat on a chair on the sidewalk. Accompanied by loud music, the women on the screen danced barefoot, leaning forward, their long, dark, wavy hair cascading in circles. Half watching the video, I kept my eyes open for Mohammed, whom I knew would pass.

From my vantage point, I watched Mohammed cross the street, but he was too far away to see me. He passed a second time wearing his jacket. I ordered another tea. After the thrill of drinking tea alone wore off, I paid for the teas and left.

Cars drove slowly, probably wondering why a woman was walking alone. Nobody stopped. I did not see anyone on the street. Footsteps behind me sounded like a warning, and I picked up my pace. The footsteps belonged to Mohammed. "What were you thinking?" he demanded. I did not answer but was relieved to have his company on the dark stretch of road coming up ahead.

"You could have been hurt," he said.

"But I wasn't," I answered.

"Were you drinking wine?" he asked accusingly.

"I wish the teashop had wine," I replied and turned off the paved road and followed a desert trail that led to the hotel.

"Stop!" he ordered.

"You can't stop me," I yelled. "You can't tell me what to do." At that instant, a wild dog jumped out of a bush, growling. "Mohammed," I screamed. The dog bared its fangs. I backed away. Mohammed squatted on the side of the road, his automatic rifle laid across his knees. "Did you know that dog was there?" I asked him.

"He sleeps there at night," he replied.

"How did you find me?" I asked.

"Men at the tea shop recognized you and told the military," he said.

"Then why didn't you come to the teashop?"

"I watched you from the corner," he said. "You were safe."

54

PACKING ZHARA

What is not started today is never finished tomorrow.
—JOHANN WOLFGANG VON GOETHE

"I would like to buy Rafallah's family fudge," I said to Mohammed. We walked to the candy store. The clerk sliced a brick of brown-and-white fudge and wrapped it in waxed paper. "May I have a sample?" I asked and pointed to a pan of orange-colored candy worms. "They taste like gummy bears," I told Mohammed.

Since we were in the suq, Mohammed bought qat. "I'm meeting friends in the garden this afternoon," he said. "Will you need me?"

"No, I'm packing," I answered. "But I need a box to carry Zhara." Just thinking about transporting Zhara to Sana'a made me uneasy. We stopped at the store for a box, and I bought two rolls of extra-strong packing tape.

"Are you one of the lucky ones to leave Marib?" the storeowner asked when I paid for the tape. "I've seen you collecting boxes."

"Thursday," I answered, "inshallah."

"And him?" he nodded to Mohammed. I answered by shaking my head no.

In my room, I piled clothes on the bed to give to the shepherds who tended the goats. There were books for the hotel lobby. I would give Daood the camera when I saw him in Sana'a. Mohammed had hinted that he wanted the cassette player—it would be his.

I rolled up the carpets and leaned them against the wall. Zhara sharpened her claws, and the carpets fell, sending her into orbit. The framed prints and mirror I stacked on the desk. I had not yet worked out how I would get to Sana'a.

Mohammed knocked at the door and asked if I needed anything before he joined his friends. "No, I'm fine," I said. "Do you think I should invite Dr. Mustafa to lunch on Thursday?"

271

"Dr. Mustafa's in Sana'a. He won't return until Friday," he answered.

"Solves that," I said.

Zhara ran into the bathroom when I put her traveling box on the bed. Such a suspicious cat—she knew something was coming. "Come kitty-kitty," I coaxed as she hid behind the toilet. I tugged her legs. That did not work. "Okay," I said and placed the box on the bathroom floor, drumming my fingers on its side, thinking she might jump in on her own. Any other time and she would be in and out of the box a dozen times.

While I sat beside the box on the bathroom floor, I thought about luxury in the West. People owned big houses and fast cars, but they tended to be cut off from intimate relationships because of a lack of time. Our bee-like behaviors developed in the age of high-speed technology, fast food, and express checkout lines. We lived attention-deficit-disordered lives, jumping from one thing to another. Multitasking was a badge of honor. In Yemen, there was the luxury of time of sitting together with family and friends. Taking life slow. Enjoying the moment. Being present. Maybe material goods would be missing in Mohammed's life, but he had great wealth.

The telephone rang. "Hello," I answered. "Sitting on the bathroom floor convincing Zhara she should get in the cardboard box."

"Ask Waheeb to help you," Daood suggested. "How will you get to Sana'a?"

"I guess I'll ask Mohammed to hire a taxi and go with me," I replied. "I can't think of any other way."

55

GRADUATION LUNCH

I am still learning.
—MICHELANGELO

Thursday morning, I picked flowers from the garden and arranged them in water glasses. The mid-January sun was warm on my shoulders as I walked to the hotel lobby to speak with the chef. Mohammed owned the cassette player, and I heard Yemeni *oud* music floating from the guardhouse window. "May I put the flowers on the table?" I asked the chef. "Our graduation lunch is at one o'clock."

"How many people?" he asked and seemed surprised when I mentioned lunch.

"Altogether, seven," I said. "Didn't Hisham tell you?" I was not completely shocked because planning, it seemed, was missing in Marib. Missing in all of Yemen, I suspected. The diplomas were not yet framed; they would be delivered to the governor's office later in the month for the students to pick up.

Dictionaries were wrapped in festive paper, and I set one at each place setting. The three women would be at one end of the table, with me in the middle and the three men at the other end.

I returned to the room and finished packing, except for the long, black velvet dress and princess shoes. I would wear them to the party along with my baltu. After I showered, I dressed. Zhara sniffed the packed boxes. Her carrying box was in the bathroom, but she would not go near it. Finally, I managed to coax her inside the bathroom and shut the door. "Don't get in the box while I am away," I said to Zhara, hoping that reverse psychology might work.

Ahmed and Khalid were the first to arrive. They sat on the sofa in the lobby. "I thought Dr. Mustafa was in Sana'a," I said, noticing his car parked outside the hotel.

"He came to Marib late last night," Ahmed replied. "I'm driving his car."

"Should I invite him?" I asked.

"He won't say good-bye to you because you're coming back to Marib," Ahmed answered.

Mohammed arrived a few minutes later, dressed in a clean white thobe, navy blue sports jacket, and black-and-white checked shawl hanging neatly over his shoulders. He sat between Ahmed and Khalid. The three looked uneasy, as if they expected examinations.

"The women are coming," Mohammed said and turned around, jabbing both men with his elbows. Three women entered the lobby, walked to the opposite side of the room, and sat on a sofa. "Congratulations," I said to the women and shook black-gloved hands.

"Let's have lunch," I said to the women and led the way to the dining room. The men followed.

Entering the dining room, Amal whispered that she could not sit with men. The other two agreed. "What if we make two separate tables?" I asked. "Is that okay?" I moved the flowers and gifts to another table. "I'll sit at the women's table," I said to the waiter.

"No," Jamila said. "We can't be in the same room with men."

"What about waiters?" I asked.

Asma shook her head slowly. "A young boy or woman must bring food." The waiter understood. He explained in Arabic that behind a door to the right was a room exclusively for women. I had been in the dining room a hundred times but never noticed the door.

"Excuse me," I said to the male students. "I'll be back."

The women's dining room was pitch black. "Can I open the blue drapes just a little to let in light?" I asked but knew the answer before the words left my mouth. I switched on overhead fluorescent lights and returned to get the flowers and gifts.

In the main dining room, the men were eating salads. "Can you sit with us?" Khalid asked.

"Sure," I answered and sat in the chair next to him. "Congratulations to you for completing the course." The waiter stood beside me, wanting my attention. He pointed to a tray of salads. "Excuse me," I said and picked up the tray and delivered it to the women's dining room. Carrying the tray with two hands, I could not knock before entering and I backed into the room. The women scrambled for their face veils.

"We need bread," Amal said.

I went to the kitchen. Passing the men's table I asked, "How's everything?" They were busy eating and looked to be enjoying themselves. "I'll be back."

"To a job well done," I said to the women. Our water glasses were empty so we could not toast. "You've taught me so much."

"We've learned a lot," Asma replied. She passed me a tray with fish, and I took a piece with my fork and put it on my plate. There was a knock at the door. The women replaced their veils.

"Thanks," I said to the waiter, who was standing with his back to the door. I took bottled waters from his hands and filled the women's glasses. "Please pass the potato salad," I said to Amal, and I put a scoop on my plate. "How's the food?" I asked, taking my first bite.

"It's good," they answered.

"I'd better check on the men," I said and left the room. The men were dipping chunks of bread into *salta*, a vegetable meat stew that I had not ordered.

"In Yemen we need salta for lunch," Mohammed said. "We asked the waiter to bring it."

"Of course," I apologized. "Order anything I forgot."

I found the waiter in the kitchen. "Could you ask the chef to make salta for the women?" I asked.

"No problem," he said.

Within a few minutes, salta bubbled in a blackened stone dish. The waiter passed me the sizzling dish on a thick piece of cardboard. I carried the salta to the women's dining room.

The men were eating cream caramel and peeling bananas the next time I passed. "Are you having tea or coffee?" I asked, carrying a tray of bananas to the women. I peeled a banana, put it on my plate, cut it into slices, and ate it with a fork. The women watched in amazement. Eating a banana with a knife and fork seemed strange even to me.

After lunch, the women wanted to take photos by the pool. "Please stay inside," I asked the men. If they had glanced out the windows, they would have seen three figures completely covered in black and one (me) with only hands and face showing.

"Thank you," I said to the women. "It's beautiful," I held the gift of a silver watch encrusted with jewels. "Matches my princess shoes," I said, and lifted my baltu to show them. We said good-bye on the steps of the hotel, the women eager to leave. Coming to the Bilquis Hotel for lunch could damage reputations. They were courageous in breaking tradition by sitting with men in class and today entering a hotel.

I opened gifts from the men: Yemeni silver, a ring, a necklace with an amber pendant, and two bracelets. "Thank you, I'm delighted with the jewelry," I said, and shook hands with Ahmed, Khalid, and Mohammed.

Waheeb met me in the lobby, and we walked to my room. "Zhara is locked in the bathroom," I explained. I had already poked holes in the sides of the carrying box and lined it with a white towel." The tape was ready. Waheeb opened the bathroom door, but Zhara hid behind the toilet.

"Here kitty-kitty," I called. Zhara stayed behind the toilet. I carried the travel box and put it on the bed. "When she comes out, close the bathroom door," I whispered to Waheeb. Usually the can opener got her attention, but not this time. Waheeb and I sat on the bed.

Mohammed knocked at the door to tell us he was walking to Marib to hire a taxi. "Sorry, I can't open the door because of Zhara," I said. "Make sure the taxi is big enough to hold the wooden chest."

Zhara ventured out of the bathroom and jumped on boxes stacked by the door. Waheeb closed the bathroom door. I tried to grab her but missed. She hurtled through the air, aiming for Waheeb. "I'm sorry," I said. "Maybe I can do this alone. Wait outside."

"Zhara, you'll have to get in the box," I said calmly, but my stomach was in knots. "I can't leave you in Marib." Finally, I got my hands around her body, her feet paddling the air, and I tried unsuccessfully to stuff her in the box. Holding Zhara was difficult because she squirmed and tried to bite. I could not shut the box lid, and I did not want to let her go.

"Waheeb, come quickly," I yelled. Thankfully, he had not run away. He held the box and I stuffed her inside. Together we taped the box closed.

Mohammed returned. "Is Zhara inside the box?" he asked, seeing the box on the bed.

"Yes, she's finally quiet," I said.

"She can't breathe. The holes are too small," he shouted. Mohammed used scissors to punch bigger holes.

"Don't push the scissors in so far—you'll hurt her." Zhara had not made a sound. I peered through holes but saw only black.

"She's fine," Mohammed said.

Mohammed and Waheeb loaded the wooden chest. Boxes came next. "Be careful with the mirror," I said as I sat in the taxi with Zhara beside me on the backseat. Mohammed sat in the passenger's seat. "Thanks for everything," I said to Waheeb and shook his hand through the car window.

"Good-bye Marib," I thought as the taxi bumped along the dirt track and neared the hotel gate. I held my breath, half-expecting the metal fence and massive wooden gates to be shut and Dr. Mustafa to be waiting with a gang of armed men, telling the taxi driver to turn around, but we passed through the open gate.

Before the first checkpoint leaving Marib, Mohamed turned to me. "The driver doesn't like driving at night," he said. "It'll be dark before we reach Sana'a. He thinks we should wait until tomorrow."

"Then tell him to drive fast," I replied. Zhara jumped around inside the box and pushed the top with her head. "Mohammed," I yelled, "she's coming out." Zhara was frantically ramming her head against the top of the box, loosening the tape.

"Give her to me," he said and reached over the seat for the box. I remembered Daood's words about Mohammed dumping her in the desert.

"Here's the tape and scissors," he said. "Cut long pieces." I cut the tape and handed them to Mohammed. He held the box on his lap until the al-Jawf turnoff and then passed her to me. Mohammed got out of the car and left his Kalashnikov with his friend, the mechanic. "When are you returning to Marib?" I asked.

"Maybe next week," he replied but said no more. We rode the next two hours in silence, lost in our own thoughts.

"Are you going to AIYS?" he asked when the taxi neared Sana'a.

"No," I answered. "But close—behind Parliament." Since we had not discussed our futures, I had neglected to tell him about renting Michael's apartment.

From Tahrir Square, I directed the taxi driver to turn right and then left. He drove into a narrow lane until he stopped in front of the five-story, mud-brick tower house. Michael had left the keys with the next-door neighbor.

Mohammed went to ask for the keys and unlocked the outside gate. He and the taxi driver carried boxes and the heavy wooden chest into the dusty courtyard. "Six thousand rials for the driver," I said, counting rials into Mohammed's hand.

Mohammed carried a stack of boxes up three flights of stairs to Michael's apartment. I carried Zhara in her box. We returned downstairs, but Mohammed asked me not to carry any boxes. He hoisted the heavy wooden chest on his back and walked slowly, stopping at each landing to rest. I walked behind him.

"The bathroom light doesn't work," I said to Mohammed as he stacked the last of the boxes in the hallway, "I want to let Zhara out of the box but keep her locked inside the bathroom."

"Does she need a light?" he asked.

"No, but I will later," I replied.

He stood on the rim of the tub and unscrewed the bulb. "It's the kind with pins—do you have extras?"

"I don't know," I answered. I looked in the kitchen cupboards but did not find any bulbs.

"Give me the keys and money," he said. A half hour later, he returned with a package of light bulbs and a blue plastic washbasin for Zhara's litter box.

"Thanks for buying the light bulbs and litter box," I said, filling the pan with sand that we had brought in a plastic bag from Marib.

Mohammed replaced the light bulb. I stayed in the bathroom and closed the door. I peeled tape from the box, but she stayed inside and would not come out. By the time I finished filling her water bowl, she had hopped out of the box. I quickly closed the bathroom door and stepped into the hallway, listening to her rake the sand in the litter box.

56

GIFTS OF THE DESERT

The end is not apparent
From the very onset.
—Herodotus

"Any service?" Mohammed asked as we stood in the hallway. The question required no answer. Mohammed pressed the light switch, which controlled the timed lights on all floors. I followed him down the stone steps. Lights went out before we reached the first floor landing. "My life will be boring," he whispered, standing in the dark. I waited on the stair until he located the light switch.

When we reached the first floor, Mohammed slid the heavy wooden bar, and the door swung inward. In the courtyard, we shook hands as the *mueddin* finished the final call to prayer. He turned the lock on the black metal gate and stepped into the dark alleyway, disappearing into spills of dappled light. "No more following Mohammed," I thought, closing the gate and locking the wooden door. I retraced my steps up the staircase and remembered to push the light switch on each floor.

Inside the apartment, I inserted the large metal key in the lock and slid the wooden bar. I let Zhara out of the bathroom. She slunk around the apartment, her belly touching the floor as she explored the unfamiliar surroundings. She jumped sideways at the slightest sounds and bristled when she saw her reflection in the full-length mirror.

I stood at the window and watched the flickering lights of Sana'a and wondered how life would be on my own without Mohammed.

The first Wednesday in Sana'a, I was to give a talk at the Taj Sheba Hotel for the International Women's Association about my time in Marib. Standing before fifty women—wives of ambassadors and oil company executives—I took a deep breath:

Whenever I shut my eyes, the desert looms before me. The amber-colored sands, plum-colored mountains, and bright blue skies, but something is far more important than colors, images, and words. I went to Marib to teach—to say thanks to the Bedouin who gave me so much. Believing that my way was superior. Even with the best of intentions, what I had to give was lacking. It was arrogance on my part. In fact, I had nothing to give and everything to gain. Living in the desert, losing my freedom, mistrusted as an outsider, suspected of spying, and being unable to write taught me humility, and the hardships brought me closer to truth. Marib turned everything I thought or thought I knew upside down. Not a day will pass in all my life that I will not remember the gifts of the desert.

But none of this I said.

My audience knew stories of Marib's lawlessness, which included tales of unruly Bedouin. Some had visited the historical sites in a day, surrounded by armed military police. They wanted confirmation that the stereotypes they knew were true. I desperately wanted to share my experiences, but that was not meant to be.

The audience witnessed a disappeared woman. A pale outline, a shadow stood before them. Her lips quivered as she held back tears. Pity and embarrassment was apparent in their eyes and faces. The meeting ended. I did not stay for tea.

Although I had stopped following Mohammed, I was not sure which way to go. Like a prisoner freed from jail, I did not have my bearings and could not trust my judgment. The confrontational desert had challenged my beliefs; its sand scoured my soul. Since my path was not evident—or faintly visible— I waited for answers. I reached an oasis but was not ready to travel onward. Bedouin crisscrossed deserts following tariqah. With time, a path would surely be revealed. Then I could continue my journey, seeking further destinations— inshallah, God willing.

Acknowledgments

I started writing this book in 2004. It has been long in gestation, which means there are many more people than mentioned here to thank. Thank you all who have added to the book. Hilary Claggett, senior editor at Potomac Books, for her enthusiasm and belief in this project deserves applaud. Thanks to Aryana Hendrawan, production editor, and her colleagues at Potomac Books for lifting this book with their skills. For Nancy Elmer, my dear friend in Hawaii, I am forever grateful and indebted to you for shouldering my responsibilities the past years. A special thanks to Dr. Tom Stevenson for his encouragement with words and deeds, and a friendship that blossomed in Yemen. Most heartfelt thanks to my friend Richard Beeler, an unrelenting critic who read numerous drafts and offered invaluable comments. Thanks so much to my dear friend Brid Beeler for her precious gift of friendship and refuge in Sana'a, Yemen. Thanks to Dr. Maria Ellis and Dr. Chris Edens of the American Institute for Yemeni Studies for their votes of confidence. Above all, I want to record my love for my father, Paul Everett, who passed away before he could hold the book in his hands. With gratitude to my mother, Helen Everett, whose love has allowed me to follow my somewhat unusual path. *Shukran*, thank you, to the many Yemenis who without any thought of reward generously offered kindness. *Shukran jazeelan*, thank you very much, Mohammed.

About the Author

For twenty-five years, between teaching assignments, Carolyn Han has traveled the Silk and Incense Roads listening to and writing stories. She believes tales give us insights into diverse cultures. Perhaps by understanding others we may come to know ourselves. In 2000 Carolyn traveled to Yemen to study Arabic. She found a rich cultural heritage and collected folk stories, some of which were eventually included in her book *From the Land of Sheba: Yemeni Folk Tales* (Interlink Publishing, 2005). Later she journeyed by camel across the *Ramlat as-Sab'atayn*, Yemen's desert, with Bedouin, and in 2004 she quit her lecturing position in Hawaii, sold her house, and moved to Yemen. Han is also the author of three collections of Chinese folktales published in the 1990s by the University of Hawaii Press. She received a BA in English from the University of Hawaii at Hilo and an MA in comparative literature from San Diego State University.